Celtic Cornwall

Celtic Cornwall

NATION • TRADITION • INVENTION

An illustrated Gazetteer

Alan M. Kent

with additional photography by Jan Beare

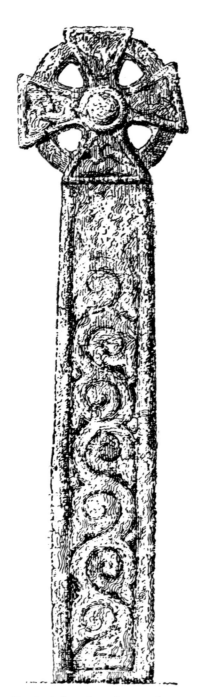

Lanivet churchyard cross, face.

First published in Great Britain in 2012

Copyright © 2012 text Alan M. Kent
Additional photography © 2012 Jan Beare

British Library Cataloguing-in-Publication Data
A CIP record for this title is available from the British Library

ISBN 978 0 85704 078 7

HALSGROVE
Halsgrove House,
Ryelands Business Park,
Bagley Road, Wellington, Somerset TA21 9PZ
Tel: 01823 653777   Fax: 01823 216796
email: sales@halsgrove.com

Part of the Halsgrove group of companies
Information on all Halsgrove titles is available at: www.halsgrove.com

Printed in China by Everbest Printing Co Ltd

Contents

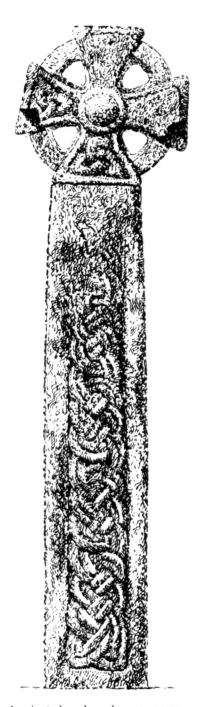

Lanivet churchyard cross, verso.

St Helen's Oratory
near Cape Cornwall.

Acknowledgements

Many friends and colleagues have assisted in the development of this book. Most of the translations contained within this volume are by Tim Saunders and myself. Those from *Bewnans Ke [The Life of St Kea]* are by Graham Thomas and Nicholas Williams. Tim, and Nicholas were, as always, most helpful with assisting with these.

My understanding of Celtic Cornwall has been enhanced over the years through the discussions and debates I have had with a number of people. Among this group are Charles Thomas, Philip Payton, Caradoc Peters, Neil Kennedy, Bernard Deacon, Derek Williams, Clive Boutle, Brian Murdoch, Craig Weatherhill, James Whetter, Julie Tamblin, Frances Bennett, Andrew C. Symons, Michael Everson, Cheryl Straffon, Jim Pengelly, Matthew Spriggs, Steve Patterson, Andy Norfolk, Cheryl Hayden, Paul Broadhurst, Kenneth MacKinnon, Garry Tregidga, Gage McKinney, Cath Camps, Chris Nancollas, Briar Wood, Michelle Brown, Mick Paynter, Paul Newman, Gwyn Griffiths, Hildegard L.C. Tristan, Adrian Rodda, Brian Stevens, Ken George, Les Merton, Andy Phillips, Audrey Randle Pool, Ann Trevenen Jenkin, Mark O'Sullivan, Martin Philp, Loic Rich, Michael Chappell, Tony Leamon, Ian Stevens, Danny Merrifield, Dean Nolan, Jason Semmens, Evelyn Newlyn, Myrna Combellack, Paul Annear and John C.C. Probert. My thanks to Neil Kennedy for allowing me to quote from his poem '*An Brennik* [The Limpets]' and to Hilary Coleman and Neil Davey for answering my musical enquiries, and to Colin and Alison Roberts for the photographs of hurling at St Columb. Thanks also to Carl Thorpe for the drawings of the incised pictorial slates from Tintagel. My on-going thanks to my copy editor Rachel Bourgoin.

My continued thanks to the staff of the Cornwall Centre, Redruth, the Penlee House Gallery and Museum, Penzance, Truro Library, Angela Broome and staff of the Courtney Library, Royal Institution of Cornwall, the St Ives Museum, the Morrab Library, Penzance, the Halls of Chivalry, Tintagel, the British Library, the British Museum, the National Library of Ireland, and the National Library of Wales.

Many of the historic photographs first appeared in volumes published in the award-winning Halsgrove Community History Series and grateful acknowledgement is given to their authors and contributors. Etchings of holy wells are taken from John Blight's antiquarian works, while the drawings of stone crosses which appear throughout this book are taken from *Old Cornish Crosses* by Arthur J. Langdon. Aerial photography is by Jason Hawkes. I am of course indebted to Jan Beare for his superb colour photography which accompanies the text.

Alan M. Kent

Morning light, Roche Rock.

8

Introduction
The Mist & the Stone

In termen ez passiez…
thera an newl ha'n mean.

[In the time that is past…
there was the mist and there was the stone.]

Many people are intrigued by Cornwall's Celtic heritage, but where can they find it and what is it? In the pages that follow I have sought to answer those two questions, allowing people to visit a number of key locations, as well as offer an explanation of why such a place is significant. I have chosen just over five hundred entries, but there could have been so many more. This volume is therefore a hand on the pulse of what makes Celtic Cornwall tick but inevitably also, the tip of a vast iceberg. It is incredible just how much of past Celtic Cornwall has survived, but also more incredible how present Celtic Cornwall continues: a future Celtic Cornwall is clearly guaranteed.

Cornwall has not always found it easy to be recognised as 'Celtic'. For a long time, the discipline of Celtic Studies was dismissive of Cornwall's status. On occasions, it was seen as rather a footnote in the field. In literary and cultural studies, apparently Cornwall did not live up to the mythological epic narratives found in other territories but, as we shall see, such a view was misguided. For others, Cornwall had for too long been another English 'county' which had completely lost its innate Celticity. This is another view that can be dismissed. When compared to many other Celtic territories, Cornwall is seen as small and lacking clout. Although still a problem, it is a view that is gradually being overturned. Centrally, the fact that Cornwall continues to recognise its Celticity (the values and ideology that make a people Celtic) shows its tenacity and drive to make the world aware of its heritage. Potentially, the fact that it has not had 'nation' status has paradoxically heightened its Celticity. Gradually, observers and academics have come to recognise that Cornwall's geo-political status is a highly suitable case for treatment, and that its on-going Celticity is one of the most interesting cultural and social phenomenons in Western Europe. It is something I have described before. Cornwall has what I have termed an 'unresolved duality of place'. It is one aspect of this duality of identity that this volume investigates: its Celticity.

Several observers have tried to debunk Cornish Celticity over the years, claiming that after the Anglo-Saxon invasions and the Norman Conquest then, in effect, Cornwall ceased to be truly Celtic. This assertion is wrong on several levels because fundamentally it seems to lack recognition of the resistance of Cornish people over time to reconfigure and re-negotiate their Celtic identity. It is also assumes a kind of assimilation and integration into England which has clearly not fully occurred. Resistance has been there in many different ways across the centuries, and it is still there in the twenty-first century. The entries in this book confirm this. They also deny the sceptics.

Cross base, King Doniert's Stone, St Cleer.

The Longstone stands near Mount Charles, St Austell. The standing stones of Cornwall were, for the most part, not erected by Celts.

Of late, Celticity has been the subject of much deconstruction, with various scholars lining up to seemingly expose the myth of Celtic Studies and somehow reground the field. This is a view to which I am broadly sympathetic. Celticity has needed deconstruction. The observations of scholars such as Malcolm Chapman and Simon James have helped to open up debate about the term 'Celtic' and subsequently allowed us to understand the processes and cultural changes which have shaped the field. None of the early peoples of south-west Britain whom we now describe as 'Celtic' would have self-ascribed themselves as 'Celtic'. The term was first applied in the eighteenth century on language groups and it has come to represent particular ethnic groups. James asks the question as to whether the Celts of the Atlantic periphery are 'an ancient people or a modern invention'? Clearly, like any living group, they are somewhere between these two extremes. Quite correctly however, Chapman has noted the mismatch between perceived popular imaginings of the Celts and the reality. He cites the association between standing stones and Celtic peoples, which is an historical anomaly. The megalithic standing stones of Cornwall were, for the most part, not erected by Celts. In fact, they were built by cultures operating some two thousand years earlier. However this has not stopped their association with Celtic peoples, and sometimes Celtic groups have even promoted or encouraged the link (one only has to look at the Cornish Gorseth).

This book looks at a number of different phases of Celticity in Cornwall. It does not argue that any one phase was more or less significant. Instead, it views Celticity in Cornwall as a continuum where subsequent declines and revivals inevitably take place, and in which the archaeological past is re-interpreted for contemporary need (be it in the eighteenth or twenty-first centuries). Nothing should surprise the reader about this. It is how all complex societies have developed throughout the centuries. It is not my wish in this introduction to offer yet another detailed historical analysis of just how the Celts 'came to be' in Western Britain. Numerous volumes have already elucidated this and the interested reader should peruse the suggested further reading.

Some background is useful however. When the Celtic-speaking peoples first appear in history books, they are noted by the Greek and Roman historians, as having their heartlands in the British Isles, Gaul, parts of the northern Iberian Peninsula and northern Italy. In Antiquity, a tribal group called the Celtae were based in south central Gaul (France) and were the only group who self-identified in ancient times as Celts. The Gaulish historian Sidonius Apollinarius was one of them. Earlier views that Celts came from Eastern Europe were misinterpretations of invasions of Eastern European areas by Celts as if they had always been Celtic. There are no accounts (at least in Antiquity) of invasions of Britain by Celts as a new, incoming people. The early records all point to Britain as Celtic-speaking and there is no need to speculate about a pre-Celtic Britain, except in the sense that people populated Britain at all.

It was from 43CE to the early fifth century that the Romans occupied Britain. Cornwall appears to have been part of the military zone of the province in the sense that it had military forts and the exploitation of resources such as tin, iron and sea salt. From about 500BCE to the early fifth century, the Celtic Britons on the island of Britain spoke the Brythonic language (a forerunner of Cornish). Celts elsewhere, such as those in Ireland, parts of Scotland and the Isle of Man, altered linguistically, and spoke a Goidelic language. Thus, for around a thousand years, despite the Roman invasion, the British Celts developed and prospered.

Archaeology has shown that the subsequent Anglo-Saxon 'invasion' of Britain was not really what occurred. Broadly, the British Celts were pushed in a westerly direction by the accumulation of land and property. This military project did not necessarily mean that people physically moved but were instead culturally changed. Initially, battles were fought, but later it appears that intermarriage and

Land's End, or Pedn an wlase.

integration of Anglo-Saxon and Celtic cultures occurred. Ethnic cleansing evolved over successive centuries into a negotiated settlement though, as this volume shows, not without on-going tension.

A series of events then occurred which resulted in the formation of Celtic Cornwall today. The west (the South-West, Wales and Cumbria) of the island of Britain seemed to resist the Anglo-Saxon encroachment more than other areas, and there followed centuries of conflict. A decisive battle at Dyrham near Bath in 577 had a devastating effect however. It created a barrier between the British Celts of Wales and those of the south-west peninsula. The Anglo-Saxons captured the valley of the River Severn. From this period, the south-western Celts were in permanent retreat from the Anglo-Saxons moving in a south-westerly direction down the peninsula, prompting many of the Britons to leave, crossing to Brittany.

In the aftermath of the Roman invasion the Celtic peoples who survived were part of the wider Celtic kingdom of Dumnonia. It provided a bulwark against the Anglo-Saxons for centuries. However, Dumnonia finally fell to the Anglo-Saxon armies during the first decade of the eighth century. We know that King Geraint of Dumnonia, was killed in battle and, by 710CE, the Saxons had reached the old Roman city of Exeter. In 721 or 722CE a decisive battle is said to have taken place at a location named Hehil (perhaps somewhere on the Camel Estuary), with the invading Saxon army pushed back to the east. For around a century, this ended Anglo-Saxon incursion into Cornwall.

In this phase we know that Cornwall was seen as a distinct political territory. In the late eighth century Bishop Kentsec is granted the title of the Bishop of Kernow. Kernow is the Cornish word for Cornwall and it translated to the 'land of the promontory people' – a name which fits given their geographical location, but also their propensity to dwell on cliff castle promontories. The name Cornwall in its Latin form (*Cornubia*) was first mentioned in a letter from Bishop Aldhelm of Sherborne around 700CE. The English name Cornwall is first recorded in 891, and it is derived from the Anglo-Saxon *Kearn Weahlas* ('the horn or promontory of foreigners'). In fact, however, the Cornish were now established as the native people, with Anglo-Saxons as the foreigner. Consequently, in the Early Medieval period, the Cornish were still often known as the West Welsh; *Weahlas* also being the Anglo-Saxon term for Wales [*Cymru*].

Exeter was perhaps operating as a frontier town between the western Celts and the Anglo-Saxons, with pockets of Celtic peoples living there. This must have been dangerous for them because, by 815, King Ecgberht of Wessex ravaged Cornwall 'from east to west'. A Cornish-Danish alliance tried to fight back against the Anglo-Saxons at Hingston Down near Callington in 838, but perhaps the writing was on the wall for wider Cornwall. By 939, King Athelstan had expelled the Cornish from Exeter and fixed the boundary of the east bank of the Tamar as the border between Cornwall and Wessex. Cornwall was therefore oppressed but delineated. Although these events took place many centuries ago, they still have ramifications in the cultural and history of Celtic Cornwall.

Since this period, Celtic Cornwall's history had been a series of resistances against more powerful occupiers. The Norman Conquest of 1066 is an interesting case. Generally it is accepted that this conquest was the real starting point for Cornwall being integrated into the English nation state. An alternative view does emerge however. Many of the Norman occupiers may well have had a sympathetic view of the Cornish for, in fact, many of them were expelled Bretons whose folk memory carried an idea of the south-west of Britain being their ancestral homeland. This so-called 'Breton Return' may well have reignited the link between the two territories. That said, the Norman Conquest still became another method of controlling Celtic Cornwall.

It seems that for a long period in Early, Middle and Late Medieval culture that English centralism accommodated Celtic Cornwall, and even valued its separateness. This was completed along linguistic lines, but also through tin and metal production, via the guarantee of the Stannary system. Cornwall also contributed to wider British battles. For example, the power of Cornish miners and archers were valued by the campaigns in France in 1415 of Henry V, who used a number of Celtic troops in his 'English' armies. Undoubtedly, Medieval Celtic culture flourished in Cornwall, in response to the Age of Saints, the development of cults, the proliferation of literature and theatre, and an affirmation of a Celto-Catholic Cornwall. Although much of this has been lost, a good deal has survived into the modern era.

The Age of Saints. The well of St Carantocus.

The Tudor period and the powers of the Reformation, of course, put an end to this Celto-Catholic construction of Cornwall, and ushered in not only the English language, but a change in religion and identity. The wider British state seemed unable to tolerate a separate Celtic Cornwall that did things differently from everywhere else. For some observers this is where the rot sets in within Celtic Cornwall: the destruction of institutions such as the Collegiate Church of St Thomas at Glasney, the restrictions on the Prayer Book and traditional practices, and the destruction of saintly culture prompted the permanent decline of Celtic Cornwall. As this book will show, however, while such events did have devastating effects on Celtic identity, cultural, political and religious defiance continued into the Early Modern era. Cornish Celtic difference was still noted at home in Cornwall and 'abroad' – in particular, by playwrights on the London stage, who still celebrated Cornish Celticity on the periphery of Britain. The Civil War has also prompted much new debate along ethnic lines. A general consensus has come to recognise that Cornish support for the Royalty in the war was due to the King's protection of Cornwall's innate difference and 'Celticity' – a very different view to that held in the standard Roundhead and Cavalier narrative of the past.

Traditional notions of Celticity may be harder to find in eighteenth and nineteenth-century Cornwall. However, many practices did carry on – if re-invented for the modern era. Methodism has had to endure some hard knocks for destroying and eroding Celtic practice. It is true that Methodism had sceptical views of some aspects of Cornwall's Celtic heritage, but likewise, as will be seen in this volume, it was also prepared to engage with it. We only have to see John Wesley's use of holy wells, or the especial Christian significance (centred around Creegbrawse) of the parish of Gwennap. Likewise – although not working along the traditional lines of Celtic social and cultural behaviour, Cornwall has good claim to be *the* industrial Celtic society – using innovation, invention, engineering and sheer bravery to complete several centuries of hard-rock mining. One may even argue that it was ever thus: that Celtic Cornwall and mining are inextricably linked. The language of mining-procedures, practices and solutions are in essence, Celtic-derived. Many recent publications, notably those by John Rowe, Allen Buckley and Peter Hancock – all express the influence of 'Celtic' mining practices. Continuities still exist: South-Crofty offers a range of knotwork-inspired jewellery created from tin mined there. The other famous 'Celtic' jewellery manufacturer, St Justin, whose work can been seen in shops throughout Britain, use Cornish metals in their manufacturing processes.

Many Celtic practices travelled with Cornish emigrants wherever they went. The mining spirits, the Knockers, were found in far-flung locations around the globe. Sporting events, festivals, literature, and even aspects of the Cornish language travelled with the Cousin Jacks and Jennies (Cornishmen and women working overseas). Most Cornish Festivals around the globe – whether the 'Kernewek Lowender' festival in South Australia or the Gathering of Cornish Cousins in Grass Valley, California – have strong Cornish-language elements to them, and are often populated by men and women wearing Cornish tartans. More than this, imaginings of the ancient Celtic past (however anachronistic) are expressed at locations such as Collumcille Megalithic Park in Pennsylvania, USA, and at the standing stones at Glen Innes in New South Wales, Australia.

Cornwall provided the world with miners and surveyors. From Stithians, Richard Randall Knuckey (holding theodolite) poses with a survey party during the Northern Territory Expedition of Australia, 1869.

Cornwall had its own Celtic Twilight so to speak – in the early part of the nineteenth century. Then perhaps was a true low point of Cornish Celticity. However, despite the moves to modernisation, various antiquarians and folklorists had been keen to collect the Celtic heritage of Cornwall. Among these were collectors such as William Bottrell, Robert Hunt and Margaret A. Courtney, whose ambitions later continued in the shape of the Federation of Old Cornwall Societies 'gathering up the fragments so they may not be lost'. Other writers – such as Robert Stephen Hawker, John Harris, John Dryden Hosken and Katherine Lee Jenner – drew on Cornish Celticity and Arthuriana for their inspiration. The Celtic Revival in Cornwall has its ignition point here with these collectors and writers, but also with the centenary in 1877 of the death of Dolly Pentreath – one of the last speakers of the Cornish language. Since that time, various scholars, folklorists and activists have sparked a huge revival in interest in Celtic Cornwall. Many of them – such as Henry Jenner, Robert Morton Nance, A.S.D. Smith, William Paynter and Enys Tregarthen – are featured in this volume. All of them point the way to an incredible process of cultural recovery, perhaps unequalled elsewhere in the modern era. It also resulted in a new flowering of literary production in Cornish, Cornu-English and Anglo-Cornish.

Contemporary Cornwall is very aware of its Celtic past, present and future. It is able to work as a cultural magpie, picking and choosing what aspects of its past it wishes to preserve. It also seeks genuine response to the needs of a new generation of Cornish people, very aware of their Celtic heritage and actively resisting accommodation into bland globalisation. Invariably, present Celtic Cornwall is based on new readings of the past colluding and colliding with the needs of the present. We should therefore expect fusion, borrowings and hybridisations – actually in just the same way that the past operated. No one can say that a moment in present-day Cornwall is any less Celtic than an occurrence in Post-Roman or Medieval Cornwall.

There are, however, some major strands and themes which we recognise as markers of Celtic Cornwall. The Iron Age, Romano-British and Post-Roman Celts of Cornwall were a people who seemingly loved large-scale construction projects. Although not responsible for standing stones, quoits (dolmens) or burial mounds, they did inhabit a landscape that contained these objects. They must have engaged and responded to them. Indeed, could it be that standing stones were merely adopted as ritual space from previous communities? Perhaps they were. However, it is to hill forts and cliff castles that the Celts of early Cornwall really applied themselves. Logistically, building castles on cliff-side promontories is a wholly appropriate place to live if your community is considering responding to any kind of attack. This legacy is best seen in the location of Tintagel, The Rumps or on The Lizard peninsula. Virtually inaccessible from the sea, the narrow neck of land at the head of the promontory meant that a small but intensive set of fortifications could be constructed which would be relatively easy to defend. Some of these cliff castles may also have served a ritual purpose judging from the archaeological evidence, perhaps because they occupy the liminal space between land and sea. There is a proliferation of such structures across Cornwall, indicating much about the lives of the early Celtic occupants of Cornwall.

Likewise, in Cornwall we find an intensive legacy of hill forts, positioned in ideal defensive locations across the territory – often above rivers and with significant views of the surrounding countryside. Although such hill forts are found elsewhere in South West Britain, many exist in Cornwall. Clearly, these constructions were major developments which required the movement and repositioning of tonnes of earth, not to mention the creation of palisades and the timber-buildings inside the hill forts. Such was their impact that these hill forts continue to be integrated into narratives and were even used as defensive positions in later conflicts. To this day the hill forts of Celtic Cornwall are used for gatherings, ritual and performance. Their significance in the landscape is on-going. Standing

Dolly Pentreath's memorial at Paul.

stones are not excluded in this book, but for those observers, who wish to find out more about them, Craig Weatherhill's *Cornovia: Ancient Sites of Cornwall and Scilly 4000BC–1000AD* (published in Halsgrove's Discover Series) will make a useful companion to this volume. We also note here the proliferation of Romano-British courtyard houses, such as those found as Carn Euny and Chysauster. These communities seem to say so much about imagined Celtic lifestyles in this period. The majestic spread of hill forts and cliff castles is mirrored by the intimacy of beehive huts and fogou chambers.

The lives of saints continue to dominate expressions of Celticity in Cornwall. Obviously relevant in their 'great age' (lasting broadly from the fifth to seventh centuries CE) of sea-crossings, missionary works, and miracles, they continued to be celebrated throughout the Medieval period. The place-names, holy well, chapels, oratories and churches named after them show their importance. Their presence and continuum is intensely felt. Although the Reformation brought down severe destruction of their icons, statues and community practices, somehow an interest and awareness of their lives has persisted. Perhaps the modern era has come to see saints as near prophets or even Pagan figures – local deities merely Christianised. Maybe the interest in saints gives us clues into a wider pre-Christian druidic culture, which again has been subsumed by Christianity. Whatever we think of saints in Celtic Cornwall, they were clearly powerful figures – touchstones into an earlier spirituality. Previous studies by writers such as Gilbert W. Doble and Catherine Rachel John have now been succeeded by the work of Nicholas Orme. Still however, the lives of the saints continue to fascinate us. John Betjeman, for one, is an example of an English writer who was somehow drawn to the Celto-Christian past. Cornwall's patron saint, St Piran, seems to be recovering the status he once had in Early Medieval Cornwall. His life and deeds are celebrated more and more on St Piran's Day (5th March) every year. A contemporary promenade play (another echo of earlier times) attracts thousands of people to the dunes at Penhale Sands. The discovery of a new dramatic *Life of St Kea* [*Bewnans Ke*] in 2000, re-invigorated long-term enquiry into saint's lives and their connection with the Cornish landscape, still attested by surviving place-names featured in the text.

It is impossible to conceive of the saints in Cornwall without referring to the numerous holy wells and baptistries connected to them. The hunting and cataloguing of holy wells was an obsession for many nineteenth-century and early twentieth-century antiquarians whose studies of folkloric practices and rituals indicated links to the Celtic-Christian past. In some communities wellhouses and baptisteries somehow survived the onslaught of time. In others we have but fragments left, but they still evoke a kind of magic. The significance and importance of wells has been claimed by Neo-Pagan groups who see them as representing key aspect of the pre-Christian past in Cornwall. Debate over their use and significance is still seen in the newspaper columns of present-day Cornwall. Dual use and respect now seems to be the way forward.

The Reverend Robert Stephen Hawker at St John's Well, near Padstow.

Related to the saints and their lives are the vast array of what we may broadly term 'Celtic' crosses in Cornwall. These wayside wheel-headed crosses are indelibly stamped on our visualisation of Celtic Cornwall. Many of them are tall and powerful reminders of the Celtic heritage of Cornwall, adorned with carvings and knotwork which testify a Celtic past. We know that many different societies used scroll and knotwork decoration in their material past and, on occasions, it is hard to determine both the dating and origins of such crosses. Many 'Pagan' menhirs were merely Christianised. Crosses in Cornwall often have a mystifying history: why they were erected, why they were taken down – and in some, cases destroyed, mutilated or simply used as gate-posts or in the fabric of buildings – and why they have been restored and re-erected? Scholars, such as J.T. Blight and Arthur Langdon in the nineteenth century, and the more recent work of Andrew Langdon and Charles Thomas, have done much to re-assert the symbolic place of these monuments in our minds. Spectacular crosses and monuments continue to be found. At the same time, communities throughout the twentieth and twenty-first centuries have used the Celtic cross as both memorials to individuals and major conflicts, and as celebrations of identity and place. The significance of carved stone is enduring.

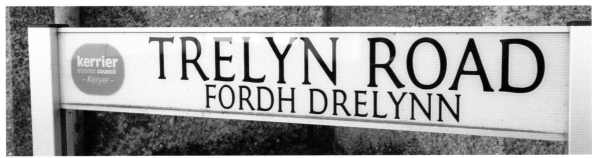

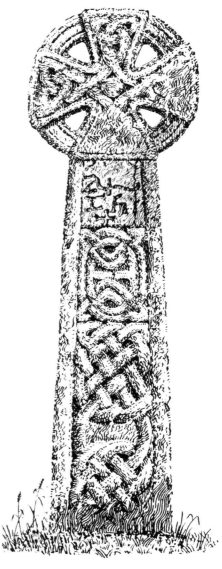

Celtic cross in Cardinham churchyard.

One strand of Celtic identity across the centuries has been the Celtic language group. The Cornish language is a key marker of Cornwall's Celticity and many of the entries in this volume are concerned with it. At first sight the history of the Cornish language might appear as a kind of terminal and unstoppable decline into oblivion. Much of its early modern and modern literature seemed to be about preservation and conservation – against the unstoppable juggernaut of English. However, the fact that at the start of the twenty-first century, Cornish is one of the few Celtic languages in ascension, proving that it will not go away, and that actually it forms a dynamic part of multi-cultural Britain. Generally Cornish is seen as part of the Brittonic or Brythonic (often called P-Celtic) family of languages, which also includes Welsh, Breton and the now defunct Cumbric language. The earlier Brythonic language was the language spoken at one time by the Celtic Britons (in different dialects and variations) from Land's End to Glasgow. The Brythonic language itself had its root in an earlier Proto-Celtic language (of which little is known), from which the Goidelic group of languages also emerged (the so-called Q-Celtic group), including Irish, Manx and Scottish Gaelic. Like the people of western Britain, the language also retreated into the West. There are generally seen to be four phases of Cornish: Old Cornish (c.800–1250), Middle Cornish (1250–1550), Late Cornish (1550–1850) and Revived Cornish (1850 onwards). In recent years, there has been some debate about the spelling of Revived Cornish, a debate which has affected many languages over time, and may be viewed as an internal discussion over the best system to use. The debate has recently resulted in a standard form for public and educational purposes though inevitably, as we would expect, there are

Tintagel - inextricably linked with Arthurian legend.

An early 13th century manuscript depicting the story of Tristan and Yseult.

still variations and different 'dialects' of the language. This dialectical variation actually demonstrates the vibrancy of the language.

Clearly, Cornwall's Celtic literary heritage is different from most other Celtic territories. This book will show that the predominant literary form was community-based, populist, liturgical drama, often looking at the lives of saints. In effect, the *'bewnans'* or *'The Life of'*-style dramas formed origin stories for local communities, building to an apex of performances in the Late Medieval period. Considering Cornwall's relatively small size, the proliferation and distribution of the theatre spaces for such performances – playing places (or the *plain-an-gwarry*) – show that the territory had one of the most advanced theatrical cultures in the world. Theatre unfortunately has generally been ignored by Celtic Studies in the past, but the profusion of these dramas in Cornwall indicates much about how a broadly illiterate society engaged with and watched their own saint's life or celebrated a fusion of the Bible on to a Celtic landscape. This is not to say that other forms did not exist. The literary records shows that the *englyn* (a three-lined unit of rhyming verse) or multiple *englyns* called *englynnyon* were extremely important and that various revivals of writing have picked up on this genre. It is also true that various modern writings in Anglo-Cornish and Cornu-English (Cornish dialect of English) have developed and re-energised traditional forms and concerns of earlier writers.

As mentioned above, epic mythological narrative from Cornwall seems to have been broadly discounted by earlier scholars of Celtic Studies. Cornwall's mythological narrative base is quite clearly founded on two legends however – that of Arthuriana and that of Tristana. Throughout this volume, the reader will find numerous locations associated with the corpus related to King Arthur. Arthur will be encountered in various formats but, for the Celts of Cornwall, he will always be symbolic of resistance against Anglo-Saxon advancement in the island of Britain. Various other characters – from Uther Pendragon, Gorlois and Igraine, to Merlin and Mordred – also form a metaphorical base in which the Cornish have come to understand themselves. Over time, various versions have been re-told to re-ignite the original Celtic edge of the narrative, despite considerable embellishment from elsewhere. In effect, however, Arthur is Celtic Cornwall's key mythological cycle.

The related corpus of Tristan and Yseult is the other major mythological cycle which the territory has good claim upon. The writers Béroul and Thomas of Britain, though writing in French, have made a considerable contribution to literary construction of Celtic Cornwall. This internationalism is important to note, since European influences impacted on writing there, as well as Cornish influences spreading to the rest of Europe. More pan-Celtic in feel, moving often between the Isles of Scilly (Lyonesse?) and Cornwall, Ireland and Wales, and then on to Brittany, the Tristan narratives represent the ability of the Western Britons to travel and to take the story across Europe. It is a narrative which still engages, still fascinates and is still to be found in the cultural geography of contemporary Cornwall. Clearly, although some narratives seem to have been lost, there are also curious survivals to be found – indicators of the subject-matter of past bards and storytellers. They will also be found in this volume.

There is not the space in this book to consider all the surviving folktales and folklore which in numerous ways have a Celtic origin to them. A few are considered here, when appropriate, but such a field really requires another volume. The folklore often holds a living connection to earlier Celtic practice. There is also a revival of interest in pre-Christian, Pagan Cornwall and that revival is also noted in the pages which follow. This is another indicator of the layeredness of Celticity both in past and present Cornwall. Indeed, there have been many studies which say that the 'spirituality of place' leads the way in both attracting visitors to Cornwall, and in the indigenous Cornish people continuing to connect with their space and place in a world which seemingly seeks to stop this unique interdependence.

Music, song and dance may also be encountered in this collection. Such elements are important for most cultures in defining identity and celebrating community. Very often, the precise origins of

Furry dance at Boscastle, 1947.

song and dance elements are lost in the distant past but contribute a great deal to feelings of Celticity in Cornwall. Gradually ethno-musicologists are beginning to understand more about Cornwall's distinctive musical heritage, and have re-created past instrumentation. Bagpipes, always attached to Scottish culture, actually have a continuum in Cornwall. The mystery play cycles of Cornwall also offer a unique glimpse into Medieval Celtic musical culture, as scholars such as Mervyn Davey, Harry Woodhouse and Richard Rastall have shown. Music, song and dance are also symbiant with the many festivals of Cornwall which have Celtic origins. Some, like May Day at Padstow, appear to have had a long continuum through recent centuries. Others, such as Golowan and Montol in Penzance, have been re-invigorated over the recent years – what the archaeologist Simon James describes as 'ancient people' and 'modern invention' at work.

Sport too, is a useful thermometer into a culture's history. Cornwall has a very active sporting year – with many of its sports either having a Celtic pedigree or shaping one in the modern era. Clearly,

Cornish 'wrasslin'.

rugby, wrasslin' (Cornish-style wrestling), and hurling are the former, whilst surfing and pilot gig rowing have shown a new agenda. Sport is clearly an area where passionate Celticity is still aroused in Cornwall, not least in surfboard designs but also in the singing of the Cornish national anthem 'The Song of the Western Men' or as it is better known – 'Trelawny' - at rugby matches. There is also a delicate balance at work to ensure that Cornwall retains interest in wrasslin' and hurling, whilst embracing the global power of surfing.

We are living in an increasingly devolved Europe and Britain and, since the 1997–2010 Labour Government's reform of the political structure of the United Kingdom, there have been frequent calls for Cornwall to have its own devolved assembly. This is not a new claim. Since at least 1201, the Stannary Parliament and its jurisdiction had represented Celtic Cornwall's unique geo-political identity. More recent pressure groups and political parties such as *Cowethas Kelto-Kernuak*, *Tyr ha Tavas*, *Mebyon Kernow* and the *Cornish Nationalist Party* have also worked to secure a more devolved power for Celtic Cornwall. At the time of writing Cornwall can only gaze enviably at Wales, Scotland and Northern Ireland, with an understanding that perhaps only its small size has prevented a similar devolution of power. This volume demonstrates that the push for devolution for Celtic Cornwall is unlikely to stop.

I hope in the following gazetteer entries that the reader and the walker will be able to find something of their own Celtic Cornwall. In their own ways all of the entries build an overview of a culture and a community that, despite centuries of change, remains resolutely different, defiant and hopeful. The entries also show how Celtic Cornwall has been defined by three interconnected strands – that of its nationhood, its traditions, and its invention.

May these locations – many from the distant past, yet made of enduring stone – emerge slowly out of the mist for you.

Alan M. Kent
Lanbrebois/Probus
Truru/Truro
Kernow/Cornwall

Beltane 2012

A note on the text

Whilst every endeavour has been made to check access and availability of the locations in the gazetteer, neither the author nor the publisher can guarantee that sites included here allow public access or will remain accessible indefinitely. The reader is advised to check access before visiting and to treat historical monuments and locations with deep respect. Map references given to the sites are approximate and use of Ordnance Survey maps is recommended.

To assist the reader in making choices about the locations to visit, the following colour codes are used throughout the text:

● Holy Wells

● Playing Places and Theatres

● Hill forts, cliff castles, enclosures, field systems, fogous, round houses and courtyard houses

● Stones and Celtic crosses

● Cornish Language, Cornish Literature, Anglo-Cornish Literature, and History

● Arthuriana and Tristana

○ The Lives of the Saints

● Folklore and Legend

● Sport and Music

● Contemporary features

Cross head in St Buryan's churchyard

The Gazetteer

penwith

● *Cara Clowse in Cowse*, St Michael's Mount

SW 515299. *The Mount is located off Marazion on the eastern side of Mount's Bay.*

In the seventeenth century, St Michael's Mount was known in Cornish as *Cara Clowse in Cowse*. This means the 'grey rock in the wood' and demonstrates that the location was submerged relatively late, and that at one point it still stood in a woodland area now underwater as part of Mount's Bay. Stories still speak of parts of preserved trees being washed ashore, demonstrating the possibility of a comparatively recent rise in sea level. Such a story is of course attached to the story of Lyonesse, in which are many Arthurian and Tristan associations.

St Michael.

For many centuries, the Mount has been a tidal island dedicated to the warrior angel Saint Michael. In the Celtic territories, islands seem to have a particular affiliation with Michael – as in Mont St Michel in Normandy and *Sceilig Mhichil* [Skelling Michael] off the Kerry coast in south-west Éire. A St Michael's Chapel is also found at the top of Glastonbury Tor, and another atop Rame Head in east Cornwall. The name of St Michael was given to the island on 8 May 495 when he appeared as a vision to some fishermen. Some observers such as Hamish Miller and Paul Broadhurst suggest that a powerful St Michael ley line runs across an alignment of ancient sites in Britain. It begins at Carn Lês Boel, comes to the Mount, the Cheesewring in east Cornwall, Brentor in Devon, travelling on to Glastonbury and Avebury ending at Hopton in East Anglia. Clearly, the Mount is a very powerful icon of Celtic Cornwall – a point recognised by the German ambassador to Britain, Joachim von Ribbentrop, who planned to live at the Mount given a successful invasion of Britain by the Nazi army during the opening years of the Second World War.

● *Ictis*, St Michael's Mount

SW 515302. *The harbour is reached by the causeway at low tide. Alternatively, there are boats which regularly cross from Marazion.*

Numerous classical writers (among them Pytheas) comment on the island of Ictis off Cornwall, which was used by Greek and Gaulish traders to dock their ships in order to load tin. Presumably, considering the size of their vessels, they kept to a slightly deeper water offshore. A causeway running to an island would have made a lot of sense. Many of the legends surrounding the journey of Joseph of Arimathea and the child Christ to Cornwall (and later to Glastonbury after his crucifixion) are rooted in an understanding of Ictis. Other suggestions for the location of Ictis have also been proposed – among them St George's Island near Looe – but this seems less likely. The islands of Britain were known as the Cassiterides [the tin islands], and were thought to have been visited by the Phoenicians, and some antiquarians have connected them to Ictis in particular.

The Giant's Well.

St Michael's Mount.

● The Giant's Well, St Michael's Mount

SW 515298. *The well is found just below the 'Giant's Heart' stone.*

Five years before the island was visited by St Michael, it was St Keyne and her nephew Cadoc, who in 450, had crossed over to the Mount. The moment she set foot on the island, a spring gushed forth, and this same spring is perhaps the one now known as the Giant's Well. As well as saintly lore, the Mount has a wide range of giant-related stories, one of which says that the Mount was built by the giant Cormoran's wife Cormelian carrying stones from the mainland across to the island in her *towzer* [apron]. Cormoran is later dealt with by Jack the Giant Killer. We know that giants feature in many Celtic narratives, so it is not surprising to find them here.

● Crosses, St Michael's Mount

SW 514298. *Several crosses can be found on the Mount.*

Looking inland over St Michael's Mount.

A wheel-headed cross known as St Michael's Mount Cross is on the south-side, below the castle (SW 514298). Sins Barton Cross (SW 514298), a Lantern Cross can be observed from the National Trust's property on a rocky outcrop. Another Lantern Cross may be seen at the northern entrance of the church on St Michael's Mount (SW 514298). A cross shaft is also found at SW 514298.

● Treryn Dinas Cliff Castle, Treen

SW 397222. *Treen is found off the B3315 where there is a large car park. Follow the track south through the fields to the site.*

The headland is a spectacular site to explore. There are both inner and outer defences, with another line of defence at the narrowest neck of the headland. The major phase of construction is generally noted as being from the Iron Age. On the middle pinnacle of the headland sits the *Logan* or 'rocking stone'. Treryn Dinas means 'farm by the cliff castle'.

A Victorian visitor to Treryn Dinas attempts to rock the Logan stone.

Treryn Dinas aerial view.

● The Minack Theatre, Porthcurno

SW 387220. *Climb the hill at Porthcurno and turn left into the car park of the theatre.*

The Minack theatre is an iconic representation of Cornish 'difference', developed in tandem with the wider Celto-Cornish revival of the early twentieth century. It was founded by the Derbyshire-born Rowena Cade (1893–1983), who moved to Cornwall during the First World War. After her family built a house at Minack [*Minack* meaning 'rocky' or 'stony place'], and following an early in-land production at Crean of *A Midsummer Night's Dream* with the Penzance Orchestral Society, Cade facilitated a production of *The Tempest* at the site in 1932. This production allowed her to see the potential of the venue, looking as it does out on the headland hill fort of Treryn Dinas, and close to the beach at Porthcurno ['cove of horns'].

Celtic inspired design at the Minack Theatre.

The Minack Theatre from the air.

Premier performance at the Minack, the cast of The Tempest, *1932.*

The Minack theatre.

The Tempest has often been read as a play about English colonial oppression of the 'Celtic' periphery, so it was appropriate that this was the first production at the site.

Carved – often with the tip of a screwdriver into wet concrete – the architecture of the theatre is much inspired by Cornwall's Celtic heritage, and throughout the site are found Celtic knotwork, spirals and plaits. This work was completed throughout the middle of twentieth-century by Cade, and her co-workers Billy Rawlings and Charles Thomas Angove. The theatre is thus almost a combination of a classical fifth-century Athenian theatre set within Celtic space.

The venue has presented a number of Celtic-themed dramas throughout the years. In 1939, the Warwick Players presented John Masefield's version of *Tristan and Isolt*, while in 1951, Nora Ratcliff's version of the same story was played. Ratcliff's *Arthur of Britain* was developed in 1953, while in August 1955, the Cornish Religious Drama Fellowship presented the story of *St Ursula*. The story of St Ursula is one of several 'lost' Cornish narratives – and it is very likely that in the Medieval period, a stage version did exist in the territory. The cult of St Ursula was certainly large. The life of the saint apparently involved a pan-European journey of some eleven thousand Cornish virgins to Cologne. The Minack was thus offering continuity back to this period.

Other Arthurian-themed plays were produced in the 1980s and 1990s, as well as folklore-based work such as *Tregeagle* (almost a Cornish variant of the Faust theme) produced on several occasions by Kneehigh Theatre. More recently, the venue has hosted contemporary theatre companies such as Bish Bash Bosh Productions who are resoundingly influenced by Cornwall's Celtic heritage. Their plays presented at the Minack Theatre include *A Mere Interlude* (2010) – based on a short story by Thomas Hardy, and Alan M. Kent's *Surfing Tommies* (2011), with the company committed to *Gwaryjy*

Kenedhlek rag Kernow [a National Theatre for Cornwall]. The Minack Theatre's season lasts from May to September, though the theatre is open to the public throughout the year.

● Coastal Path from Porthgwarra to Land's End

SW 373215 to SW 343252. *The cliff path is well-signposted.*

There is poetry in the landscape here; the place names retaining their Cornish language origins. Begin walking at *Porthgwarra* ['high up cove'] and progress to *Tol-Pedn-Penwith* ['the holed headland of Penwith'], then meet *Carn Guthensbras* ['outcrop by the large sunken reef']. *Ardenswah* meanwhile, means 'silver stream' with *Zawn Kellys* translating to 'lost chasm'. Particularly spectacular are the lichen-encrusted rock masses found at *Carn Barra* [Bread Carn], which resemble loaves of bread. *Nanjizal* is a beautiful cove. It means 'low valley'. *Carn Lês Boel* translates to 'ruined fort at an axe-shaped outcrop' and not surprisingly, this is the site of an Iron Age cliff castle. *Trevean* Farm holds a ruined farmhouse with outbuildings but one can almost hear traditional Cornish language still being spoken at such as spot. Further inland is *Raftra* Farm, where the nineteenth-century folklorist William Bottrell was born.

● The Cornish Chough, Porthgwarra to Land's End

SW 373215 to SW 343252. *Choughs can sometimes be seen in this area.*

The Chough [*Pyrrhocorax pyrrhocorax*] is a member of the crow family, with a distinctive red beak and legs. It has an excitable, high-pitched call which sounds like 'chi-ow' which is probably from where it gains its English-language name. In Cornish it is known as *Palores-palor,* in Cornish being 'to dig'. The chough is a significant symbol of Celtic Cornwall. It is included in the Cornish coat of arms, along with the miner and the fisherman, and it is said that King Arthur was transformed into a chough when he died; the red beak and feet representing his bloody and violent end. The chough was often caught and eaten by Cornish people – so in effect cannibalising their own identity – and consequently their numbers declined significantly in the nineteenth century. Past over-eating, egg-collecting and a decline in habitat meant that the last pair nested in Cornwall in 1952. The chough was extinct in Cornwall until 2001, when three took up residence in West Cornwall. In 2002 a pair began nesting and a clutch of eggs hatched. The Lizard now also has a breeding community. The chough's survival is dependent on having suitable feeding habitats and, in turn, this is reliant on traditional forms of livestock grazing on coastal pasture.

Miguel de Cervantes Saavedra (1547–1616), the Spanish novelist, writes about the associations between the Cornish Chough and King Arthur in his epic work, *Don Quixote:*

'Have you not read,' cried Don Quixote, 'the Annals and History of Britain, where are recorded the famous deeds of King Arthur, who according to an ancient tradition in that Kingdom never died but was turned into a crow by enchantment and shall one day resume his former shape and recover his Kingdom again.

In the ceremonies of the bards of the Gorseth of Cornwall, this same legend is extolled during Section XIII of the order of service where the Deputy Grand Bard declaims the following:

An als whath Arthur a with,
Yn corf Palores yn few;

Chair ladder rock, along the coastal path.

The chough.

Y Wlas whath Arthur a bew,
Myghtern a ve hag a vyth.

[Still Arthur watches our shore,
In guise of a Chough there flown;
His Kingdom he keeps his own,
Once King, to be King once more.]

The rest of the bardic order respond with *Nyns yu marow Myghtern Arthur!* [King Arthur is not dead!].

St Levan's Church, near Porthcurno

SW 381223. *From the Minack Theatre, follow the road south-west to St Levan's church. There is a car park on the hill above the churchyard.*

St Levan – or more accurately Selevan (probably a Byrthonic Celtic form of Solomon), was a warrior-prince of the late fifth century who is likely to have hailed from Cornwall, although some conflicting evidence points to an Irish origin. He is the brother of St Just and the father of St Cuby. Selevan first came to live at Bodellan before becoming associated with this location. Many stories have come down to us about Selevan. So it was said, Selevan only ate one fish a day, but refused to fast, even on a Sunday. One day, a local woman by the name of Joanna, who was working in her garden, soundly chastised him for putting to sea on the Sabbath in order to catch fish. His response to this was to call Joanna a fool, and that picking herbs was just as sinful as fishing. The result of this story is that to this day, no child born in the parish is baptised Joanna.

Bench end at St Levan's Church.
The Grim and Happy Fools.

St Levan's Church.

Other stories persist: once, aiming to feed his sister and her child, the saint caught a chad, but deciding it was too small he threw it back. He kept catching the same fish on three occasions so reluctantly had to feed his extended family with it. When his nephew took a bite of the fish, he immediately choked upon it. Selevan took this as a sign of retribution from God that the saint had been dissatisfied with what his Maker had provided. Until recently, the bony chad was still known locally as the 'chuck-cheeld' [choke child]. Curiously enough, on one of the highly ornate bench-ends within the church are carved two fish – possibly chads or 'chuck-cheelds'.

The church itself remains intimately Medieval in feel. Much of the rood screen survives containing fantastical images of wyverns (a winged two-footed dragon) associated with wickedness, disease and pestilence. Panels of the rood screen also show numerous instruments of the Passion: the Flail, the Pillar, the Hammer, the Spear and the Crown of Thorns (wooden representations of images that would else-

Cornish language inscription at St Levan.

where in Medieval Celtic Cornwall have been presented in Passion plays). Other bench-ends include Alpha and Omega, a Grim Fool and a Happy Fool, facing heads and a Santiago de Compostela pilgrim. The pilgrim is an important image – representing as he does the pan-Celtic route from Cornwall to Brittany and through the mainland of France and Spain, or otherwise the trip across the Bay of Biscay to Ferrol, or La Coruña. Galicia, if not having a surviving Celtic language, at least has many folkloric and musical traditions (bagpipes among them), with similarities to Brittany and Cornwall.

On the parclose screen on the north side of the chapel, in the 1930s-constructed lower screen, an inscription in Cornish runs along its length:

Rag carensa dew ha rag cov sans selevan cryst agan bara terrys ragon ny.
[For the love of God, and in memory of St Selevan, Christ our bread broken for us.]

Although clearly written in a form of revived Cornish of this period, the author of these words is not known. It is, however, a powerful reminder of the on-going nature of Celtic Christianity in this part of Cornwall.

In the churchyard, is to be found a very large boulder, from which it is said, the saint used to preach. Legend says that one day Selevan hit the rock with his fist, splitting it in two, and supposedly made the following prediction:

When with panniers astride,
A packhorse one can ride
Through St Levan's stone,
The world will be done.

Chuck-cheeld bench end.

Thankfully, given the size of the rock and the slow speed in which the crack has moved, it is unlikely that the world will end in the near future. However, the boulder is a powerful centre of energy and may have once been the location of pagan ritual; Christianity later imposing its faith on this site.

The wheel-headed cross, St Levan.

● Crosses, St Levan's churchyard, near Porthcurno

SW 380221, SW 380222, SW 380222, SW 378223, SW 382223.

There are numerous crosses in and around St Levan's church. Their origins are mixed. The main wheel-headed cross in the churchyard (SW 380221) dates from the period of incorporation into Anglo-Saxon 'England', but there are numerous other Celtic-inspired more modern crosses in the churchyard. A wheel-headed wayside cross (probably more 'Celtic' in origin – SW 380222) is found at the north-east entrance to the churchyard and close to this is a mutilated cross slab or wheel-headed cross (SW 380222), on which is a crucifix figure. On route to Ardensaweth (SW 378223) is to be found a wheel-headed wayside cross, and at Rosepletha Farm (SW 382223), another cross of this type can be seen.

● St Levan's Well, near Porthcurno

SW 382218. *The well is found along a footpath going down from St Levan's Church towards the cove at Porthchapel.*

The well is not as spectacular as some others in Cornwall, it being a fairly simple stone structure. Folklore tells us that it was famed for the relief of toothache and sore eyes. Just below the well are the remains of a saint's cell. It was custom for any sufferers of the above conditions to take water from the well, and then perhaps spend the night in the cell, resting and recuperating. The cell has a spectacular view of the Channel and the headland of *Pedn-men-an-mere* ['the great stone headland']. Presumably, the cove is named after this small cell or chapel.

St Levan's well.

● John of Chyanhor by Nicholas Boson, St Levan

SW 378248. *The house of Chyanhor is presently marked by a thatched cottage located between Bottoms and Trebehor.*

Nicholas Boson (1624-1708) was born in Newlyn and he was a merchant, writer and Cornish literary and language scholar. Boson was forbidden to speak Cornish at home and it was only when he had to negotiate business with local fishermen that he could use Cornish. Between 1674 and 1708 he wrote *A Few Words about Cornish* and sometime in the 1660s, *The Duchess of Cornwall's Progresse to see the Land's end and to visit the mount*, both in English and Cornish. One of the few surviving prose texts in Cornish, *John of Chyanhor,* is a morality tale, giving advice to the reader and listener on how best to live. The story begins at a house called Chyanhor [the ram's house] in the parish of St Leven, but then moves further east, finally returning through St Hilary Downs, Penzance, Coose Cornwilly near St Buryan, and back to St Levan once more. It begins thus:

1. *En termen ez passiez thera trigaz en St. Leven, dên ha bennen en teller kreiez Tshei an hÿr.*
2. *Ha an huêl a kÿdhaz skent: Ha medh an dên dhÿ e urêg; me a vedn mÿz dha huillaz huêl dhÿ îl; ha huei el dendel 'gÿz bounaz ÿbma.*
3. *Kibmiaz têg ev kÿmeraz, ha pel dha êst ev a travaliaz, ha uar an dûadh e ' ryg dhÿz dhÿ tshei tîak; ha 'ryg huillaz ena huêl dha 'uîl.*

St Levan's cell.

The view from St Levan's Well.

[1. In the time that is past, there were living in St Levan a man and a woman in the place called Chyanhor.
2. And the work fell scarce. And said the man to his wife, "I will go to seek work to do, and you can earn your living here."
3. Fair leave he took, and far eastwards he travelled, and at last he came to the house of a farmer, and did seek there work to do.]

John is given three points of advice by the farmer he works for: take care not to leave the old road for a new road, take care not to lodge in the house of an old man married to a young woman, and be struck twice before striking once. This advice allows him to outwit robbers, prove the innocence of some accused murderers, and learn that while he has been away, his wife has given birth to a son. The story is also known across Europe as *The Servant's Good Counsels*, and as Brian Murdoch has argued, the tale may have links with the eleventh-century Latin poem from Tegersee in Germany called the *Ruodlieb*, thus suggesting that Cornish was used for the transmission of wider folk culture. Boson learnt the story from one of his family's servants. Boson's original version is lost, and only a few verses survived written down by his son, John. Fortunately however, Edward Lhuyd transcribed the work in his own phonetic version of Cornish. Based on the tithe map of 1838, where there is a field marked Chyanhor, the 'imagined' home of John used to exist close to this spot. It is presently marked by the thatched cottage, probably built sometime after this date.

⬤ Ithell Colquhoun, Lamorna Valley

SW 447245. *Drive on the B3315 from Newlyn through Sheffield. Just before Boleigh Farm, turn left into Lamorna Valley.*

Ithell Colquhoun (1906–1988) was an artist, poet, novelist and practising magician who became highly attuned to the Celticity of Cornwall. Colquhoun was born in India of British parents and received her formal training in art at the Slade School in London. Joining a group of experimental painters in London, her art took the direction of surrealism, influenced, for example by the need for automatism. In her writing and research Colquhoun developed ideas surrounding what we might now call Goddess Spirituality, and became a member of several occult societies including the Ordo Templi Orientis, the Order of the Keltic cross, various Druidical orders and a branch of the Theosophical Society.

During the 1940s, she spent more and more time in Cornwall, initially purchasing a primitive dwelling in the Lamorna Valley which could only be inhabited during the summer months. She then moved to a permanent studio in Paul in 1959. Her book *The Living Stones* (1957) is both an autobiographical account of how she came to live in Cornwall but also set the agenda of a sacred landscape in the territory, profoundly influenced by Celtic notions of space and place. Here, she found a kinship with the Celto-Cornish landscape, viewing stone circles, holy wells and other landscape features as 'geysers of energy'. *The Living Stones* became a profoundly influential book for other writers on the sacred geometry of Celtic Cornwall including John Michell (1933-2009) in his *The Old Stones of Land's End* (1974) and *The New View Over Atlantis* (1983).

Celtic cross near Lamorna.

⬤ Modern Celtic Cross, cliffs, near Lamorna

SW 449238. *The cross is found a short distance along the coastal footpath from the car park beside the harbour.*

The tradition of locating crosses in spectacular locations continues here, with the cross looking out to Carn du.

● Lamorna Artistic Colony, Lamorna

SW 452242. *Complete a walk around the harbour.*

In the late nineteenth and early twentieth centuries, Lamorna became popular with artists of the Newlyn School. It is particularly associated with the artist S.J. 'Lamorna' Birch, Alfred Munnings, Laura Knight and Harold Knight. Many of the paintings of this group capture a romanticised vision of on-going Celtic culture and landscape. Several paintings by the group are to be found in the Penlee Museum and Art Gallery in Penzance (SW 469301). The granite quarries are still visible on the eastern side of the harbour. Granite from here was taken to build St Buryan Church. The host community is also imagined in Anglo-Cornish song in the popular ballad 'Lamorna'. Although in English it nevertheless reflects the Celtic isolation of this tiny village, not to mention the attraction of the girl in question! Albert Square probably refers to Albert Square in Penzance:

'The Bathing Pool' by the Newlyn School artist S.J. 'Lamorna' Birch.

'twas down in Albert Square,
I never shall forget,
Her eyes they shone like diamonds
And the evening it was wet, wet, wet;
And her hair hung down in curls,
She was a charming rover,
And we roved all night
In the pale moonlight
Away down to Lamorna.

Lamorna Valley, late 1800s

Keigwin House today.

● The Keigwin House [or Arms], Mousehole

SW 469264. *Close to the harbour, past the The Ship Inn public house.*

In the seventeenth century, one of the most important scholars of the Cornish language was John Keigwin (1641–c.1710), the grandson of the Squire Jenkyn Keigwin killed by the Spanish in the notorious raid on Mousehole, Newlyn and Penzance in 1595. Keigwin thus came from a Cornish-speaking family and was one of a number of writers and scholars who foresaw the rapid decline of the Cornish language in the Early Modern period, and wished to prevent further loss.

Keigwin's father Martin was a merchant who had spent time in Brittany and Wales, and thus had knowledge of these Celtic languages too. His mother was Elizabeth Scawen, the sister of another important Cornish writer and translator, William Scawen. In 1678 Scawen had been passed a copy of the passion poem, *Pascon Agan Arluth [The Passion of Our Lord]* and asked John and his father to translate it. Keigwin completed the work in 1682. In 1693 he then began translating the Helston-based play, *Gwreans an Bys [The Creation of the World]*. Keigwin was supposedly a master of five languages (Greek, Latin, Hebrew. French and Cornish) and on the request of Sir Jonathan Trelawny, the Bishop of Exeter, had been passed three Cornish manuscripts which he duly translated in 1695. These were the three plays of *Ordinalia*. In a brief poem entitled 'On the Death of Mr. John Keigwin' another writer of this phase, John Boson, was to observe:

> *En Tavaz Greka, Lathen ha'n Hebra,*
> *En Frenkock ha Carnoack desks dha,*
> *Gen ol an Gormola Brez ve dotha*
> *Garres ew ni, ha Neidges Ewartha.*

Keigwin House, Mousehole 1880s

[In the Greek, Latin and Hebrew language,
In French and Cornish well-learned,
With all the praise of mind was his
We are left while he has flown upwards.]

Keigwin also translated into Cornish Charles I's famous *Letter of Thanks* to the Cornish people for their support during the Civil War, the English language version of which can still be found in several churches in Cornwall. The Keigwin House [or Arms] is now a private house, but it was the residence of this famous family who spoke and saved the Cornish language.

Merlin's Island, Mousehole.

● Merlin Island, Mousehole

SW 474263. *The island is directly opposite the main harbour entrance.*

Known now as St Clement's Isle, this island used to be called Merlin Island. It is obviously the inspiration for the Cornish-language place-name of the harbour at Mousehole: *Porthynys* [island harbour]. A supposedly ancient Cornish-language prophecy is associated with the island: *Ewra teyre a war meane Merlyn, Art lesky Penzanz ha Newlyn* [They shall land on the Rock of Merlin, Who shall burn Paul, Penzance and Newlyn]. This prophecy is forever attached to the Spanish attack on West Cornwall in 1595, and though purported to be ancient, it was probably devised much closer to that date. The isle's original name of Merlin is probably a romantic interpretation of a possible hermit-like existence on the rock for Early Modern imaginings of the often pan-Brythonic prophet and enchanter.

Dolly Pentreath memorial plaque.

● Dolly Pentreath memorial plaque, Mousehole

SW 469264. *This is located a short distance from the Keigwin Arms, back down to the west side of the harbour.*

Dorothy or Dolly Pentreath (1692–1777) is one of the most famous of the apparently final generation of Cornish speakers in the eighteenth century, though there is now plenty of evidence that Cornish continued to be spoken well into in the nineteenth century. Dolly is something of an iconic figure however, and when Daines Barrington (1727–1800), the writer, antiquary and lawyer came to Cornwall in 1768 looking for traces of the Cornish language, he came to meet her. Apparently Dolly swore at him several times 'in a language which sounded very like Welsh' and initially he became convinced she was the last surviving speaker. Dolly claimed that she never spoke any English until she was twenty years old. This may have been the case, since she worked in the fishing community as a fish-seller or jowster, married to a Jeffrey. Towards the end of her life, she made a living by fortune telling and chattering in Cornish to anyone who would pay her to do so. She claimed to be 102 at the end of her life, but in fact, she was just 85 years old. One of her residences in the village is marked by a plaque. It reads 'Here lived Dolly Pentreath, one of the last speakers of the Cornish Language as her native tongue. Died Dec. 1777'.

● Cornish language, Mousehole

SW 471264. *For a good view of the village, walk along the eastern wall of the harbour to the 'mousehole' entrance to the harbour.*

A number of other Cornish writers and speakers are associated with the village. Oliver Pender lived in Mousehole in around 1711, and he corresponded with William Gwavas (1676–1741). Gwavas's family originally came from near Sithney, but he was born at Huntingfield Hall in Suffolk, becoming a London barrister. Gwavas corresponded with a number of speakers in West Cornwall in order to improve his own understanding of the language. Pender wrote back explaining how he had been busy with the pilchard industry and also commenting critically on the work of the Welsh antiquarian Edward Lhuyd. Around 1728, Gwavas also wrote a small poem to his Mousehole neighbour Nicholas Pentreath – probably a relative of Dolly Pentreath - about the importance of paying tithes:

Dolly Pentreath, from an engraving dated 1781.

Contravack Nicholas Pentreath,	[Neighbour Nicholas Pentreath,
Pa reffo why doaz war an dreath	When you come onto the beach
Gen puscas, comero whye weeth	With fish, take care
Tha geel cumpas, hedna ew feer;	to do fairly what is wise
Ha cowz meaz, Dega, Dega,	and speak out, 'Tithe! Tithe!'
Enna ew oll goz dega gweer.	That is your true tithe.]

Another famous piece of Cornish language writing comes from Mousehole. This is a letter by William Bodinar written in 1776. Bodinar was a fisherman who died in 1789, and he may well have been paid to write this letter for Daines Barrington. It is widely regarded as the last surviving example of 'native' Cornish prose. We know from the writer William Pryce that Bodinar was a 'very old man' and that in a conversation with him, the fisherman explained that how in Morlaix he was able to make himself understood by Breton speakers. This says much about the on-going similarities between the Cornish and Breton languages.

William Bodinar's Letter

Bluth vee eus egance a pemp. Thearra vee dean boadjack an poscas. Me rig desky Cornoack termen me vee mawe. Me vee de more gen care vee a pemp dean moy en cock. Me rig scantlower clowes eden ger Sowsneck cowes en cock rag sythen warebar. No riga vee biscath gwellas lever Cornoack. Me deskey Cornoack mous da more gen tees coath. Nag es moye vel pager pe pemp en dreav nye ell clappia Cornoack leben, poble coath pager egance blouth Cornoack ewe oll neceaves gen poble younk.

[My age is three score and five. I am a poor fisherman. I learned Cornish when I was a boy. I went to sea with my father and five other men in a boat. I hardly heard a word of English spoken in the boat for as much as a week together. I never saw a Cornish book. I learned Cornish going to sea with old men. There are no more than four or five in the village who can speak Cornish now, old people four score years old. Cornish is all forgot by the young folk.]

'Tom Bawcock's Eve'.

Tom Bawcock's Eve, Mousehole

SW 470264. *The procession ends on the beach, seen only on 23 December each year.*

Although Cornish is no longer operating as a widespread community language in Mousehole, the village still has a very strong sense of Celtic identity. This is borne out in a contemporary festival called Tom Bawcock's Eve. The festival has its roots in an oral narrative about a fisherman named Tom Bawcock, who during a period of famine in the community because of bad weather, eventually sails out to bring home seven sorts of fish, thus saving the community from famine. Various origins for the festival have been suggested, and the narrative may have its origins in Cornish-language oral narrative or a more modern pedigree. The scholar and folklorist Robert Morton Nance learnt about the festival in the 1920s and wrote a Cornu-English song 'Tom Bawcock's Eve' – which has come to be traditionally sung at the event:

> *A merry plaace, you may believe*
> *wuz Mouzel 'pon Tom Bawcock's Eve.*
> *To be there then who wudn' wesh,*
> *To sup o' sibm sorts of fesh!*

In the late twentieth and early twenty-first century, interest in the festival has been enhanced by the popular children's book *The Mousehole Cat* (1990), written by Antonio Barber and illustrated by Nicola Bayley. The festival has evolved to include willow and paper lanterns built in the shape of Tom Bawcock, his boat and fish. The night-time festival now culminates in the release of the lanterns on to the harbour water and into the air. A popular food associated with the festival is star-gazy pie, a fish pie which has the heads of the fish poking through the crust, 'gazing at the stars'.

St Paul Church, Paul

SW 464271. *In the middle of the village of Paul.*

Saint Paul or Pol is one of the major Celtic saints associated with both Cornwall and Brittany. A life of the saint was written by a Breton monk in 884, drawing on an earlier account which had already embellished

Dolly Pentreath memorial.

his life. Apparently Paul, surnamed Aurelian, was the son of a Welsh chieftain named Perphirius and was educated at the monastic centre of Saint Ilitud at Llantwit Major. He responded to a call to travel across the sea and so headed south to Brittany via Cornwall. His sister Saint Sativola was living in West Cornwall, leading a life of prayer with other women, but apparently they had no residence. Accordingly, it was Paul who found for them an area of dry land on the edge of Newlyn. This is possibly near the village of Paul, which holds his name. In Brittany, Paul was given the Island of Batz, located close to Roscoff and the town of St Pol de Léon, where he was consecrated as bishop. On the Island of Batz, he was said to have expelled a dragon or 'certain serpent', but he also had a practical nature in helping to found Christian Brittany. The cathedral at St Pol de Léon dedicated to the saint, may have helped inspire the design for Truro Cathedral, part of the Cornish revival's 'Breton gaze'.

● Dolly Pentreath Memorial, Paul

SW 464271. *In the middle of the village, the memorial is embedded in the churchyard wall.*

Although Dolly is associated with Mousehole, she actually originated from nearby Paul. In 1850 the scholar Louis-Lucian Bonaparte (1813–1891), a nephew of the more famous Napoleon, erected a granite memorial to her in the wall of the churchyard at Paul. Bonaparte had come to settle in Britain, and had become an expert on the minority languages of Europe. His special interest was Basque, but he was also greatly intrigued by the surviving remnants of the Brythonic language of Cornish. Bonaparte completed the task with the help of the Reverend John Garrett, the vicar of St Paul. The Memorial holds a Cornish-language translation of Exodus, XX, 12: '*Gwra perthi de taz ha de mam: mal de dythow bethenz hyr war an tyr neb, an arleth de dew ryes dees*' ['Honour thy Father and thy Mother: that thy days may be long, upon the land which the Lord thy God giveth thee']. The memorial is constructed as an echo of earlier Celtic wheel-head crosses. Another tribute was written to Dolly around 1777 by a mining engineer from Truro named Thomson (or Thompson):

Coth Doll Pentreath can ha deau
Marrow ha kledyz ed Paul pleû
Na ed en Egloz, gan pobel braz
Bes ed Egloz-hay, coth Dolly es.

[Old Doll Pentreath, aged 102,
Deceased and bured in Paul parish too,
Not in the Church with people great and high,
But in the churchyard doth old Dolly lie.]

Icon of Sancreed holding a piglet

● Sancreed church, Sancreed

SW 422294, *On the A30 turn right at Drift and head toward Sancreed. The church is located in the middle of the village.*

Sancreed church has a very ancient feel to it. The saint associated with the area was probably called Sancred. Very little is known of his life, but a Medieval story persists that he accidentally killed his father, and as part of his remorse and penance, went to work as a swineherd. Celtic saints have a habit of leading such lives and are often linked to particular animals. Boars and pigs also have a considerable presence in early Britain. In a nook in the south church porch is a small, modern terracotta image of the saint cradling a piglet.

Detail from the mss Pascon Agan Arluth.

● *Pascon Agan Arluth*, **Sancreed Church**

SW 422294. *The church is in the middle of the village.*

Pascon Agan Arluth is one of the central texts of the surviving canon of Cornish language literature. It is variously also called *The Cornish Passion Poem*, *The Poem of Mount Calvary* and *The Passion of Our Lord*. The name of the author or authors is not known. Several later manuscripts of the poem exist, but the oldest and best known is the one presently held in the British Library (MS Harl, 1782) which is said to have been found in Sancreed church. This manuscript dates from c.1450 though it is thought to be a copy of an older original.

Scholarship now generally believes that the manuscript pre-dates that of the *Ordinalia* and that it may have actually provided the writers of that text some of their material for the second play, *Passio Christi* [The Passion]. Written in seven-syllabled lines assembled into eight-line stanzas with alternating rhymes, the work is proof of the skill of poets of this period. The manuscript also includes a number of illustrations – something rare in Cornish language texts. One of the leading scholars of the poem, Brian Murdoch, describes the work as 'not a versified Gospel as such… but rather a treatment of the Passion as the central incident in the divine economy of fall and redemption'. For the Celtic Medieval mind, reading such a work probably facilitated individual salvation whether read aloud for an audience or as a solitary experience. Sancreed was obviously a significant literary and theatrical space and place, considering the survival of this manuscript as well as information about the nearby *plen-an-gwarry*. The text below gives an example of the poem. This passage is based on Matthew 27:51 and Mark 15:33 when at the time of Christ's death, there was an eclipse and an earthquake. Meanwhile, graves opened and the bodies of the saints rose:

Nango hanter dyth yn wlas	[Then at midday or after
po moy del yma scryfis	in the country, as it is written
dorgris esa ha lughas	there was an earthquake and lightning
han tewolgow kekyffyrs	and darkness also
veyll an tempell a squardyas	The veil of the temple was torn
yn tre dew zen dor cozys	in two and fell to the ground.
ena yn weth y torras	And there also broke
en veyn o creff ha calys	stones that were strong and hard.]

For a people used to a landscape of stones that were 'strong and hard', this must have been a terrifying, yet very real prospect.

● Wheel-headed crosses, Sancreed churchyard

SW 420293.

There are two tall wheel-headed crosses in the churchyard here. The first (SW 420293), stands to the right of the south porch of the parish church. A triumphant Christ with arms outstretched and a halo is found on the head of the cross. Two panels are found on the shaft. The decoration has been erased on the top panel, but the lower one features eight interlacing knots. The name Runho appears as an inscription in a small panel. Runho may well have been the mason responsible for the carving. Other zoomorphic work on the cross may be dated to the 10th century. A second cross is stands beside the path on the south side of the churchyard (SW 420293). Another Christ with arms outstretched can be seen on the head of the cross. The sides of the monument display zig-zag designs in a triangular pattern.

● Wayside crosses, Sancreed

SW 420293 and adjacent

Known as the Anjarden Cross, this wheel-headed wayside cross was moved in 1914 to its present location overlooking the road (SW 420293). Another called the Sellan Cross is found nearby in the north of the steps leading to the new churchyard, and a further wheel-headed cross is to be found in the western boundary wall. This is called Trannack Cross, since it was found on the local Trannack estate in 1887.

Sancreed wheel headed crosses.

● Playing Place, Sancreed

SW 419295. *Walk northward up the hill from the church. The former playing place is now under the houses of 'Beacon Estate'.*

According to Peter Pool's study of the *Penheleg* manuscript, dated 1580, there were miracle plays which were performed at Sancreed. An observer notes that 'It fortuned within a while after there was a miable [miracle?] play at Sankras Parish. Divers men came to the play…'. This disposition also notes that some time between 1498 and 1505 – when the miracle play culture seemed to be fully operational – a murder took place during the performance, committed by a Mr Trevrye. Events surrounding the authorities dealing with the murder were left until the performance had ended, which suggests that the play (possibly a life of St Sancreed) was quite engaging. The fact that the observer of this event (a Mr Veal) who was then aged around ten, called the parish Sankras, suggests that Cornish language was still being used at this date. On the north-western edge of the Beacon Estate a curve in a hedge is still visible, indicating the enclosure of the Round. A field to the west was once known as Plain Gwarry.

● William Rowe, Sancreed

SW 419295. *Rowe would have known the Playing Place at Sancreed.*

William Rowe [or *Wella Kerew*] originally of Bojewyn in St Just-in-Penwith, and later of Hendra, Sancreed, was a farmer who was interested in helping to save the Cornish language. He began c.1675 a set of Biblical translations – among which was Genesis III. Rowe also made translations of St Matthew II 1-20 and IV. The British Museum holds the religious writings of Rowe, copied from the originals by the Reverend Henry Ustick, the Vicar of Breage. Rowe's Cornish tended to follow that of previous generations, but according to Nance, he wrote 'his Cornish in an English spelling usually given to place-names'. Ustick, whose Cornish was weaker than that of Rowe, copied a few letters incorrectly (corrected in the brief sample here):

1. Lebben an hagar-breeve o moy foulze a well onen vthell an Bestaz an gweale a reege an Arleth Deew Geele: Ha e a lavarraze tha an Vennen. Eah! reeg Deew lawle, Chen a raze debre a kenevrah gwethan an Looar?
2. Ha an venen a lavarraz tha an hagar-breeve, ni a ell debre a thore oll an gweth an loar.
3. Boz thort an gwethan a ez en crease an Loar, Deew a lavarraz why nara debre anothe na narewa e thotcha, lez why a varaw.

[1. Now the serpent was more subtle than any beast of the field which the Lord God had made. And he said unto the woman, Yea, hath God said, Ye shall not eat of every tree in the garden?
2. And the women said unto the serpent, We may eat of the fruit of the trees of the garden.
3. But of the fruit of the tree which is in the midst of the garden, God hath said, Ye shall not eat of it, neither shall ye touch it, lest ye die.]

In 1908 a pamphlet was published in Boston, Massachusetts which was titled 'The Worthies of Pow Kernow: Memories of the Kereve [*Kerew*] Family also Select Works of the Same'. The pamphlet contained a history of the Rowe family back to William, and was published by John Rowe Needham in the United States of America. The manuscript is now lost but is thought to have contained some of William's works. The Rowe family in America might have formed the correspondents of William Gwavas, and raises the distinct possibility of Cornish being spoken there.

● Chapel Downs Well, Sancreed

SW 418293. *The well is located by following a footpath opposite the church.*

For most observers, Chapel Downs Well is one of the most magical places in West Cornwall, and the well site is particularly unspoilt, nestled in a holly and pine grove. The well was 'rediscovered' quite late (in 1879), so this may be one reason for its aura. Unlike many other wells in Cornwall, there is relatively little folklore associated with it, but in the contemporary era, the site has been much claimed by both Christian and Neo-Pagan groups. A spectacular set of *jowds* [rags] or clouties decorates the well, and offerings are often left. Put in context with the other activity at Sancreed, and the observer will realise that the area is a centre-point of Celticity over a number of centuries.

Chapel Downs Well.

Chapel Downs Well near Sancreed.

● Carn Euny courtyard houses and fogou, near Sancreed

SW 403288. *Follow the signs from the A30 at Drift. A narrow lane leads to the car park just below the site. Care is advised on this lane.*

For many observers, this location is indicative of Celtic Cornwall, though as a site it has been occupied since the Bronze Age. Here can be seen four connected courtyard houses, which sometimes feel as if the residents have just vacated. In each of the courtyards, a central roof post support hole can be seen and there are numerous rooms and chambers. There are two spectacular elements to the site: the first is a long fogou with a creep passage leading to the surface. Secondly, off this is a corbelled underground room, holding on its walls luminescent moss. The inhabitants here would have been farmers and the village seems to have been abandoned around 400.

● Chapel Euny Wells, near Carn Euny, Sancreed

SW 399288. *The two wells are located close to Carn Euny settlement on either side of the path.*

Saint Euny or Uny was the brother of Saint Ia and Saint Erc (Erth) and therefore one of the Irish missionaries led by Gwinear, who landed in the Hayle estuary. The proliferation of dedications to him would indicate that he was a man of some influence. Traditionally, it is said that his hair was shaved at the front though he wore the back of it in long tresses down to his waist. He was said to have carried a hand bell and was clothed in white robes, perhaps showing druidical affiliation. As well as the parish of Sancreed, he is also associated with Crowan and Redruth (where he is patron saint). In his *Popular Romances of the West of England* (1865) Robert Hunt (1807–1887) wrote about the two wells' healing properties: 'On the first three Wednesdays in May, children suffering from mesenteric [intestinal] disease are dipped three times, against the Sun, and dragged three times round the well over the grass in the same direction'.

● Caer Brân hill fort, Sancreed

SW 408290. *The site lies between Carn Euny and Grumbla.*

This is an Iron Age hill fort which contains the remnants of a single round house. It appears to have inner and outer defence embankments.

● St Buryan Church, St Buryan

SW 409257. *The church is in the middle of the village on the B3283.*

St Buryan Church c.1890.

According to the early *Medieval Exeter Calendar* or *Martyrology*, Buryan or Beryan appears to have been an Irish maiden, through whose prayers the son of King Gerent was cured of paralysis. Typical of the Celtic church in Cornwall, a Celtic monastery had grown up at St Buryan, the surrounds of the churchyard, probably matching the original enclosure. King Athelstan (c.893–939) established a different style of religious house during his rule, in which a community of priests and canons lived, studied and worked together (the eventual model for the proto-university College of St Thomas at Glasney near Penryn). The likelihood however, is that the original monastery was founded on the site of the young Irish maiden saint. Veryan on the Roseland peninsula to the east, may also take its name from Buryan or Beryan.

The observations of scholars such as Thomas Taylor (1858–1938), author of *The Celtic Christianity of Cornwall* (1916), have been crucial in helping us to understand the earliest Christian communities in Cornwall. Taylor likens them to 'pioneer settlements' probably built on existing pagan sites. He believes they were most likely to consist of congeries of 'beehive-style' cells made of wood. The whole monastery must have looked very much like a farmstead. Charles Thomas has revealed in various publications that there was in fact, little evidence for Christianity in Romano-British Cornwall and that the earliest signs of Christianity (inscribed stones) suggest that Christianity was introduced from three sources: the Mediterranean and Gaul, and from Wales. Of these, the latter was most influential and the archaeologists Ann Peston-Jones and Peter Rose believe that 'the most important early Christian settlements in Cornwall originated in the late fifth and sixth centuries as daughter houses of Welsh monastic communities'. They also note that 'with Christianity came a whole package of ideas, not merely that of faith, but also the associated site-types, place-names, monuments, and presumably the method by which parts of large estates could be alienated to provide support for the new religious communities'. In this way, they argue 'enclosures [such as the one at St Buryan] also served to delimit the sacred, consecrated area'. The present churchyard wall may be one such surviving boundary.

We know that by the early tenth century, Athelstan had reached the Isles of Scilly and that religious reform was on its way. Some observers view Athelstan and his achievement positively, praising him for founding both the Cornish bishopric at St Germans and for altering the monastery model at St

Churchyard cross St Buryan.

Alsia Well (see opposite).

Buryan. This view might be termed 'Anglo-apologist' for observers such as John Angarrack, who views Althelstan rather as a ruthless tyrant subjugating the Celtic people of Cornwall. Thus the church was used as an instrument of colonisation, alongside a wider supplementation of indigenous Celtic church documents, literature, laws and charters. Despite the thousand years between then and now, the debates over the control the Anglican church has over Cornwall, and Cornwall's need for an independent Celtic church (modelled along the Church of Wales) continue to this day. Many of the founding principles of the early Celtic church in Cornwall have recently been both revived and reconstructed with the organisation *Spyrys a Gernow* [Spirit of Cornwall] and the Newlyn-based Reverend Andy Phillips pushing for a realignment with these principles of worship. Despite the centuries in between, this is another way in which Celtic Cornwall shows a remarkable continuity.

● Churchyard and Churchtown Crosses, St Buryan

SW 408257, SW 408256.

The churchyard cross head at St Buryan (SW 408257) is one of the most distinctive in Cornwall. Set on a base stone, the western side shows a figure of a triumphant Christ with arms outstretched wearing a skirted tunic. The reverse face is a cross with five distinctive bosses. Such bosses were commonly said to represent the five wounds that Christ received at the Crucifixion. It is theorised that the cross head may have been constructed shortly after King Athelstan granted land to the religious community at St Buryan. A second market or church-town cross is found a short distance away

(SW 408256). This again shows a triumphant Christ but it is much cruder in design and was probably hewn several centuries later. Such a position in the market place would make the local populace aware of their Lord during daily life.

● Ann Wallis and Jane Barnicoate - Late Speakers of Cornish, St Buryan

SW 408256. *This is the traditional market location in St Buryan.*

One Matthew Wallis of St Buryan wrote a certified statement for Louis Lucien Bonaparte in 1859 which read as follows:

> I, Matthew Wallis, do certify that my grandmother Ann Wallis have spoken in my hearing the Cornish language well. She died about 15 years ago and she was in her 90th year of age. Jane Barnicoate died 2 years ago and she could speak Cornish too.

This shows that traditional Cornish was still being spoken in this community in 1857. Edwin Norris' version of the *Ordinalia*, which he called *The Ancient Cornish Drama* and published in 1859, was published around the same time as part of the late nineteenth-century revival of interest in the language. This shows a remarkable continuity, considering the difficulties the Celtic language of Cornish has faced. The German linguist Georg Sauerwein (1831–1903) was writing poetry in Cornish in around 1865.

Nineteenth century photograph of Boskenna Cross near St Buryan.

● Alsia Well, Alsia, near St Buryan

SW 393252. *Just after St Buryan, take a minor road to the north west, to find Alsia Mill. Just after the mill is a small stone stairway in the hedge. Follow the signs to the well.*

The name of this well is probably from the Cornish word *alsyow* [slopes] and it is located at the bottom of a slope. Around the well are roughly-hewn granite boulders and the roof is made of oblong granite blocks. An old, gnarled hawthorn grows above the well. The past inhabitants of Alsia used the well waters for a variety of medicinal cures, but would often become enraged if too many strangers came to imbibe them.

● Boskenna Crosses, near St Buryan

SW 425242, SW 41924, SW 420240.

There are three crosses around Boskenna, all within close proximity. The most famous and distinctive of these is located upon an old granite roller fastened to a millstone (SW 425242). One side of this cross displays an arms-outstretched Christ figure, while the reverse displays a cross with small bosses. A second cross is located beside the public footpath (SW 419241) on the way from Boskenna Gate to St Buryan churchtown. It probably functioned as a wayside marker. A third wheel-headed cross is on the B3315 road (SW 420240), opposite an entrance to Bokenna Manor. This one has a Latin cross on both faces of the head.

Boskenna Cross today.

Boscawen-Ûn stone circle.

An insert which came with
The Cornishman *newspaper in*
September 1928, celebrating the
first modern Gorsedd.

● The first modern Cornish Gorsedd, Boscawen-Ûn stone circle

SW 412274. *The circle is reached from the A30 by a footpath leading south.*

Boscawen-Ûn [meaning place of 'elder trees on the downs'] is one of the most spectacular stone circles in Cornwall. It is composed of nineteen upright stones with a central stone leaning to the north-east. The stone circle was the chosen site of the ceremony of the first modern Gorsedd in 1928. The site seems to have been selected because the *Trioedd Ynys Prydian* [the Welsh Triads] suggests that 'Beisgawen' in 'Dyfnwall' was one of the three main Gorsedds which gathered in Britain. Dyfnwall would most likely be Dumnonia (wider Devon and Cornwall), whilst Beisgawen is purported to have been Boscawen Ûn. Clearly, this suited the aims and objectives of the founders of the modern Gorsedd in Cornwall since it offered a longevity and continuity across the centuries.

If this were the place where a bardic order in Cornwall chose to meet then there may well have been, as Lyon suggests, 'ceremonies and contests for music, singing and literature'. In fact, the circle at Boscawen Ûn is dated to around 2000BCE, so is not from the period when Celts and Celtic languages are attested in Britain. However, as Malcolm Chapman observes, this has not stopped generations of observers making connection between Celtic culture and such structures. It could even be the case in Cornwall that stone circles may well have operated as proto-*plain-an-gwarry* ritual space, so they are part of a wider tradition of performance of Celticity. Such evidence seemed less important for the founders of the modern Gorsedd of Cornwall, which via 'Welsh' reinvention, courtesy of the scholar Edward Williams (or, as he preferred, Iolo Morganwg [1747–1826]) in 1792, eventually found its way to revival – or complete invention – in 1928.

Candidates for admission into the bardic order of Cornwall should 'exhibit a manifestation of the Celtic spirit' and in contrast to the Welsh Gorsedd, it was decided early on that all members of the Gorsedd should be treated equally and wear one colour: blue. Senior bards or holders of office should then have a different style of head-dress, or wear plastrons (ceremonial breastplates). The first ceremony took place on the 21 September with Henry Jenner as Grand Bard and Robert Morton Nance his deputy. Jenner had already been initiated in the bardic order in Brittany in 1902 and Wales in 1904, while Nance, alongside A.M. Bluett, J.S. Carah, Gilbert H. Doble, Annie Pool, Trelawney Roberts, J.C. Hambley Rowe and W.D. Watson had been made bards at Treorchy in Wales earlier in 1928. This formed the nucleus of a group who could return to Cornwall and begin the Gorsedd structure there. The twelve bards initiated during this first ceremony at Boscawen Ûn were Michael Cardew, Charles Henderson, W.B. Tregonning Hopper, James Dryden Hosken, A.K. Hamilton Jenkin, Sir Arthur Quiller Couch, E.A. Rees, G. Slogget, T. Taylor, Herbert Thomas, J. Thomas and J.C. Tregarthen.

Since 1928, the Gorsedd ceremony has evolved and developed and travels to different locations each year (alternating between sites in west, mid and east Cornwall). The language of the ceremony itself, though part-based on the Welsh model and part-rooted, ironically (considering the Gorsedd is part of the wider Celtic territories 'writing back' at English colonial control), in the ceremonies of the Church of England, is highly ritualistic and displays considerable theatricality. Nance himself was keen to distance himself from the 'Pagan' elements of Celticism. Important elements of the ceremony presently include the *Offreyn Frutys an Nor* [The Offering of the Fruits of the Earth], *Arta ef a Dhe* [He Shall Come Again] and *Cledha Myghtern Arthur* [The Sword of King Arthur] – the latter a staged moment when all bards unable to reach the sword (possibly a symbolic representation of Excalibur) lay a hand on a shoulder with one who is in contact with it. Recently the Gorsedd movement, having realised that its expansion has taken it away from some of the ancient sites of Cornwall have developed a new and more intimate *Awen* [Inspiration] ceremony which will return to venues such as Boscawen

Ûn. Whether or not past Gorsethsow took place in Cornwall, the contemporary performance of Cornwall's 'manifestation of Celtic spirit' is an important and established past of the ritual year.

● Pedn an wlase, Land's End

SW 34325. *Land's End is found at the end of A30. Park in the main car park. Alternatively, walk around from Sennen Cove on the coastal footpath.*

In Cornish, Land's End is know as *Pedn an wlase* ['end of the land'] and it has surely had a spiritual dimension to the Celtic people of Cornwall for centuries. The early revivalist Cornish-language writer Nicholas Boson (c.1624-1793) wrote *The Dutchesse of Cornwall's progresse to see the Land's end & to visit the Mount* in around 1665. It is an absurd and fanciful piece, composed of an admixture of folklore, classical learning, mythology, invention and satire for his children, John, Thomas and Katherine. There has been some confusion over the centuries over the exact location of Land's End, with some sources suggesting that present-day Cape Cornwall was thought of as the location. However, by the time of Norden's map in 1610, it was fixed at the present location. The gaze into the west and the end of the land is no better emphasised than in the writer Robert Walling's set of hand-drawn Cornish language magazines from the First World War. This he titled *An Howlsedhas* [The West] and filled the magazine with snippets of traditional literature in Cornish, as well as descriptions of modern inventions, such as military tanks as used on the Western Front. Walling lived between 1890 and c.1976. The Anglo-Cornish poet James Dryden Hosken (1861-1953) also noted the especial effect of gazing into the west.

Land's End, Pedn an wlase.

The Land of the West by James Dryden Hosken

She hath an ancient story,
    And stricken fields of fame,
A bright historic glory,
    A halo round her name.

Her heart's a moorland vastness,
    Her zone it is the sea;
A light above a fastness
    Her lure to liberty.

Maen castle entrance.

● Maen Cliff Castle, Sennen

SW 348258. *The castle can be reached on the coastal footpath from Sennen to Land's End.*

This a very old site, probably first dwelt in during the fourth century BCE. It was re-worked and reconstructed during the Iron Age. The surrounding field systems were adjusted to include the cliff castle.

○ Sennen Church, Sennen

SW 356255. *The church is located on the main A30 towards Land's End.*

Sennen obviously had an origin saint associated with it, but little information has survived. We do know of the Irish Saint Senan, who was abbot of the monastery of the Inis Cathaig in the Shannon Estuary. His fame later spread to Brittany, so it is possible he may have travelled to Cornwall. The Medieval records present a problem too – because surviving documentation points to a feminine form of the name.

The ditch at Maen Castle.

Sennen church in the late nine-teenth century.

Celtic cross at the entrance to Sennen church.

● Crosses, Sennen

SW 356255, SW 357255, SW 361266, SW 364255, SW 356251, SW 357246.

A number of crosses may be found in the parish of Sennen, showing its significance as a place of Celtic Christianity. On the north side of Sennen churchyard is Trevear Cross (SW 356255) and near the South Gate (SW 357255) is an equal-limbed cross with splayed ends. Escalls Cross – originating in a hedge at Escalls farm – is now to be found in the private garden of Carn Towan (SW 361266). Mayon Cross meanwhile stands in a field north-east of Sennen Churchtown (SW 364255), with Sennen Green Cross located beside a public footpath in south-east of Mayon Farm. At SW 356251 is Trevescan Cross, while at SW 357246 is Trevilley Cross. The latter has a cross with a figure of Christ upon it.

Chapel Carn Brea, etching

● Chapel Carn Brea, near Sennen

SW 38528. *On the A30 at Crows-an-wra, turn into the minor road which leads to a car park on the eastern side of the hill. Follow the footpath to the summit.*

This location is not to be confused with Carn Brea, near to Redruth. Considering the location of this hill, it is not surprising that it would have had not only pagan affiliations in the distant past, but also

Sennen Cove with a distant view of Sennen village and church

Plain-an-Gwarry, St Just-in-Penwith.

Christian ones. Chapel Carn Brea looks over most of the surrounding landscape of this far tip of Celtic Cornwall. Two chapels once stood at this spot – one as an appendage to a manor house, and the other as a separate chapel on the summit dedicated to Saint Michael. It is said that in the chapel on top of the great stone cairn, there once lived a hermit or holy man. He apparently kept lit a beacon to help guide shipping around the Land's End. The location is now an important Neo-Pagan site.

● Arthuriana, Bosworlas, near St Just-in-Penwith

SW 378303. *The farm is found just off the B3306 from Sennen to St Just-in-Penwith.*

Igraine's husband was Gorlois, the Duke of Cornwall, and this location translates to the 'house of Gorlois'. Jenner believes that the Cornish form of the name was 'Gworlos'. Although interesting, such translations can broadly be dismissed as well-intentioned but nevertheless as invention.

● Dick Angwin, St Just-in-Penwith

SW 371315. *St Just-in-Penwith is on the B3306.*

The traveller and naturalist John Ray (1627–1795) was aware of Cornish in St Just-in-Penwith in 1667. One man he spoke with told of a Dick Angwin, who could write Cornish.

● Plain-an-gwarry, St Just-in-Penwith

SW 371315. *The plain-an-gwarry is just to the east of the main Market square in the middle of the town between Cape Cornwall Street and Market Street*

Like the plain-an-gwarry at Perran Round, the one here at St Just-in-Penwith has a good claim to be one of the oldest theatres in continual use in Britain. The Reverend George Hadow, vicar of St Just, wrote in 1860:

The old structure still remains in St Just Churchtown, close to the principal inn; the clear outline of the circus is quite apparent, being formed externally by a stone wall of about four feet perpendicular in height, whilst a green bank slopes inwards; there is now no outside ditch, nor are there any steps... a pathway leads right through it from the town to the market-place.

However, writing earlier in 1754, William Borlase noted that the playing place was better preserved:

It is an exact circle of 126 feet diameter, the perpendicular height of the bank, from the area within, now seven feet; but the height from the bottom of the ditch without, ten feet at present, formerly more. The seats consist of six steps, fourteen inches wide, and one foot high, with one on the top of all, where the Rampart is about seven feet wide.

Haddow and Borlase's observations would suggest there has been considerable erosion of the steps across a century. In comparison, to other plain-an-gwarrys, the encasement of the Round in a stone wall is quite unusual, but this may match its more urban location. There is little evidence of a capella

Cross shaft discovered lying horizontally, incorporated in the wall of the church at St Just-in-Penwith (see page 63).

or conveyor (as found at Perran Round, and mentioned independently in William Jordan's *Gwreans an Bys*). The plain-an-gwarry here hosted a production of the full cycle of the *Ordinalia* in 2001. There is, however, no evidence that the *Ordinalia* would have been performed here in the Medieval period. It is much more likely to have been a life of the local Saint Just. Continuity back to this Medieval period of performance is provided by the many contemporary theatre companies who still make use of this performance space. The plain-an-gwarry at St Just-in-Penwith is indicative of the lasting nature of Cornwall's premier Celtic literary form: popular community-based drama.

⬤ St Just Church, St Just-in-Penwith

SW 372315. *The church is just to the east of the main Market square in the middle of the town.*

St Just is known in Cornish as *Lannyust* [The Holy site of St Just]. There are contradictory stories about the saint's origin. Some observers view him as Justus, who was sent to the island of Britain by Pope Gregory in 596 to convert the Anglo-Saxons, eventually becoming Archbishop of Canterbury in 616. However, a more likely explanation may be that he was the Yestin or Justin who was one of the sons of Gerent, and of a wider family of Celto-Cornish saints. William of Worcester informs us that in the fifteenth century the church at St Just enshrined his relics, which would be concurrent with a Cornish-language drama celebrating his life and works.

An image of Christ of the trades.

St Just-in-Penwith church.

Market cross, St Just-in-Penwith church.

Celtic carving on the cross shaft, St Just-in-Penwith church.

After renovation in 1865, builders at the church discovered a significant wall painting of Christ surrounded by tools – known as Christ of the Trades. Some observers view the naked and wounded figure of Christ simply surrounded by the tools of husbandry, fishing, cloth and metal-working trades. Alternatively, it is perhaps, a message about man's sins and the continuing Passion of Christ. Certainly such images were painted alongside a residual Medieval Celtic Christianity. There is also an image of St George and the Dragon – with the dragon's claws found in the bottom left-hand corner of the picture.

Interestingly the church also houses a very ancient tombstone with a Latin inscription and one of the forms of the cross known as a Chi-rho monogram. This is known as the Selus Stone since on the edge of the stone are caved the words SELVS IC IACIT [Selus lies here]. Clearly, Selus was a significant figure in post-Roman west Penwith sometime in the 5th or 6th Centuries. The original inscription may have been completed by an illiterate carver, since another hand has added an 'I' and an 'N' to complete the name Selinus. Situated at the end of the north aisle is a cross-shaft. Located in one panel is a spectacular example of interlace Celtic knotwork, formed by two concentric circles.

A number of other crosses are to be found in the vicinity of the church. A Market Cross is located in the south-western corner of the churchyard (SW 371314). This has a figure of Christ on the reverse. Just outside the south porch of the church are the remains of a wheel-headed cross head, while in the vicarage garden is another example (SW 378314). Two further crosses are to be found at nearby Boscean House (SW 365317) but unfortunately there is no public access.

Wider Celticity in St Just-in-Penwith is celebrated in the Lafrowda Festival, which has been running since 1996. Lafrowda is the ancient Cornish name for the church lands where the community of St Just-in-Penwith stands today. Lafrowda Day itself is always held on the third Saturday of July. The festival integrates music, literature, theatre and community arts.

● The poetry of John Tonkin, St Just-in-Penwith

SW 372315. *The Market square is in the middle of the town.*

John Tonkin often walked these streets and was a man of letters writing in Cornish in St Just-in-Penwith around 1695. Tonkin was a committed Protestant and championed the work of William III. Because in the early twentieth century, Henry Jenner and many of the early Cornish revivalists were committed to a more Celto-Catholic construction of the past (partially based on saints' lives and holy wells), in the early phases of the revival his work was somewhat ignored. Indeed, Jenner, a neo-Jacobite, called Tonkin a 'violent Whig' in response to one poem titled *Menja Tiz Kernuack buz gazowas* [If Cornish people would but listen]. Tonkin's poetry, however, is rather good, as in 'A Cornish Song, to the Tune of the Modest Maid of Kent'.

A Cornish Song, to the Tune of the Modest Maid of Kent by John Tonkin

An Prounter ni ez en plew East
grouns a broaze carra Apostle Chreest
magga pel ter el eve heathes
ha nenna Dewe e vedd'n e worras

[Our vicar in the parish of St Just
may he act like an apostle of Christ
as far as he can manage it
and God help him with the rest.

hi ni an Poble ul dale gweel
an peath eggee e Lal tha ni da zeel
ha rie gun gwella scovarn dortha
na dale ni gurra ul thal gotha

And we the people should all do
what he tells us to do on Sunday
and give our best ear to him.
We should not let it all drop.]

● Edward Lhuyd and the famous Englyn, St Just-in-Penwith

SW 372315. *The church is just to the east of the main Market square in the middle of the town.*

In 1700, the parish clerk of St Just-in-Penwith offered a visiting scholar, Edward Lhuyd, a triplet or *englyn* which has since been regarded as very famous metaphor for retaining the Cornish language:

An Lavor gôth ewe laver gwîr,
Ne vedn nevera does vâs a tavaz re hîr;
Bes dên heb tavaz a gollas e dîr.

[The old saying is a true saying,
No good will counted to come from too long
 a tongue;
But a man without a tongue lost his land.]

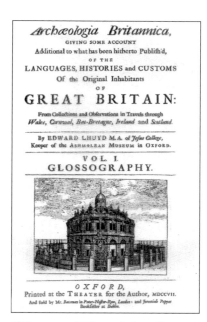

Title page of Edward Lhuyd's Archaeologia Britannica.

This *englyn* was given to Lhuyd (1660-1707) while he was in Cornwall collecting material for what would become his *Archaeologia Britannica: An Account of the Languages, Histories and Customs of Great Britain, from Travels through Wales, Cornwall, Bas-Bretagne, Ireland and Scotland*. Lhuyd was born in Loppington, Shropshire, attended grammar school at Oswestry and went up to Jesus College, Oxford in 1682 but later dropped out before graduating. He was first assistant to the Keeper of the Ashmolean Museum, and then finally became Keeper in 1690, holding this post until his death. In May 1697 Lhuyd and his assistants, David Parry, Robert Wynne and Williams Jones, began their tour of Great Britain, and following a request from John Keigwin, the party eventually arrived in Cornwall in 1700. Not all parishes were recorded in depth, but both Jones and Lhuyd spent considerable time in Cornwall. Despite being handed the above text from the parish clerk of St Just-in-Penwith, paradoxically, the parish was not studied in as much depth as others in Cornwall. Lhuyd's work on the language had often been dismissed by some scholars, but more recently his work has been re-appraised as being an important study of Late Cornish, it differing considerably, as we might expect, from Medieval or Middle Cornish. The work of Lhuyd has been of great interest to writers and scholars such as Richard Gendall (b.1924), who has proposed a Late Cornish variant of the Revived language.

Lhuyd realised that the *englyn* was a possible form for his own poetry. In 1703, he composed a long poem titled 'On the Death of King William III, a British Song in the Cornish Dialect; according to the pattern of the poets of the sixth century'. It is written in support of the Protestant cause in Ireland; Cornish soldiers having fought for William III at the Battle of the Boyne. In the elegy he addresses the native occupations of the Cornish as fishermen and miners, asking them to take up the Protestant fight:

Kosgardh an dowrm squattyow goz rwzow, [Fellows of the water, scat your nets,
Goz golow, goz revow, goz oll skaphow; Your sails, your oars, all your boats,
Seith mledhan ne dhibryw vor-bozow For seven years do not eat sea-food.

Kosgardh at Stên, rowmann goz bolow; Fellow of the Tin, abandon your mines;
Gwlezow, ravow, palow, pigolow: Picks, shovels, spades, pick-axes:
Komero' gostanow, marhow, ha kledhow. Take shields, horses and swords.]

Lhuyd's feelings about the native nature of the *englyn* were perhaps proven to be true, when in 2000, a previously undiscovered Cornish text came to light. This was *Bewnans Ke* [The Life of St Kea]. In that play King Arthur talks exuberantly about his guests being entertained:

Dun, ow amors ha'm cuvyon, [Come, my friends and dear ones,
gans solas hag englynnyon with entertainment and verses,
ha meth aha melody whek. and mirth and sweet melody.]

It may be that the *englyn* and *englynnyon* (multiple triplets) are the *de rigeur* verse form for anyone constructing poetry in Cornish from the sixth century to the Medieval period.

● Various Crosses and memorial stones, St Just-in-Penwith

SW 392330, SW 39630, SW 364306,

On Carnyorth Common, around half a mile, north east of St Just-in-Penwith may be found Boslow Stone (SW 392330). On its western face is an inscription: the words TAET and UERA, making Taetuera, which Charles Thomas has suggested might be the name of a local priest. It may have acted as a boundary marker in the past. At SW 396300 is Leswidden Cross, a mutilated wayside wheel-head cross. The cross may again have been a boundary stone – probably between the manors of Bartinney, Leswidden and Carnglaze. A stranger story is associated with Penvorder Cross which is located in private garden in Cot Valley (SW 364306) just below St Just-in-Penwith. It can be viewed from a nearby path. Hailing originally from St Breward Parish in North Cornwall, following movement to Blisland in 1902, it was then sold on in 1990 to arrive at its present position in the west of the territory.

Boslow stone.

● Kenidjack Cliff Castle, St Just-in-Penwith

SW 355326. *This can be found close to the end of Nancherrow Valley, off the B3306 at Kenidjack Farm.*

Representative of those 'corner-dwelling' Celts of Cornwall, at Kenidjack can be observed a triple Iron Age defensive structure. There are also the surviving remains of three roundhouses here.

● St Helen's Oratory, Cape Cornwall

SW 352318. *Park at the top car park, and walk down the hill to the Cape Cornwall peninsula. The oratory is on the right-hand side in a field owned by the National Trust.*

*Overlooking Kenidjack with
St Just in the distance*

St Helen's oratory, located in the field named Park an Chapel, is an iconic symbol of Celtic Cornwall. Clearly the oratory is some kind of early Christian chapel. The granite Greek-style cross atop one of the gable ends of the structure has not always been there. It was found in 1984, when it was ploughed up in a neighbouring field. The following year, it was fixed to the chapel. It may have originally been intended to be a gable cross. Supposedly, an ancient chi-rho cross was also found here in the late nine-

An aerial view of Cape Cornwall.

St Helen's Oratory.

An aerial view of the landscape around Pendeen

teenth century, but was disposed of by local vicar John Buller, who threw it into a well. Buller was probably aware of the ancient tradition of Cape Cornwall being known as 'The Promontory of Helenus, so called because of the landing there of Brutus, accompanied by Helenus' (found in Harrison, writing in 1580) but also offered an alternative – that the name may be derived from Cornish. Although not marked on maps, the area was once known as *Pen Hailen* [the great stone head]. From *Hailen* is thus derived Helen, but as we know in Celtic Cornwall, stories sometimes merge and collide to make meaning.

● Boscaswell Holy Well, Pendeen

SW 376347. *Off the B3306, follow the road to the bottom of Lower Boscaswell. The well is located on a footpath to the west.*

This well originally had a well house with a rounded roof, but is now only lined with granite blocks. According to local tradition, the Well housed a number of leeches used to cure sickness in cattle and horses.

● Pendeen Vau Fogou, Pendeen

SW 384355. *From the B3306 follow the signs to the lighthouse. On the eastern side, see the track to Pendeen Manor Farm. Permission is needed to visit the fogou.*

This is an Iron Age fogou located close to Pendeen Manor, the birthplace of Dr William Borlase (1696–1772), often viewed as the 'Father of Cornish Archaeology'. Unlike other local fogous, this one is not located close to a surviving courtyard village.

Boscaswell Holy Well.

● Porthmeor Courtyard House Settlement, near Gurnard's Head

SW 434371. *This is found on Porthmeor Farm off the B3306. Permission to visit is required.*

This is a settlement of Romano-British houses linked to the local field system. There are three houses in total, and to the south-west is a further house, next to a ruined fogou.

● Arthuriana, Bosigran, near Gurnard's Head

SW *This is a short distance along the coastal path from Gurnard's Head.*

It is hard not to make a connection here with Arthur's mother Igraine since the location Bosigran could mean 'the dwelling of Igrain'. This was again, Henry Jenner's well-intentioned suggestion. Iolo Morganwg (not always a reliable source) notes that there was one Eigron, one of the sons of Caw (the father of Gildas), who mentions that Eigron founded a church in Cornwall. However other convincing explanations can be found. The form *igran* here might translate to Gerran or Geran - so perhaps 'Geran's House', or according to Oliver Padel, 'the house of the crane, or heron'.

The view across Gurnard's Head

● Tregaminion Well, Morvah

SW 401358. *Follow the loop road through Morvah village and locate Tregaminion Farm. Follow the bridle path to where it meets the coastal path. In a triangular field is the well structure.*

The field here is called Chapel Field and at one point probably contained a baptistry. Previous observers noted 'hewn stone' at the site. Now there is a modern pump house on top of it. The well was known for its healing qualities, and according to local tradition was used by John Wesley for baptisms.

● Fenton Bebibell, Morvah

SW 429352. *The well is found quite near to the famous Mên an tol on Nine Maidens Down, near a windswept thorn tree.*

Translated from Cornish, *Fenton Bebibell* means 'Well of the Little People'. This is a magical name for a magical well site on the downs. The moors of Penwith are filled with legends and stories of 'little people'. In the parish of Morvah there was a tradition of baptising dolls on Good Friday. Near to Fenton Bebibell is another well at a farm (SW 428354).

● Mên Scryfa, Morvah

Men Scryfa in the late 1800s.

SW 426354. *This inscribed stone is further along the path leading to Mên an tol.*

Mên Scryfa translates to 'stone of writing' and on the stone is inscribed a dedication in Latin: RIALO-BRAN-CVNOVAL-FIL [Rialobran, Son of Cunoval]. *Rialobran* equates to 'Royal Raven' while *Cunoval* means 'Famous chieftain'. The lettering equates to the style in use in the sixth century. Rialobran was obviously an important prince.

> **The Road to Rialobran** by Alan M. Kent
>
> *Find on your path from Morvah to Madron*
> *'Grave of Rialobran, Cunoval's son.'*
>
> *This is the translation of stone's scroll*
> *set up for the good of a royal soul*
>
> *named 'The Raven', his father - 'Worthy Fame'*
> *set immortality and chiselled name*
>
> *of his son, who once ruled Carn Bran's skyline*
> *but now is watched by mute Greenbarrow mine.*
>
> *At the start of the road to Rialobran*
> *alone, sits inscribed school-house, spick and span.*

Plaque placed on in eighteen eighty two,
a late structure according to stone's début,

and though England's past and poetry feature
stone's name and words are untouched by teacher.

Latin/Cornish, like Raven, buried in earth,
killed young, not given life's pennyworth.

Oh pilgrim of this sixth century tomb
consider the truth of culture's heirloom:

a more fitting test of literature
heeds well the Raven mourner's signature.

But the message isn't carved or written.
instead, hidden history of Britain.

scratched on the road to Rialobran
true continuum is left without Kinsman,

such is the sweep of civilisation,
the poet comes to realization

how while stone has stood as time's icon,
two languages came, written, now are gone.

So like Cunovel, find hope dashed by Death's logan
taken at the end of the road to Rialobran.

But dear Cunovel, at son's setting, do not cry.
A thousand years on, we've unearthed the reason why.

⬤ Chûn Castle hill fort, near Morvah

SW 405340. *The castle is located on a hill close to Trehyllys Farm. The farm is found down a lane on the Penzance to Morvah road.*

This is a stone built Iron Age hill fort, with commanding views of the surrounding countryside and ocean. Inside the substantial walls are to be found buildings and a stone-lined well. Two large gateposts mark the south-western side of the construction. It was occupied again in the sixth century CE. Close by, may be found the Chûn Quoit chamber tomb, and although thought by many to symbolise Celtic landscape, it is in fact, much earlier.

The famous mermaid bench end

● Bosullow Trehyllus, courtyard house settlement, near Morvah

SW409342. *The settlement is located north east from Chûn Castle.*

This is a Romano-British settlement. It contains a complex of three courtyard houses, each next to tiny fields and gardens.

● Zennor Church and the Mermaid of Zennor, Zennor

SW 455385. *From St Ives, turn right off the B3306. The church is in the middle of the village.*

Unfortunately, little is known about St Senara. She does however, have a holy well which is to be found a short distance away – under Zennor Carn. Zennor church is perhaps more famous for its carved bench-end in holy-oak depicting the community's most famous icon – the Mermaid. The bench end is actually now part of a smaller chair and although the mermaids' face is somewhat disfigured, she can still be seen holding a comb and mirror. The scales of her fish-like tail are also clearly visible. Mermaids appear to be very important figures in the mythology of the Celtic people of Cornwall, for there are several other mermaid narratives, relating to Morvah, Padstow, Seaton and Cury. However, the most famous mermaid narrative is found at Zennor with a version recorded by the folklorist William Bottrell (1816–1881) in 1873. The longevity of the story is not known. It could be that it has its origins in older Medieval or early-modern Cornwall. Certainly during Bottrell's time the people of Zennor viewed the narrative as accounting for their famous bench-end.

In Bottrell's version, hundreds of years ago, there was a very beautiful and richly attired lady who regularly attended services at Zennor church. The lady's origins were unknown. As well as this, she never seemed to grow old. The best singer in the parish was Mathey Trewella, and one day he followed her. He never returned and neither did the lady. One Sunday morning a vessel put to anchor about a mile from Pendower Cove. The captain of the ship was greeted by a mermaid who asked if he could raise anchor for it was resting on the door of her dwelling and she wanted to get in to her children. So it was said, the men 'worked with a will' to remove the anchor for the sailors knew she could bring bad luck. When local people heard this, they concluded that it was this sea-lady who had visited the church and who had enticed Mathey to her underwater abode.

Such narratives embody the Celtic folk narrative of Cornwall, and yet there are other imaginings of mermaids in the literary canon. In the Passion play of the *Ordinalia*, two doctors are philosophising how Jesus Christ can be both God and Man, One of them replies that by way of comparison, they should look at the mermaid, which is both woman and fish:

Doctor nynsy henna man	[Doctor, that is not right at all,
n any il bos yn della	not can it be so,
de the uerwel yn certan	that a man should die
awos cous lauarow da	for saying such things.
myreugh worth an vorvoran	Look at the mermaid,
hanter pysk ha hanter den	half fish and half man
y vos dev ha den yn wlan	Let us believe the same thing of him
the'n keth tra-na crygyans ren.	that he is clearly God and man.]

The *Ordinalia* was probably performed around Penryn, and yet this sequence shows that mermaids folklore extended elsewhere across Cornwall during the Medieval Celtic period.

● John Davey and the Cornish Language, Zennor

SW 455385. *Follow the steps up to the church. The plaque is to the left of the porch.*

John Davey memorial plaque.

On the wall of the church is a memorial plaque erected by St Ives Old Cornwall Society and dedicated to John Davey (1812-1891). Davey was a farmer and schoolmaster who was one of the last people to have some traditional knowledge of the Cornish language. Hailing from nearby Boswednack, his knowledge of the language was recorded by the St Ives-based historian John Hobson Matthews who found that Davey could 'converse on a few topics in the ancient language', with him apparently learning Cornish from his father. Legend has it that he kept his Cornish alive by speaking to his cat. There has been some debate as to whether Davey learned 'book' Cornish rather than traditional Cornish, but the one piece of Cornish poetry recorded by Matthews, known as *The Crankan Rhyme*, is not recorded elsewhere suggesting that he did learn traditional Cornish. Matthew could not make sense of the rhyme but later scholarship has understood the poem to be a piece of humour about how the road between Penzance and Marazion is more fertile than the rocky fields of Cranken:

Robert Morton Nance's headstone.

A grankan, a grankan,	[O Crankan, O Crankan!
A mean o gowaz o vean	Beyond the fields of the spring
Ondez parc an venton	you give but little
Dub trelawza vean	- only three shoots by the stone.
Far Penzans a Maragow	The road between Penzance and Marazion
Githack mackwee	is very green
A githack macrow	and a whole lot fresher
A mac trelowza varrack.	- three shoots grow for every passing horseman.]

● Robert Morton Nance's grave, Zennor

SW 455385. *The grave is found in the middle of the churchyard to the east of the church.*

Robert Morton Nance (1873-1959) was a significant activist in the modern Celtic Revival in Cornwall and he is buried in Zennor churchyard, an inscription on his grave reading *Oberow vewnans yu y wyr govath* [His life's work is his true memorial]. Nance was a writer, artist, activist and linguist. His parents belonged to the Cornish community of Cardiff which gave him an interest in Cornish culture. Nance trained as an artist under Sir Hubert von Herkommer and his drawings were featured in the short-lived but influential *Cornish Magazine*, edited by Arthur Quiller Couch. Upon his marriage to his second wife, Annie Maud Cawker, he settled in nearby Nancledra and spent the rest of his life working for Cornwall.

Many of the institutions of the Celtic Revival in Cornwall are attributed to Nance such as the foundation of the Old Cornwall Societies, the Cornish Gorseth, and the revival of both spoken and written Cornish. His vision for Cornwall was to synthesize popular culture with antiquarianism. However, his model for the revival of Cornish which he termed Unified Cornish, was somewhat romantic, it being based in the Medieval period but also unifying different historical periods of the language, a project which has since been critiqued. However, many observers now see that Nance's model was relatively accurate and had its merits.

One of Nance's achievements was the founding of the first Old Cornwall Society in St Ives in 1920. This gave communities a mandate for collecting, preserving and promoting Cornish culture rather than allowing it to be lost. His model was ultimately based on old-style European nationalism which used folk culture and language as the basis for nationhood. The philosophy of the Old Cornwall Societies was 'to gather up the fragments so they may not be lost'. As preservers of Celtic culture in Cornwall, the Old Cornwall Society movement has been highly effective and the Federation still exists today. It was Nance who was one of the motivators of the Gorseth movement in Cornwall, eventually becoming Grand Bard between 1934 and 1959.

Nance's interest in the Celtic folk culture of Cornwall also resulted in his interest in Mummers and Christmas Plays. He was a prolific playwright with his *Cledry Plays* having a vision of undamaged Celtic culture still operating in West Cornwall. His 1932 play *An Balores* [The Chough] is an allegorical play based on the death of the Cornish language and its causes. Along with his co-worker A.S.D. Smith, Nance completed numerous translations, Unified Cornish versions of the *Ordinalia*, as well as several dictionaries. In the post-war period, Nance remained inspirational to a new generation of writers and activists involved in the Celtic revival in Cornwall. These included E.G. Retallack Hooper, P.A.S. Pool and Richard Jenkin. Nance observed that 'one generation has set Cornish on its feet. It is now for another to make it walk'.

From *An Balores* [*The Chough*] by Robert Morton Nance

An Kensa Den: Nep choca keth garow yo, yn-sur; rag an ydhyn drokna prest ymons ow-cut aga nythow yn clegrow an als, le mayth esa trygys an balores voghosak. Ha pupteth oll y a-wre hy ladra, orth-hy-herdhya mes a'y nyth hy-honen, kepar del wruk an Sawson dh'agan hendasow, orth aga-helghya mes a'ga fow bys y'n cona tyr Kernow-ma!

An Nessa Den: My a-bref bos henna gow – Ny agan-honen yu dhe vlamya! Ny, an dus Kernow, yu, re-s-ladhas! Hy res-ombrederas, "Pandr' a-dal dhern bewa, ynnof ow-quthya yn-few spyrys Myghtern Arthur, aban na-vyn tus Kernow kewsel Kernewek na-moy? – Pandr'a-dal bos Arthur bew, marow mar pe y davas?"

[1st Man: It is some rough command aw, surely, for those wicked birds are ever building their nests in the crags of the cliffs, where the poor chough lived. And every day they robbed it, thrusting it out of its own nest, even as the accursed Saxons did to our forefathers, driving them out of their country into the peninsular of Cornwall!

2nd Man: I will prove that to be false. We ourselves are to blame! We, the people of Cornwall, it is who have killed it! It thought within itself, "What good is it for me to live, keeping the spirit of King Arthur alive in me, since the folk of Cornwall won't speak Cornish any more? What is the use of Arthur being alive, if his tongue is dead?"]

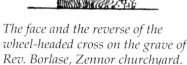

The face and the reverse of the wheel-headed cross on the grave of Rev. Borlase, Zennor churchyard.

● Wayside wheel-headed crosses, Zennor churchyard

SW 454385. *These are situated on the Borlase grave on the north side of the churchyard.*

● Tregaminion Well, Morvah

SW 401358. *Follow the loop road through Morvah village and locate Tregaminion Farm. Follow the bridle path to where it meets the coastal path. In a triangular field is the well structure.*

The field here is called Chapel Field and at one point probably contained a baptistry. Previous observers noted 'hewn stone' at the site. Now there is a modern pump house on top of it. The well was known for its healing qualities, and according to local tradition was used by John Wesley for baptisms.

● Fenton Bebibell, Morvah

SW 429352. *The well is found quite near to the famous Mên an tol on Nine Maidens Down, near a windswept thorn tree.*

Translated from Cornish, *Fenton Bebibell* means 'Well of the Little People'. This is a magical name for a magical well site on the downs. The moors of Penwith are filled with legends and stories of 'little people'. In the parish of Morvah there was a tradition of baptising dolls on Good Friday. Near to Fenton Bebibell is another well at a farm (SW 428354).

● Mên Scryfa, Morvah

SW 426354. *This inscribed stone is further along the path leading to Mên an tol.*

Mên Scryfa translates to 'stone of writing' and on the stone is inscribed a dedication in Latin: RIALO-BRAN-CVNOVAL-FIL [Rialobran, Son of Cunoval]. *Rialobran* equates to 'Royal Raven' while *Cunoval* means 'Famous chieftain'. The lettering equates to the style in use in the sixth century. Rialobran was obviously an important prince.

Men Scryfa in the late 1800s.

The Road to Rialobran by Alan M. Kent

Find on your path from Morvah to Madron
'Grave of Rialobran, Cunoval's son.'

This is the translation of stone's scroll
set up for the good of a royal soul

named 'The Raven', his father - 'Worthy Fame'
set immortality and chiselled name

of his son, who once ruled Carn Bran's skyline
but now is watched by mute Greenbarrow mine.

At the start of the road to Rialobran
alone, sits inscribed school-house, spick and span.

At the grave of the Reverend William Borlase (a descendant of the more famous Dr. William Borlase) are fixed two wheel-headed wayside crosses. Borlase, who died in 1888, was a former vicar of Zennor. The shorter of the two crosses was found at nearby Tregerthen Farm. It is holds an equal-limbed cross with expanded ends. A Christ figure is found on the reverse face. The taller cross was built into the floor of the cottage presently housing the Wayside Museum, but was rescued by Reverend Borlase. The cross is similar in design to the shorter one, with a cross and a Christ figure on the reverse of the head. Another cross – originally built into a stile at Trevega – is to be found in the churchyard, while Wicca Cross is found outside the Wayside Museum (WW 454383).

The grave of Reverend William Borlase.

● Zennor Holy Well, Chapel Jane, near Zennor

SW 434383. *On the B3306, park at Treen and walk north toward Gurnard's Head. The chapel is a short distance along the coast.*

Here can be found the remains of a twelfth-century chapel, known for many years as Chapel Jane. On the east side of the chapel is a small spring and it is thought that this once provided water for the chapel. In its day, the well here had a reputation as grand as that of Madron.

Looking eastwards over Gurnard's Head towards Zennor, far distant.

● Round houses at Sperris Drift and Wicca, near Zennor

SW 473384, SW 473385. *Sperris Croft lies to the south of the B3306 on a ridge. Wicca Round is located just below.*

Sperris Croft consists of seven Late Bronze Age/Early Iron Age round houses in a row. Wicca may actually consist of three huts. The Wicca here has nothing to do with Gerald Gardner's modern witchcraft and is probably derived from the local de Wycke family.

● D.H. Lawrence, Higher Tregerthen, Zennor

SW 465388. *From the car park at Wicca, follow the track to Lower and then Higher Tregerthen.*

Higher Tregerthen, Zennor.

As we shall see in this volume, sometimes visiting writers and observers can offer important insights and understanding of Cornwall's Celtic heritage. One such writer is D(avid) H(erbert) Lawrence. Lawrence (1885–1930) was born at Eastwood, Nottingham but between 1916 and 1917, he and his German-born wife Frieda lived at Higher Tregerthen near Zennor. Dissatisfied with England, Lawrence had come to Cornwall to seek what he termed his 'Ranamin' – a planned Utopian and alternative community, and yet he and his wife were both persecuted as German spies. His experiences in Cornwall were later fictionalised in the novel *Kangaroo* (1923) and in a short story titled *Samson and Delilah*, first published in the United States in 1922. *Samson and Delilah*'s theme is a returning Cornishman from overseas and is set in an imagined Tinner's Rest public house in Zennor. In a revealing chapter in *Kangaroo*, titled 'The Nightmare' Lawrence has his central character, Richard Somers, reflect on the Celticity of the Cornish:

> *Queer it was. Right and wrong was not fixed for them as for the English. There was still a mystery for them in what was right and what was wrong. Only one thing was wrong – any sort of physical compulsion or hurt. That they were sure of. But as for the rest of behaviour – it was all a flux. They had none of the ethics of chivalry or love.*

Whether we believe this to be true or not, what Lawrence does note is a very different identity still persisting in Cornwall. In the novel, Somers then reflects further on Cornish Celticity:

> *And as Somers sat there on the sheaves in the underdark, seeing the light swim above the sea, he felt he was over the border, in another world. Over the border, in that twilight, awesome world of the previous Celts. The spirit of the ancient, pre-Christian world, which lingers still in the truly Celtic places… The old Celtic countries have never had our Latin Teutonic consciousness. in the blue-eyed, or even in the truly Roman, Latin sense of the word. But they have been overlaid by our consciousness and our civilization, smouldering underneath in a slow eternal fire, that you can never put out till it burns itself out.*

To some extent here, Lawrence conflates and confuses different periods of Celtic history. As this volume shows, much of Celtic experience in Cornwall has been connected to Christianity, and yet here, he appears to be referring to a pre-Christian pagan Celtic Cornwall, which he deems as preferable. Lawrence never quite found his 'Ranamin' in Cornwall, yet Cornwall's pagan Celtic past has continued to inspire both native and visitor alike. Indeed, there are a high number of Neo-Pagan groups and gatherings in Cornwall, who use ancient sites for both ritual and celebration.

Aerial view of the Penwith Moors and field systems.

● Field Systems, near Zennor

SW 455385 – 495405. *A stop along any part of the B3306 will provide an excellent view.*

The field systems here make for spectacular viewing and seem to epitomise much of the Celtic flavour of the Penwith landscape. Many of the fields were laid out during the Iron Age period, and they have continued to be used in much the same way into the contemporary era. Many of the individual fields have Cornish language names.

● Towednack Church, near St Ives

SW 487381. *The church is located by leaving the B3306 between St Ives and Zennor, and turning south.*

The church here is dedicated to St Tewennocus and it was built sometime in the thirteenth century. It is supposedly one of the last churches in Cornwall to have had a service in traditional Cornish (in 1678). Saint Tewennocus is probably the same saint as St Winwalo who is also commemorated on The Lizard at Gunwalloe, Landewednack and at Landevennec in Brittany. There, he is Saint Gwennole. One major piece of folklore is attached to the Church, relating to the parish feast day on 28 April. In winter (which was seemingly colder and longer in the past) a local farmer took a stump of a tree to burn on his fire. It began to blaze while they sang and drank. Suddenly from out of the stump came a cuckoo, crying 'Cuckoo! Cuckoo!' The bird was kept and the farmer resolved to celebrate this annually as 'cuckoo feast'. The resultant feast was in the past also called Crowder feast because the procession was led by a *Crowder* [Fiddler]. In 1987 Towednack was the site of major Celtic pilgrimage event with the monks of Landevennac and Cornu-Celtic singer Brenda Wotton (1928–1994) in attendance. One of the hymns sung celebrated Celtic saints:

> *All these Cornish shores are holy*
> *Here the saints did in prayer did dwell,*
> *Raising font and altar holy*
> *Preaching far with staff and bell.*
> *Piran, Petrock, Paul Aurelian,*
> *Euny, Sampson, Winwaloe.*

● Crosses, Towednack

SW 487380.

Tredorwin Cross is located on the right hand side of the south porch of Towednack Church. It is a wheel-headed wayside cross. On the right hand side of the same porch is a Gable cross which may have been placed here after renovations. This may connect with the folklore here: the devil was responsible for the church tower not having any pinnacles.

● Castle-an-Dinas Hill Fort, Nancledra

SW 485350. *This is best reached from the B3311 at Castle Gate.*

Holding four lines of defence, this hill fort seems to have a stone wall as its innermost ring. There were clearly two phases of construction of which the stone wall was the earliest. In the south-eastern corner is a late eighteenth century folly known locally as Roger's Tower.

● St Ia's Well, St Ives

SW 515407. *The well is found on the hill rising from Porthmeor Beach just past the Tate St Ives gallery.*

Saint Ia was Saint Euny's sister and part of the Gwinear group of saints from Ireland. Initially she

St Ia's well.

settled on the land of a chieftain called Dinan, who treated her well but she was later martyred by King Tewdrig of Trencom at Connerton near Hayle sometime around 450. Her tomb was in the church at St Ives in Medieval times. St Ives is known in Cornish as Porth Ia [Ia's harbour]. The most popular legend associated with St Ia is that she floated over to Cornwall in an enlarged leaf – a story perhaps comparable to St Piran's millstone.

The prolific Anglo-Cornish novelist Joseph Hocking (1860–1937) wrote a novel about the saint, which he titled *The Bells of St Ia* (1911). In his younger day Hocking was ultra-Protestant in his views, but this vision later softened and he became fascinated with aspects of the Celto-Cornish revival. Saints and the power of ancient monuments became important themes within his fiction. The well site, which is quite modern, is known in Cornish as *Venton Ia*, and was the main source of water for the area of St Ives known as 'Downalong'. Ia's feast day is 3 February.

● Barbara Hepworth Studio and Garden, St Ives

SX 517406. *The garden is short walk from the Tate St Ives at Porthmeor.*

Now part of the Tate St Ives, Hepworth's studio and garden displays Hepworth's interest in the native monuments of the landscape of Penwith, which she re-imagined with a modernist twist. Both Neolithic, Bronze Age and Iron Age phases of development were of interest to her. Hepworth (1903–1975), like many of her contemporaries in the community in St Ives – such as Andrew Lanyon, Ben Nicolson and Christopher Wood – felt an affinity with Celtic space and place. She was born in Wakefield, but spent much of her life in Cornwall.

St Ia's church, St Ives c.1900.

Aerial view over St Ives. St Ia's Well is sited on the corner of Porthmeor Hill and Beach Road, at the bottom left hand corner of the cemetery seen mid picture.

The Penbeagle cross.

● Crosses, St Ives

SW 518405, SW 507398.

The churchyard cross in St Ives is an impressive monument (SW 518405). It is a gothic Lantern cross, and on the narrower sides of the head may be found a Bishop with a staff, whilst on the opposing side a possible image of St Ia. Another cross is found at Penbeagle (SW 507398). According to the local historian Matthews, the cross was still whitewashed in 1890, a common practice across Cornwall.

● Cokyn-baba and Joanies, St Ives

SW 522408. *St Ives Museum is found in Downalong, at Wheal Dream, close to Bamaluz Point and Porth-gwidden. The museum is open during the summer.*

Cokyn-baba is the general name given to small 'toy' boats traditionally made by the quay boys of St Ives. To make one, a cork net-float is cut in two, one half being trimmed and shaved into a narrow hull. A small piece of roofing slate is then forced in as a centreboard. It is then rigged with chips of wood, to form a kind of three-masted lugger. Joanies are children's dolls created by fisherman when they were unable to put to sea. They are made from broken oars, masting or spars of wood, and carved into totems. This was a traditional piece of Celtic folk art which has undergone a revival in recent years. Examples of both are contained within the museum.

● The Painted Bird, St Ives

SW 517405. *The shop is located on Fore Street in the town.*

The Painted Bird is a must-stop shop for the Celtic enthusiast in Cornwall. Started in 1991, the shop not only stocks a range of Celtic-themed gifts and products, from Cornwall, but also displays items from the other Celtic nations. It has a particularly good range of Celtic music and Celtic-inspired jewellery.

● Plain-an-gwary and Cornish Drama, St Ives

SW 515493. *This sits on the hill at Stennack, leading from the harbour towards Zennor. The medical centre (once a Primary School) marks the location.*

The parish accounts of St Ives in the period 1571 to 1587 indicate a range of theatrical activity occurring in the town. A play once ran in the town for six days. Considerable construction needed to be completed for the performance because the accounts indicate payment for trees and wood, the making of Heaven and the need for half a dozen lambs' skins. There is also mention of an interlude with elm boards needed in the playing place. Funding for the play appears to have come from the ale drunk, which increases during the week-long run. By 1633, the drama seems to have shut down – replaced instead by a King and Queen of Summer, hosting 'Somer games'. Perhaps the play was an imagining of the life of St Ia, which seems to have many dramatic possibilities. Players from Germoe and as far away as St Columb Major (in mid Cornwall) also performed at St Ives.

● The Fairy Well, Carbis Bay

SW 536387. *The well is close to the cliff path above Carrack Gladden.*

It is perhaps apt that somewhere in Cornwall there is a well named in this way. A proliferation of fairy stories dominate the major nineteenth-century folktale collections of Robert Hunt and William Bottrell.

● Trencrom Castle, Trencrom Hill, near St Ives

SW 518362. *Lanes lead to the site off the A3074 where it meets the A30.*

Originally a Neolithic site, it was further developed in the Iron Age and several roundhouses can be found in the enclosure. The site may well have been occupied as late as the ninth century.

● The Giant's Well, Trencrom Hill, near St Ives

SW 520363. *The chair-shaped well is found in the Iron Age hill fort.*

The alignment of this well is interesting. It is due north of St Michael's Mount and faces the sunsets of the Spring and Autumn Equinox. It is again associated with giant lore; this time with the giant Trecobben who was in perpetual conflict with Cormoran at St Michael's Mount. In the valley to the east of the hill is the so-called Bowl Rock which is supposed to have been hurled by Cormoran against Trecobben.

The Giant's Well, Trencom Hill.

The Church of St Euny, Lelant,
overlooking the River Hayle

● Agnes Davey, Church of St Euny, Lelant, near Hayle

SW 548377. *The church is located north of the village.*

From the dispositions of the Bishop's Consistory Court at Exeter in 1572 we learn of a famous case of defamation where a local woman called Agnes Davey was called a 'whore' and 'whore bitch' – and unusually, these being spoken in 'English and not in Cornowok'. This is interesting since it suggests Cornish was the community language of the period. A recorder named William Hawysh wrote down the disposition noting that the incident happened on *dew whallon gwa metton in eglos de Lalant* [All Saints morning in Lelant church].

● Henry Jenner's grave, Church of St Euny churchyard, Lelant

SW 547377. *Follow the path between the old churchyard and the new one to the west. Turn into the modern churchyard. The grave is located on the left side close to the wall.*

Henry Jenner (1848–1934) is considered by many observers to be the father-figure of the Cornish language and Celto-Cornish revival. He was born at St Columb Major in mid Cornwall, and in the 1870s he became aware of the oral tradition of Cornish operating in Penwith. Over a long career at the British Museum library, Jenner discovered the *Charter Endorsement* (originally from St Stephen-in-Brannel) and liaised with the Reverend W.S. Lach-Szyrma (1841–1915) gathering survivals and fragments from Newlyn. On the suggestion of L.C. Duncombe Jewell (b.1866) of the Celto-Cornish Society [Cowethas Kelto-Kernuack], in 1904, Jenner completed *The Handbook of the Cornish Language*. In the book Jenner asks, 'Why should Cornishmen learn Cornish? The question is a fair one, the answer is simple. Because they are Cornishmen.' In the 1920s Jenner helped Nance in developing the Old Cornwall Societies and then in 1928 became the first Grand Bard of the Cornish Gorsedd. Over the course of his long career, Jenner wrote numerous articles on Arthuriana, Tristana and Cornish literature. Jenner was also made a bard of the Breton Goursez in 1901, being fluent in Breton. This helped to established firm ideological links between the Breton and Cornish revival. Jenner was a Stuart Royalist, and although understanding Celtic identity, he was not committed to separatism. Toward the end of his life, Jenner converted to Catholicism, which he eventually came to believe was the purest form of Celtic spirituality. Jenner's model for the revival of Cornish was actually based on late traditional texts in Cornish – it being closer to the lived contemporary speech of West Cornwall. Nance however, rejected this model. A.S.D. Smith (1883-1950) wrote of Jenner in the following englyns:

The grave of Henry and Kitty Lee Jenner.

A'n Dasserghyans Kernewek ef o tas,
Mur y garenza dhe Gernow y wlas
Py fen-ny, na-ve ef ha'y were bras?

Down o y skyans, cuf y golon hel,
Rak les Kernowyon mar a-ve y whel,
Gony pan ve tremeneys a'agan gwel.

[To the Cornish Revival he was a father, great his love for Cornwall his country; where would we be, were it not for him and his great help?

Deep was his knowledge, kind his generous heart, great was his work for the good of the Cornish people, woe to us when he passed from sight.]

Jenner was married to the poet and artist Katherine Lee Jenner [*nee* Rawlings] (1853-1936) who complemented much of his work. She is also buried here at Lelant.

From *The Old Names* by Katherine Lee Jenner

The half-forgotten music of old names
Clings to the rocks and hills,
And an intangible human fragrance gives
To senseless earth, and fills
With glamour half divine all the wild places,
Recalling the old days,
When man on earth believed that the Divine
Encompassed all his ways.

Out of the vast void of oblivion
Rings the wild melody
Of those old words, whose only resting-place
Is the vague memory
Of man, the creature so prone to forget,
Yet who forgetting clings,
Subconsciously remembering their sense,
To the old names and things.

Lelant church cross.

Crosses, Lelant

SW 547377, SW 548375, SW 548376, SW 548372, SW 548373.

St Uny's churchyard at Lelant holds several Celtic crosses of varying types and sizes. To the west of the church is six foot tall wheel-headed cross, with a carved figure of Christ on the western side (SW 547377). To the north east is another smaller cross with another carved figure (SW 548375) and on the south side is another tall wayside cross (SW 548376). On the right hand side of the south porch of the church (SW 548372) is Trevethoe Cross, which once stood locally in the gardens of Trevethoe House. An impressive cross is also to be found at SW 548373 on the western bank of the estuary.

Collurian Well, White Cross, near Hayle

SW 523347. *To reach the well, turn off the A30 at Whitecross and head north to the farm at Collurian. The well is in the left had side of the farm lane.*

This well is a little neglected but it was thought to have powerful healing properties, particularly for eye diseases.

Crosses, St Paul's Church and churchyard, Ludgvan, near Penzance

SW 505330.

Three crosses can be found in the churchyard: the first a wheel-headed cross at SW 505330 is south east of the church itself; the second – a Latin style cross - is near the south entrance (SW 505330), while the third in on the eastern side, set on a base (SW 505330). Inside the church at the foot of the belfry is a decorated knotwork carved shaft of a cross which is embedded into the step (SW 505330).

Wheel-headed crosses, Lelant.

● Chysauster courtyard house settlement, Newmill, near Penzance

SW 473350. *The site is signposted from the B3311. There is a nearby car park.*

Consisting of nine courtyard houses, this site is one of the most spectacular Romano-British villages to be found in Britain. High walls still remain and life here can be easily imagined. The community is well-organised with a central street, and a set of gardens. To the north east once stood the field systems that were managed by the residents here. At the southern end of the village is a ruined fogou – the entrance of which it is still possible to see. There are also remains of an earlier Iron Age settlement on the same site.

● Market Cross, Penzance

SW 469301. *This cross now stands beside the Penlee House Gallery and Museum in the middle of Penzance.*

This monument was first recorded to be at the corner of a house at the lower end of Causewayhead in 1829. It was then moved close to the Market House, then the Morrab Gardens and finally Penlee

The original site of the Old Market Cross, Penzance at the corner of Causewayhead. The cross can be seen at the corner of the building.

The eleventh century cross that once stood outside the Market House in Penzance from 1867-1899 is now sited outside Penlee House Museum and Gallery. It is believed to be the cross of King Ricatus.

gardens in 1953. It holds knotwork, inscriptions and two curious figures. One inscription reads in Latin PROCUMBUNT IN FORIS – QUICUMQUE PACE VENIT HIC [They lie here in the open, whosoever comes hither in peace, let him pray for their souls]. Another probably says REGIS RICATI CRUX [the cross of King Ricatus]. Charles Thomas has labelled the cross 'a Cornish wonder' and has argued for the mathematical mysticism of its construction. The larger figure on the cross is somewhat incomplete. Thomas argues that the figure on the side is a miniature of the King holding a model of the cross.

● Hurling Ball, Penlee House Gallery and Museum, Penzance

SW 469301. *This is found on display inside the Penlee House Gallery and Museum.*

Hurling (which is described in detail in the entry about St Columb [SW 913637]) was once popular in Penwith. Hurling is a kind mob football game with Celtic origins. At the Museum here can be seen a hurling ball from nearby Paul bearing the Cornish language inscription '*Paul Tuz whek Gwaro Tek heb ate buz Henwis 1704*'. This might be translated to 'Men of Paul – sweet fair play without hate to be called'.

● Golowan and Montol Festivals, Penzance

SW 473303. *Penzance is located at the eastern end of Mount's Bay. Turn left off the A30 at Chyandour to reach the town centre.*

Golowan is the Cornish language word used to mark the midsummer celebrations of the ritual year in Cornwall. Traditionally, the celebrations were conducted on St John's Eve – the 23rd June. The festivities have been revived since 1991, though there is good historical and folkloric evidence of previous centuries completing components such as a mock mayor and Penglaz – a mast type of Obby Oss. The core of the modern festival are the three days known as Mazey Eve, Mazey Day and Quay Fair Day – which is now a huge community arts celebration. Mazey Day sees Market Jew Street closed and a long parade winds through the town – composed of local schoolchildren, musicians and themed constructions of Celticity. Theatre, poetry and music events coincide. *Montol* meanwhile is the term, first recorded by Edward Lhuyd in 1700, meaning 'winter solstice' and it is celebrated in a present-day revived festival between the 15th and 22nd of December. The festival has lots of concurrent events but includes revivals of guising (disguised dancers), a Mummers' Play and a beacon lit at Lescudjack Hillfort. A Lord of Misrule is chosen and Penglaz is also paraded. Golowan and Montol are presently one of the leading representations of festival Celticity in Cornwall.

Montol Festival.

● Celtic temperament and the Brontë family, Penzance

SW 474302. *The Wesleyan Methodist Chapel is located at the southern end of Chapel Street.*

Maria Branwell (1783–1821) was the Cornish mother of the writers Emily Brontë (1818–1848), Anne Brontë (1820–1849), Charlotte Brontë (1816–1849) and the painter and poet Branwell Brontë (1817–1848). Maria was born in Penzance; her father Thomas Branwell was a successful merchant who owned several properties throughout the town. With others, they helped to develop the first Wesleyan Methodist Chapel in the town. Maria met Patrick Brontë in 1813 when visiting her Aunt Jane and Uncle John Fennell in Yorkshire after four family deaths between 1808 and 1812. A number of critics have observed traces of Celtic temperament and imagination in the works of the Brontës – supposedly derived from their Cornish roots.

Maria Branwell Brontë.

● The poetry of James Jenkin, Alverton, Penzance

SW 465302. *Alverton is on the western side of Penzance*

Jenkins lived in Alverton, Penzance and he was writing around 1700. Very little of his poetry has survived although he was regarded as being talented by his contemporaries. This short poem, written with internal rhyme, offers somewhat world-weary advice about women, relationships and life.

Ma leeaz Greage. Lacka vel Zeage.
Gwel gerres. Vell commerez.
Ha ma leeaz Bennen. Pocare an Gwennen.
Eye vedn gwrrez de gu Teez. Dandle peath an beaz.
Fleaz hep skeeanz. Vedn gweel gu Seeaznz.
Bur mor crown gy pedery. Pan dall gu gwary.
Ha madra ta. Pandrigg Seera ha Damah.
Narehanz moaz dan Cooz. Do cuntle gu booz.
Buz gen nebbes lavirrians. Eye venjah dendel gu booz dillaz.

[There are many wives worse than chaff,
Better left than taken,
And there are many women like the bees,
They will help their men to earn worldly wealth.
Children without wisdom will do their whim,
But if they think what their play is worth
And take careful note of what father and
   mother did
They would not go to the wood to collect
   their food
But with a little labour they would earn their food and drink.]

● Lescudjack Hill Fort, near Penzance

SW 476310. *The hill fort is located towards the eastern side of the town, close to the A30. Castle Road runs alongside the site.*

Lescudjack hill fort is an unexcavated Iron Age settlement. Its name probably comes from the Cornish *Lan* [enclosure] and *socsek* [shielded]. A single rampart surrounds an area of approximately three acres.

● Lesingey Round Hill Fort, near Penzance

SW 453304. *This is located just off the A3701. Coming from Penzance, turn down Lesingey Lane. The hill fort is on the right hand side, a short walk across the fields.*

Celtic energy appears to exude from this location. Lesingey is an Iron Age fort but it is enclosed in a more modern stone hedge. The interior is overgrown with trees. It once had commanding views of the landscape east of Penzance.

⬤ May Horns, Newlyn and Penzance

SW 463290. *The ceremony and procession takes place on May 1st, beginning at the Tolcarne Inn, Newlyn.*

The blowing of May horns was a traditional event in many Cornish communities, to welcome in the Summer. In Newlyn and Penzance, this tradition has recently been revived. 'Mayers' are permitted to wear white, green and all kinds of greenery. The idea is to make as much noise as possible to mark the change in the ritual year. In the nineteenth century itinerant merchants would come into towns with the specific purpose of selling children and young people May horns.

⬤ *The Pilchard Curing Rhyme* by John Boson, Newlyn

SW 464265. *This spot on the coastal road to Mousehole offers a good view of the harbour at Newlyn.*

John Boson (1665-c.1720) was the son of the merchant Nicholas Boson. In the so-called *Pilchard Curing Rhyme* (c.1710), Boson celebrates the importance of pilchard fishing to the community around Newlyn. He takes the reader through the processes of curing, storing and packing the fish, emphasising the social cohesion needed. The last lines of the poem show how pilchards were exported to Catholic countries around the Mediterranean for Lent. Although the pilchard industry is no longer significant in Cornwall, fishing remains an important occupation. Cornish survived in fishing communities for longer, and was generally used as the main method of communication when at sea.

Ma canow vee wor Hern gen Cock ha Rooz.	[My song is of pilchards with boat and net
Kameres en zans Garrack glase en Kooz.	Taken in the bay of the Grey Rock in the Wood.
Poth'u an Coocoe devithes Treea	When the boats had come home
Durt Moar Tees Por Dega dega Creea	From the sea people cried, "Tithe! Tithe!"
Ha kennifer Bennen oggas e Teen	And every woman near to her husband
Gen Kawall ha Try Cans Hern wor e Kein.	With a basket and three hundred pilchards on
Th'a gweel Barcadoes en Kenifer Choy	her back.
Gen Ganow leaz Hern, Hern, Holan moy	To make smoked pilchards in every house
	With mouth wide open, "Pilchards! Pilchards!
	More salt!]

⬤ Madron Holy Well, Madron

SW 446328. *On the B3312 just past Madron, turn right. There is a car park. The well and chapel are close by.*

Madron well is reached by a magical, tree-lined path from the car park. Little is actually known about Madron – or his or her sex. Some possibilities are the Welsh Saint Padarn or the Irish Saint Madran, who founded the abbey and bishopric at Tréguir in Brittany. A female Saint Madryn is also celebrated in the stained glass windows of Tintagel Church, so there may be connection to her. The well here is

Madron Well.

dressed and decorated to spectacular effect. The clouties tied to the surrounding branches represent an idea that as they slowly decayed, so would the illness or affliction. The well itself is difficult to reach, it lying the middle of boggy ground. This might be the reason for the nearby stone-encased water in the chapel. Among the writers inspired by the location was the Anglo-Cornish, North-Cornwall-based poet, Robert Stephen Hawker, who ties the well at Madron to the Arthurian corpus.

The Doom-Well of St Madron by Robert Stephen Hawker

"Plunge thy right hand in St. Madron's spring,
If true to its troth be the palm you bring:
But if a false sigil thy fingers bear,
Lay them the rather on the burning share."

Loud laughed King Arthur when as he heard
That solemn friar his boding word:
And blithly he sware as a king he may
"We tryst for St. Madron's at break of day."

"Now horse and hattock, both but and ben,"
With the cry at Lauds, with Dundagel men;
And forth they pricked upon Routorr side,
As goodly a raid as a king could ride.

The Bapistry at Madron.

● Madron Well Chapel, Madron

SW 447328. *The Chapel is a short distance on from the well.*

Madron Well Chapel seems to eloquently represent so much about Celtic Cornwall. The ancient chapel or baptistry is an impressive structure with a well set in one corner and a set of stone side benches for resting pilgrims. The altar at the end of the chapel says much about the layeredness of Celtic spirituality in Cornwall. The Lord's Prayer in Cornish often jostles with Neo-Pagan offerings, corn crosses, candles and crystals. In the altar a square hole may be seen, probably the position for a cross or an image of a saint. The folkloric record gives an established history of healing and miraculous cures at the site. The baptistry was partially destroyed during the Reformation when some of the icons were removed and destroyed. The Chapel is still a centre of worship for both Christian and Neo-Pagan groups.

The Lord's Prayer in Cornish: Pader Agan Arluth

Agan Tas-ny, us yn nef, Benyges re bo dha Hannow, Re dheffo dha wlascor, Dha voth re bo gwres, y'n nor kepar hag y'n nef. Ro dhyn-ny hedhya agan bara pup deth-oll; Ha gaf dhyn agan camwyth, Kepar del aven-nyny dhe'n re-na us ow camwul er agan pyn-ny; Ha na wra agan gorra yn temptasyon, Mes delyrf ny dyworth drok. Rag dhyso-jy yu an wlascor, ha'n gollan, ha'gordhyans. Bys vyken ha binary. Amen.

Inside the Bapistry, Madron.

● Crosses, Madron Parish

SW 453318, SW 453318, SW 454315, SW 447305, SW 448291.

Madron's spiritual past and present is reflected in the high number of crosses to be found in the parish. A good starting point is the churchyard at Madron church. At SW 453318, close to the tower is a wheel-headed wayside cross, with a figure of Christ on the eastern face. Rather strangely, he has no feet. A gothic cross is found nearby (SW 453318) close to the south porch. A taller and more substantial Latin-style cross is to be found a couple of fields away, south of Madron church at SW 454315. This is known as Bocathnoe Cross. Just to the south at Heamoor at SW 460313 is Heamoor Cross, supported by a three-stepped stone base. *Park an Growes* Cross ['Field of the Cross' Cross] is at Park an Growes Farm (SW 447305) and can be accessed via a public footpath. Trembath Cross is found further west close to Buryas Bridge (SW 448291).

● The Battle of Vellandruchar, near Penzance

SW 435435. *This is found just off the A3071 from Penzance to Newbridge.*

William Bottrell, Robert Hunt and Henry Jenner draw attention to the Arthurian traditions which surround the location of Vellandruchar or Vellandruchia ['wheel mill']. Supposedly, Arthur once fought a battle with Danish invaders on ground here (the Danes were more likely to be Saxons). So great was the slaughter that the waters of the mill ran with blood. Archaeology of the surrounding area has revealed a number of finds of arrow, spear and axe heads which do indicate a considerable battle. The area is also well known for its adder population. According to Thomas Malory, Arthur's last battle began because a knight was bitten by an adder, who raised his sword to kill it. Other knights mistook this sword-drawing as the signal to start the conflict. Not far off is the location of Boleigh (SW 437248) and this has also been touted as a possible battlefield. The name may mean place of slaughter but equally could mean milk place or dairy farm [*Boleath*], or even place by the slab [*Bos legh*]. Jenner also suggests that the river running through the mill – known as the Kemyel – might have been the Kemelen mentioned by Gerald of Wales or the Camlan of the continuer of Nennius. Other evidence might be derived from the place-name Rosemodress [the heath of Mordred] (SW 441237) and maybe Tregadgwith (SW444257), with one translation of this being 'battle trees' – the site of a conflict within a wood. Other Arthurian-associated place-names might be Trevorian [Morian's farm] (SW421264) with Morian mentioned in the *Gododdin* (a British poem dating from around 600). Bosjewan or Bojewan [The house of Ewan] (SW434273) might have an association with Urien of Rheged who had a son called Ewan [or Owain] – named by Malory as Sir Ewaine.

West Cornwall and The Lizard

● Davies Gilbert, St Erth

SW 549350. St Erth is to the south of the A30 near Hayle. At the causeway by Hayle Estuary, turn south.

Davies Gilbert (1767–1839) was the only son of Edward Giddy, curate of St Erth parish church, and Catherine Davies, daughter of Henry Davies of nearby Tredrea Manor. Davies Giddy would later adopt Gilbert as his surname, the maiden name of his wife, though to complicate matters, he also wrote under the pseudonym of Edward Collins Giddy. Gilbert was educated at Penzance Grammar School and Pembroke College, Oxford, later became High Sheriff of Cornwall, and later Member of Parliament for Helston, and Bodmin. In 1826 he edited John Keigwin's translation of *Passyon Agan Arluth* which he called *Mount Calvary* and under his pseudonym published *A Cornish Cantata*, a set of rhymed Cornish place-names, in an attempt to show the mystical poetry of language and place:

Vel-an drukya Cracka Cudna
Tuzemenhall Chun Crowzenwhrah,
Banns Burnuhal Brance Bosfrancan,
Treeve Trewhidden Try Trembah

Carn Kenidgiac Castle-Skudiac
Beagle-Tuben Amalvear,
Amalibria Arnal-whidden,
Skillywadden Trink Polpeor

Pellalith Pellalla-wortha,
Buzza-vean Chyponds Boswase,
Venton-gimps Boskestal Raftra,
Hendra Grancan Treen Bostraze

Perhaps paradoxically, in his introduction to *Mount Calvary*, Gilbert rejoices in the fact that Cornish was not much longer in use. However, Gilbert did study Cornish with an eye on the emergence of philology, which had traced the links between Greek, Latin and the Germanic and Scandinavian languages, and would soon come to be applied on Brythonic and Goidelic languages.

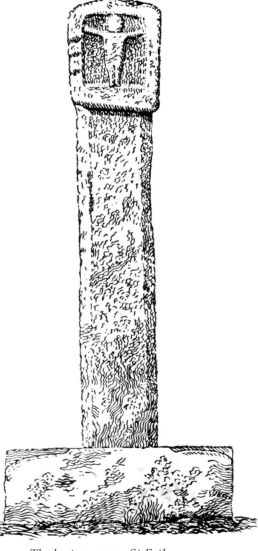

The lantern cross, St Erth.

97

Churchyard cross, Phillack.

St Phillack's Well.

St Phillack's Cross.

● Cross Head and Cross Shaft, St Erth parish church, St Erth

SW 549350. *St Erth parish church is towards the south of the village.*

Several interesting sections of Celtic crosses can be found at St Erth parish church. In the southern part of the churchyard is a wheel-headed churchyard cross, holding five bosses and a stretched image of Christ. Inside the church is a cross shaft, which is intricately decorated with knotwork and holds the remains of an image of Christ. In the main street in the village, there is also a lantern cross (SW 550351).

● St Phillack's Well, Phillack, near Hayle

SW565384. *Her well may be found close to Phillack church. Proceed up some steps and through a gate. The well is immediately on the right.*

St Felicitas (or Phillack) came to Cornwall with her sister Ia, and her brothers Euny and Erc. Her well is a circular hole surrounded by stone. It is covered with a metal gate. Felicitas received the same cruel fate as her sister Ia, at the hands of King Teudar (sometimes Tewdar, or Tewdrig).

Phillack church

The cross at Mexico Lane.

● Churchyard cross, Phillack

SW 565384. *This cross is located on the south side of Phillack churchyard.*

This impressive Celtic cross is of the wheel-headed type, though on the western side it also has an elongated figure of Christ. Somewhat unusually, Christ's legs protrude into the shaft.

● Wheel-headed crosses and Chi-Rho design, Phillack

SW 565384. *The crosses are located around the churchyard and close to the church.*

There is a small wheel-headed wayside cross situated on the south-western side of the churchyard between the lynch-gate and the church tower (SW 565384). A second cross known as the Wheal Alfred Cross (since it was used as a gatepost at Wheal Alfred mine some 2 miles south east of Phillack) is situated against an outbuilding on the south-east side of the church. Carved from granite, it holds a Latin cross. A Chi-Rho stone is located in the wall of the south porch of the church. The Chi-Rho design is one of the earliest Christian symbols (itself based on the life-giving Egyptian Ankh symbol) and this one is dated to the late 5th or early 6th century. West from the church, set against a hedge near Mexico Lane is another wheel-headed cross.

Looking past Phillack Cross towards the lych-gate, 1973.

● *The Life of St Gwinear*, Gwinear, near Hayle

SW 590393. *Gwinear is found close to the A30 and is best accessed by the minor roads leading from Angarrack.*

Saint Gwinear was an Irish Prince and a pupil of Saint Patrick, who because of his faith became exiled to Brittany by his father King Clito. When Clito died, Gwinear was asked to return to Ireland, and claim the throne. However, Gwinear rejected this, and instead, travelled with a party of some 777 missionaries to Cornwall. The local tyrant and pagan King Teudar killed many of the evangelists in Gwinear's party, and then killed Gwinear himself. The Penzance-based writer Richard Ogden (1951– 2003) has written a new mystery play titled *The Life of St Gwinear*, which was published in 2008, but first performed under his direction at Penzance Grammar School sometime in the early 1980s. The play is not a verse drama, but does move between the past and present, dramatising the Saint's life. Such a work proves the continuum of this form of drama in Celtic Cornwall.

● Crosses, Gwinear, near Hayle

SW 590373, SW594373, SW 586412.

A number of crosses can be found in and around the village. On the north side of the churchyard is a wheel-headed wayside cross known as churchyard cross (SW 590373). Located on a window sill inside the church is a fragment of a wayside cross, and moved here from close-by Polmenor is another wayside cross near the north porch (SW594373). Near the south porch of the church is another church- yard cross (SW 586412).

● St Gwinear's Well, near Barripper

SW 615387. *From the A30 junction at west Camborne, take the minor roads south to Barripper, and the Carnhell Green. Then turn north to Roseworthy Barton.*

Close to farm at Roseworthy Barton you will see a marshy area of rushes. This was the site of St Gwinear's Well, and in a field some short distance away was a Chapel. To this day this field is called Chapel Field. The well is now used for domestic water and had been cemented all around. Gwinear was clearly a major saint in the pantheon of Cornish saints, so this would have been an important Celtic pilgrimage site.

● Cheston Marchant, Gwithian, near Hayle

SW 586413. *Gwithian village is found on the B3301 from Hayle to Portreath.*

Cheston Marchant, who died in 1695, was a centenarian who could speak only Cornish and not a word of English. She lived at Gwithian.

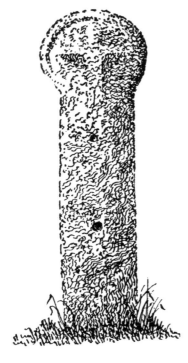

Wheel-headed wayside cross, Gwinear churchyard.

● Nine Maidens Down Cross, Clowance, Crowan

SW 633348. *The cross is situated in the ground of the Clowance Estate, four miles to the south of Camborne.*

Originally a parish boundary stone where four parishes met, the cross has been moved several times. It was re-erected at Clowance in 1989 and is highly decorated. It is one of Cornwall's most distinctive wheel-headed crosses.

● Calvadnack roundhouse settlement, Carnmenellis

SW 690355. *Travelling from Four Lanes to Helston on the B3297, take a left hand minor road to Tolcarne Wartha. The settlement can be accessed via a public footpath.*

There are four round houses here, alongside a large field enclosure. Although there was Bronze Age activity here, this probably dates to the Iron Age.

● *Bewnans Meriasek* [The Life of St Meriasek], the church of St Martin and St Meriadoc, Camborne

SW 645401. *The church of St Martin and St Meriadoc is in the middle of Camborne town centre on the A3407*

Nine Maidens Down cross.

The church of St Martin and St Meriadoc is a fifteenth-century building made entirely of granite. It was originally dedicated to the Celtic saint St Meriodoc, with St Martin being added when the church was rebuilt in the fifteenth century. *Bewnans Meriasek* [*The Life of St Meriasek (or Meriadoc)*] is a miracle play written in Middle Cornish in 1504. The recently discovered *Bewnans Ke* and *Bewnans Meriasek* are the only two surviving vernacular plays in Britain dealing with the lives of the saints. The 4568 lines, in seven- and four-syllabled verses, of *The Life of Meriasek* form an exuberant weaving together of historical and legendary characters from different centuries, with strong undertones of contemporary Cornish politics of the late fifteenth century. It was probably written at the monastic centre of Glasney College, Penryn by Radolphus Ton. The work was performed over two days in the round, offering the twin soteriological themes of conversion and healing through miracles involving Meriasek, the Pope Sylvester, and the Virgin Mary. According to tradition, St Meriasek lived in Brittany in the 7th century.

The first day of the play begins with Meriasek's education in Brittany, but his mind is soon set on rejecting worldly comforts; he travels as a Christ-like missionary to Cornwall, and comes into contact with a pagan king, the Tyrant Teudar (possibly as Philip Payton has suggested, a satirical interpretation of Henry VII in the aftermath of the rebellions of 1497). Meriasek and Teudar debate the Virgin birth, and Teudar tries to tempt Meriasek. Meriasek hides in a rock (*Carrek Veryasek* [Meriasek's rock]) where he becomes a hermit. Teudar has a number of Cornish-baiting lines, which would have undoubtedly raised the hackles of the audience:

Duke Kernov hag oll y dus	[Duke of Cornwall and all his folk,
indan ove threys me as glus	Under my feet I will crush them
poren kepar ha treysy	Just like grains of sand.]

If Teudar is a representation of Henry VII, it is an extraordinarily clever dramatic device, since the authorities may not have understood the Cornish language, or the allegory. Events shift to St Sylvester who heals a leprosy-stricken Constantine while in Cornwall, while a duke of Cornwall, reminiscent of King Arthur, challenges Teudar. As much as the play is written as an origin story for Camborne, it also extols the energy of a wider Celtic and Catholic Cornwall (and several locations mentioned in this volume), not least when the Duke of Cornwall first parades in the 'playing place':

Me yv Duke in oll Kernow	[I am Duke in all Cornwall
indella ytho ov thays	So was my father
hag vhel arluth in pov	And a high lord in the country
a tamer the pan an vlays	From Tamar to Land's End
tregys off lemen heb wov	I am dwelling now, without a lie,
berth in castel dynas	Within the castle of Dynas
sur in peddre	Surely in Pidar,
ha war an tyreth vhel	And in the high land
thym yma castel arel	I have another castle,
a vath gelwys tyndagyel	Which is called Tintagel:
henna yv ov fen tregse	That is my chief dwelling seat.]

The second day opens with Meriasek healing the blind Earl Globus and a demoniac. Meriasek is chosen to succeed as bishop, first resisting but eventually agreeing to the task. In a developed sequence, a boy is imprisoned by a tyrant, and his mother prays before a statue of Mary, taking home their image of the infant Jesus when her supplications seem of no avail. Mary, with Jesus's blessing, frees the boy, and when he returns home, his mother restores the image of the baby to the statue. In a grotesque counterpart to this miracle is a comedic black mass.

A second Sylvester sequence follows, when he is asked to dispose of a menacing dragon. The play ends with Meriasek's death. Some critics have argued that the play is too disparate, but in fact, there is substantial coherence between all the plots. An excellent English language translation of the play (*The Camborne Play*) was made by Myrna Combellack in 1988. *Bewnans Meriasek* has not been performed in its entirety in the modern era, and so is ripe for revival.

● Crosses and Celtic heritage, Camborne

SW 645400, SW 633400, SW 647400.

Inside the church may be found a carved altar stone (SW 645400), originally located at Chapel Ia, Troon. This chapel of Saint Ia was recorded in 1429 and a holy well – named *Fenton-ear* [the well of Ia] was sited nearby. This relates to the cross on the south-western side of the churchyard known as St Ia's Cross (SW 645400). The cross is decorated and inscribed but has several holes in it, probably from its location once at the well head at Crane. In the chancel wall is another cross head (SW 645400). Two other chapels are known to have once existed near the Church of St Martin and Meriadoc. One was dedicated to Our Lady and St Anne (which might fit the Mary-themed aspects of the drama) and the other chapel is found at Menadarva [derived from *Mertha-Derwa*] being dedicated to St Derwa. On the western side of the churchyard may be seen the Connor Downs Cross (SW 633400), which stands around six foot high. This originally stood at a parish boundary between Gwinear and Gwithians and was known locally as the *Maen Cadoar* ('Cador's stone'). Close by, and located in Commercial Square, outside Camborne Institute (SW 647400) is the so-called Institute Cross. A number of modern nineteenth- and twentieth-century Celtic crosses are also found in the churchyard.

● *Pradeer inta Pan drez tho those*, the church of St Martin and St Meriadoc, Camborne

SW 645401. *The church of St Martin and St Meriadoc is in the middle of Camborne town centre on the A3407.*

Oliver J. Padel has drawn attention to this couplet from c.1638 found in an account of churchwardens for Camborne. It seems to refer back to the Reformation.:

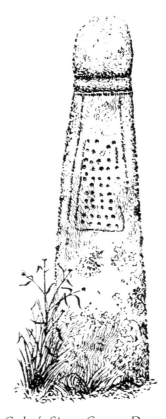

Cador's Stone, Connor Down.

Pradeer inta Pan drez tho those	[Consider well what is to come,
Ha Fay war goth gacha tho voze.	And let go of faith in the old.]

The account, dated 27 March 1638 was completed by Nicholas Hockein and Olliuer Glanfill, but the couplet was written in a different hand. The Cornish couplet is preceded by another in English: "He that doth like this Fist, Let him make a better where he list." According to Padel, potential writers in the Camborne area of this time were Richard Pendarves (died 1674) and the Reverend William Oliver (died 1681) but the evidence is inconclusive.

● Plain-an-gwarry, Rosewarne, near Camborne

SW 646414. *This is located on the northern side of the A30 close to Camborne, on the northern side of a property called 'Rosewarne Gate'.*

Local folk memory in the area talks of this field as 'Ring Close' and it was once where the people of Camborne wrestled and played sports. In this visit to Cornwall in 1700, Edward Lhuyd knew this area as being called 'Plains… Hent's one called Plain an gwari where they used to act, but no one remembers it'. It is now part of an industrial park. Tantalisingly, it is only a short distance from the church of St Martin and St Meriodoc, so was this where performances of *The Life of Meriasek* took place? Just to the north at Magor are the remains of a Romano-British villa (SW 637424). There are no upstanding remains to be found.

● Industrial Celts, Pool, near Camborne

SW 667413. *Michell's Shaft is located on the A3047.*

Much of this book has shown the agrarian nature of Celtic Cornwall. Related to this are notions about Celtic peoples having an oral tradition, being in tune with the land and environment, and being romantic and superstitious. To some extent, this traditional notion of Celticity has been turned upside-down in Cornwall, where industrialisation has walked hand in hand with Celtic identity. There has been, in fact, a close connection with mining and industry since the Bronze Age period. Thus the Celts of Cornwall may go against the grain of traditional Celtic culture, and be more concerned with controlling the environment, having a practical view of the world, and able to be industrial. Although Cornish culture has been marked by period of agrarian, oral and superstitious Celticity, it has also shown other aspects of Celticity – not least the tradition of hard-rock mining. This can be seen in numerous locations in Cornwall, but also here in particular, at East Pool. Michell's Shaft Engine House contains the last beam whim engine to be installed in Cornwall. It was built in 1887 by Holman Brothers. It has a cylinder of 30 inches. At close by Taylor's Shaft, there is a Cornish Mines and Engines discovery centre, also run by the National Trust. One of the engine houses here contains the 90 inch Harvey's Engine.

Tin Miners: Industrial Celts at work.

● Great Flat Lode Trail, Camborne

SW 695398. *The best way to explore the Great Flat Lode trails is on bicycle. Begin at Wheal Buller. Signposts and explanation boards point the way.*

The Great Flat Lode is a huge mineral bearing body located to the south of Carn Brea in West Cornwall. 'Lode' is the Cornish mining term for a vein of mineral running through the underground rock. The Great Flat Lode here has a small gradient, which has meant that successive mining enterprises have been able to access the tin. The Lode was discovered in 1870, and at that point in time was a great boost to the industry. From Wheal Buller, head east to Carnkie, Treskillard and Grenville United mines. The route then takes you through Condurrow, Higher Brea, Tuckingmill, Carn Brea and back to Wheal Buller.

Lots of Cornish-language vocabulary is embedded in the processes of mining. William Pryce (c.1725-1800) wrote *Mineralogia Cornubiensis* for 'the benefit of gentlemen adventuring in tin' so that they could understand the miners' technical vocabulary. A selection of the entries is listed below:

Astel: A board or a plank. [Lhuyd]. An arch or ceiling of boards over the men's heads in a Mine, to save them from the falling stones, rocks, or scales of the lode or its walls. To "throw the Dead to Stulls", is to throw the refuse part of the Mine on these arches or Stalls, both to save the trouble of bringing it up to grass, and because this helps to make the Mine more secure.

Cuare: [Cornish] A quarry of stones.

Dol: Pronounced Doll, is Cornish for 'a valley or dale'. Dol-côth, the old field or meadow. Dol-côth, the old valley or dale. The name of a great mine in Cornwall.

Elvan: [Elven, in Cornish, an 'element, a spark of fire']. A very hard close grained stone, thought to be a bastard limestone, but I do not find that it has any calcarious quality. A very unpromising stratum for Copper Ore.

Gad: [Gedn is Cornish for 'a wedge', Gad an 'iron wedge', Gad is Armoric (Breton) for a Hare]. A Gad is a an iron wedge to drive between the joints of rocks, in order to loosen the ground for the pickaxe.

Guag: [Hunger, emptiness; ac idem, Leary, Cornish]. Tinners holeing into a place which has been wrought before, call it "Holeing the Guag".

Huel: A work, a Mine, as Huel Stean, a Tin Mine: Huel Kalish, the hard work.

Pryan: [from Pryi, Clay, Cornish]. Pryan Ore, Pryan Tin, Pryan Lode, that which is productive of Copper Ore or Tin, but does not break in large solid stones, only in gross pebbles, or sandy with a mixture of clay.

Zigher: [Slow, Cornish] When a very small flow stream of water issues through a cranny underground, is said to Zighyr or sigger.

A group of miners at Dolcoath c.1900.

● Treslothan Cross, Treslothan Church, near Troon

SW 650378. *Treslothan is approximately one and a half miles south of Camborne. In the village of Troon, turn right to Treslothan.*

This wayside cross shows a crude figure with outstretched arms. Close to the cross is situated the grave of the Anglo-Cornish poet John Harris (1820-1884). As well as celebrating Cornwall's bardic and druidical heritage, Harris also offered a 'Romantic construction' of hard-rock mining, celebrating the 'industrial Celtic' heritage.

● Trebowland Round, Comford, near Gwennap

SW 729387. *On the A393 from Ponsanooth to Comford, take a left turn after Burncoose to Trebowland Farm. The round is on the right, a short distance up a track.*

This is probably an Iron Age settlement enclosure, composed of a single circular bank and ditch.

● St Day Old Church, St Day

SW 732423. *St Day is located off the B3298 between Chacewater and Redruth.*

Old St Day church, closed in 1956.

As early as the thirteenth century, there was a chapel of the Holy Trinity as St Day. and another even earlier – which is believed to have been dedicated to St Day as well. This is probably the same commemoration as the Breton Saint Dei. Clearly, along with St Michael's Mount and Penhale Sands, this was one of the great Medieval pilgrimage centres of Cornwall. It could be that St Day's significance is related to the legend associated with nearby Creegbrawse, and this is why is drew so many pilgrims. St Day Old Church is a surviving memory of the significance of the location: built of pock granite in 1828, it soon decayed and was closed in 1956. In 1540, we know that St Day was known as 'the town of Seynte Trynyte' and its popularity may have developed from an document of Pope Gregory in 1070 who declared the significance of the location. An ancient Christmas carol – which may well have a longer Celtic heritage – has also developed in the town. This is called the 'Saint Day Carol':

Now the holly bears a berry,
 as green as the grass:
And May bore Jesus
 who died on the cross;

And Mary bore Jesus Christ
 our Saviour for to be,
And the first tree in the greenwood
 it was the Holly.

● Creegbrawse, near St Day

SW 745435. *Creegbrawse lies between Chacewater and St Day.*

The place-name element 'Creeg' means 'barrow' – a prehistoric burial mound. The brass work in Solomon's temple was supposed to have been made from Cornish tin. Joseph of Arimathea was a tin trader from Phoenicia who made his money through intercourse with the miners and smelters of Cornwall. It has been suggested in several sources that Joseph of Arimathea brought the child Jesus (and sometimes Mary his mother) to Cornwall. He landed them at St Michael's Mount and then travelled inland to Creegbrawse which is the epicentre of the Christ in Cornwall tradition. The Christ in Cornwall legend is also connected to Lammana near Looe, with the Jesus Well in North Cornwall and with Glastonbury in England. The presence of Solomon and Joseph of Arimathea as central characters in the *Ordinalia* cycle may display a long-term connection of Cornwall to the Middle East. An old song connects this legend to the tin miners of Cornwall:

> Joseph was a tin man
> And the miners loved him well.

● Salem, near Chacewater

SW 740443. *Salem is just to the east of Chacewater.*

A similar legend connects Saint Paul to the hamlet of Salem, near Chacewater. Supposedly, Paul travelled to Britain and preached here. It is argued by some observers that the reason the Methodist leader John Wesley was keen on the spiritual significance of both the first and second Gwennap Pits was because of their connections to the Paul and Christ legends in this area.

● St Mary's Fountain, Illogan, near Camborne

SW 664437. *The well is to be found on the road from the middle of Illogan to Tehidy Country Park.*

Clearly a more ancient site, a nineteenth-century stone structure and trough now lay over the well. It is marked 'Mary's Well' and was erected in 1888 by Gustavius Lambert Basset.

● Plain-an-gwarry, Illogan, near Camborne

SW 670440. *The remains of the site are to be found some 75 metres north east of the Old Rectory and 50 metres south from the old school building (now Illogan village hall).*

The Church Terrier of 1680 includes a reference to the churchtown of Great Quintrell, where 'under the hedges [there was] a bowling green or playing place'. The above position seems the best probable location as it would have been sited originally next to the original church, the remains of which may still be seen. It unclear which saint's life or narrative might have been versified for performance here. Many Cornish theatre companies in the present era perform drama in Illogan Village Hall, so we find much continuity in this location.

Gwennap Pit.

St Euny's Well.

● St Euny's Well, Carn Brea village, near Redruth

SW 691413. *The well is located on the outskirts of the village, next to a stream.*

The Irish St Euny has dedications in Sancreed and Crowan parish, though he is patron saint of Redruth too. The well here is very beautiful with a moss-encrusted top stone. Stories say that anyone who drank from the well would avoid a hanging.

● Plain-an-gwarry, Redruth

SW 694424. *The site of the theatre is to be found on the western side of Treleigh Terrace, between the site of Heyden's Works and Colebrook.*

A 'pleyne-an-gwarry' was first recorded in this location in 1583. Whether this was a full circular structure has been the subject of some debate. In a William Borlase manuscript of his antiquarian excursions around Cornwall between 1751 and 1758, held in the Royal Institution of Cornwall in Truro, he observes that 'at a place called Penguare there is a spacious green plot at the northern end of which there is part of a Plan-an-guare, the remaining mound is high but ruinous, and shews no signs of ever having gone more than half round so that one would think it is rather a theatre than an amphitheatre.' If this were the case, then the shape makes for an interesting alternative Medieval theatre space. As St Euny is the patron saint of Redruth – and considering his well is only a short distance away – an origin drama is very likely to have been presented here.

Carn Brea Well.

● Carn Brea Well, Carn Brea, near Redruth

SW 684407. *From the B3297 coming from Redruth, follow the signs to Carnkie. At Carnkie, turn right and follow the track to the top of Carn Brea. The well is just to the north west of the modern castle.*

The unassuming well at the top of Carn Brea [Cornish: hill tor] is close to the Neolithic tor enclosure and Iron Age hill fort to be found there, and probably provided that community with a supply of water. On some maps it is marked as the Giant's well, perhaps because of on-going folkloric associations of giants living on the hill. There are no saints' traditions associated with the well.

● Carn Brea tor enclosure, Carn Brea, near Redruth

SW 686407. *Having reached Carn Brea, the enclosure system extends over much of the hill.*

At this location there are terraces from the Neolithic period, with boulder walls connecting the tors, but the outer ramparts were added in the Iron Age. Between the castle (originally a Medieval hunting lodge) and the Basset monument are eleven roundhouses

● Imagining Druids, Carn Brea, near Redruth

SW 684407. *From the B3297 coming from Redruth, follow the signs to Carnkie. At Carnkie, turn right and follow the track to the top of Carn Brea.*

The hollow rock basins on top of Carn Brea, caused by differential weathering, have long been associated with druidic altar sacrifices. The romantic invention of druidic activity on Carn Brea, is no better completed than in the work of the nineteenth-century Anglo-Cornish poet John Harris. Harris (1820-1884) who hailed from nearby Bolenowe, was much inspired by misplaced antiquarian interest in Carn Brea as a site of druidic and bardic activity for the West Britons – or western Celts of Britain. His poem *A Story of Carn Brea* (1863) considers this theme.

From *A Story of Carn Brea* by John Harris

How the great mountain like a rocky king
Stands silent in the tempest! Not a gust
With water laden, rushing with fierce front
Against his wrinkles, but he shakes it off,
Like filmy atoms from an insect's wing.
The thunder growls upon his splinter'd head,
Yelling from cave to cave, and every crag,
Carved by the Druid in the olden time,
When men were wont to worship on his crest,
Seems like a fiery pillar, as the flames
Leap from the clouds, and lick their knotty sides.
He, awful in his calmness, shakes his locks,
And gazes up into the solemn sky,
As if a strain of music shoot the air.

Rock basins on Carn Brea.

● Druid's Hall, Redruth

SW 697418. *The Druid figure is found above a doorway on Druid's Hall opposite the premises of the Royal British Legion.*

Perhaps because of the association of the place-name element 'Druth' with druids, a splendid carving of a druid – complete with sickle and oak-leaves – is found on the ruined Druid's Hall. The Hall was built in 1859 on the former Town Hall, which contained a theatre. A few remaining walls of the Hall remain, but it now operates as a garden. Perhaps aware of the figure and the historical association, in 1868 the Anglo-Cornish poet John Harris wrote an epic poem based on Druidic activity in Cornwall, which he named *Luda: A Lay of the Druids*:

Druid's Hall entrance, Redruth.

The sun was shining on the lake,
When the good palmer sought the brake.
Leaving the castle on the right,
He walked along the ledgy height
Towards an opening in the wood,
Where a rough Druid temple stood.
For well he knew by sight and sound,

From distant vale and rising ground,
And cottage nestled by the mere,
That a religious rite was near:
And hence he travelled on and strove
Before mid-day to reach the grove
Beyond the rude gorseddau-seat,
Where the wild worshippers would meet.

Both the antiquarian interest in druids as well as a Neo-Pagan revival of interest has prompted many groups to follow a druidic spirituality in contemporary Cornwall. Indeed, although the Cornish Gorsedd frequently distances itself from druidic practice, the ceremony is undoubtedly influenced by such culture. The place-name Redruth, in fact, has little to do with druidic activity and is derived from *red ruyth* [red ford].

● Cornish Studies Library, Cornwall Centre, Redruth

SW 697418. *The library is contained in the Cornwall Centre on Alma Place in the middle of Redruth.*

Housed in the old meat market and Post Office, the Cornwall Centre houses the Cornish Studies Library, which is a resource centre for anyone interested in Celtic Cornwall. The wide-ranging collection covers all aspects of Celtic Studies and includes some 30,000 published sources, 30 local newspapers on microfilm, 160,000 postcards, a large collection of maps and many oral history recordings. The library is open every day of the week except Sundays.

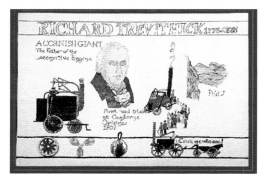

Part of the Tregellas Tapestry

● The Tregellas Tapestry, Cornwall Centre, Redruth

SW 697418. *The tapestry is found in Cornwall Centre and in Market Way below.*

The Tregellas Foundation was established by Rita Tregellas Pope to advance the knowledge and understanding of Cornwall's cultural heritage. The first step of this was to display the history of Cornwall in the form of a tapestry. This modern embroidery project was conceived under the direction of Tregellas Pope. She brought together a team comprising two designers, Joanna Tucker and Annie Corey, and a group of skilled spinners, dyers and embroiderers. The full tapestry is composed of fifty-eight panels, many of which are dedicated to Cornwall's Celtic heritage.

● The formation of Mebyon Kernow, Oates Temperance Hotel, Redruth

SW 698417. *The building of the former Oates Temperance Hotel is located close to Redruth Railway Station. From the station pass under the railway bridge on the A393 and the Hotel is the first large building on the left-hand side.*

The political party *Mebyon Kernow* [Sons of Cornwall] - now often just MK - was founded on Saturday 6th January 1951 at the Oates Temperance Hotel in Redruth. There were thirteen people present at the meeting and a further six sent apologies. Helena Charles was elected chairman, with Lambert Truran as Secretary and George Pawley White at Treasurer. The party was formed as a response to the economic and cultural changes that were affecting Cornwall in the post-war period, with an eye on political movements in the other Celtic countries. The seven original aims of the party were as follows:

1. To study local conditions and attempt to remedy any that may be prejudicial to the best interests of Cornwall by the creation of public opinion or other means.

2. To foster the Cornish Language and Literature.

3. To encourage the study of Cornish history from a Cornish point of view.

4. By self knowledge to further the acceptance of the idea of the Celtic character of Cornwall, one of the six Celtic Nations.

5. To publish pamphlets, broadsheets, articles and letters in the Press whenever possible, putting forward the on-going aims.

6. To arrange concerts and entertainments with a Cornish-Celtic flavour through which these aims can be further advanced.

7. To cooperate with all societies concerned with persevering the character of Cornwall.

Through the 1950s and 1960s, MK was in essence a pressure group with members being able to join other political parties as well, but by the 1970s the organisation was operating as a fully functional political party. Since this time, MK has contested local, Westminster and European elections. In 2011, the Party celebrated its 60th anniversary. The main aim of latter-day *Mebyon Kernow* is still to establish greater autonomy in Cornwall, through the establishment of a legislative Cornish Assembly, with the ideological agenda being Cornish, green, left of centre and decentralist. *Mebyon Kernow* is a member of the European Free Alliance and has close links to *Plaid Cymru*, the nationalist party of Wales.

● Krowji, Redruth

SW 692418. *Krowji is located close to the A3047. At the roundabout, turn back into Redruth.*

Krowji – meaning 'cottage' is a creative arts and business centre located in the Old Grammar School buildings in Redruth. It facilitates the development of the artistic community within West Cornwall, and has on its site a range of creativity – from theatre and textiles, through the web designers and jewellery makers – many of them inspired by Cornwall's Celtic heritage. It is also famed for its Melting Pot Café, in which the Cornish language can often be heard.

● Hell-Fire Corner, Redruth rugby ground, Redruth

SW 897446. *On the A30, take the main exit off to Redruth. At the roundabout on the A3047, take the minor road south. The rugby ground is around quarter a mile away from the roundabout.*

Rugby is a popular sport in Cornwall. Redruth Rugby Football Club was formed in 1875 and is the oldest club in west Cornwall. Rugby's origins were formalised at Rugby School in the late eighteenth century, but soon spread elsewhere across Britain.

There is however, a suggestion that such mass ball games were developed much earlier. Nennius's *Historia Britonum*, from the ninth century CE, for example, explains that groups of boys playing in this way were noted in southern Britain or possibly Wales. Games of this type were also well known in Brittany. The Celtic passion for sport in Cornwall is well-noted in one part of the ground at Redruth – the location known as Hell-Fire corner. This is located close to the main gate. It seems this corner of the ground was the most unsettling for visiting teams because it was where the strongest support and noise came from – perhaps resembling the noise of Hellfire Corner (a perfect target for German gunners) located close to Ypres. Redruth Rugby Football Club has had many great players. One of them was Bert Solomon (1885-1961) who was a star of the early 1900s. Although helping Cornwall to win the 1908 County Championships, Solomon refused later selection for England and the British Lions. As a working-class Celt, he seems to have felt uncomfortable amongst the upper-class English players. The Anglo-Cornish writer D.M. Thomas dramatised his life in his 2004 play *Hell-Fire Corner*.

⬤ Dalla, Tregajorran, near Illogan Highway

SW 675407. *Tregajorran at the north western slopes of Carn Brea.*

Dalla are Cornwall's premier Celtic-influenced band playing roots Cornu-Celtic music. The band's mainstays are Neil Davey (from the famous mid-Cornwall Davey family of Cornish musicians) and Hilary Coleman, and the present line-up includes Bec Applebee, Jen Dyer and Kyt Le Nen Davey. Davey and Coleman's cottage at Tregajorran forms the base for their work. Their music fuses the sounds of clarinet, bouzouki, fiddle, accordion and percussion, and often uses the talents of contemporary bagpiper Will Coleman. Although the group draw on the traditional corpus of Cornu-Celtic music and dance, they are also highly progressive, and over the past decade have researched and evolved Cornish music. Dalla can often be seen playing music at modern Cornish dance gathering known as *Nos Lowen* [Happy Nights]. Their CD releases include *A Richer Vein* (2001), *More Salt* [*Hollan Mouy*] (2004), *Rooz* (2007) and *Cribbar* (2010). Dalla have gone on to influence many new bands playing Cornu-Celtic music, including Pentorr, Radjel and Leski making for a vibrant contemporary music scene drawing on the Celtic musical traditions of Cornwall.

⬤ Bolenowe Holy Well, Bolenowe, near Troon

SW 677378. *Travel south from Camborne to Troon. At Troon, take the minor road to the east over Croft Common to Bolenowe. The well is located on the eastern side of the hamlet.*

This well is sometimes known as Vincent's Well or Chute as it is close to the house where the Vincent family have lived for several generations. There are currently two parallel blocks of granite which mark the well.

⬤ Nance Hill Fort, near Portreath

SW 664450. *The fort is found to the left of the B3300 running from Redruth to Portreath and accessed by a footpath.*

This oval-shaped fort is probably Iron Age. A line of strong defensive ramparts is found in the south west of the structure, with a further enclosed area to the south east.

● Crane Cliff Castle, near Portreath

SW 774196. Travelling on the B3301 from Portreath to Gwithian, park at the car park close to Rekajeage Downs and walk to Crane Castle in a westerly direction.

This was probably once a much larger structure but some of the northern structure has been worn away by the sea. It is an Iron Age settlement, known locally as the 'Bowling Green'. It is a short distance from the Roman-British villa at Magor (SW 637424).

● Thomas Tonkin, Noel Cater, William Allen and Edwin Chirgwin, St Agnes

SW 721516. Tonkin's house at Trevaunance is the large dwelling to the left of the cove.

Thomas Tonkin (1678-1742) was born in St Agnes and educated at Queen's College, Oxford and Lincoln's Inn. Tonkin later became the Member of Parliament for Helston and took part in the Stannary Courts. He lived at Trevaunance, St Agnes, and began to be very interested in the survivals of Cornish both around St Agnes and elsewhere in Cornwall. Eventually, he developed a manuscript titled *Archæologia Cornu-Britannica*, which was later in part published by William Pryce (under his name) in 1790. Believed lost, but mentioned in other correspondence of the period, the manuscript eventually turned up at car boot sale in Totnes in Devon in the early twenty-first century. Between 1700 and 1708 Tonkin corresponded with Edward Lhuyd, with their letters covering discussion of the problems of reviving and sustaining Cornish. Around 1698, Captain Noel Cater wrote this folk song down for Tonkin:

Ha mî ow môs en gûn lâs	[As I went on a green plain
Mî a-glowas trôs an buscas mines	I heard the noise of the tiny fish
Mes mî a-droucias ün pesk brâs, naw ê lostiow;	But I found one big fish with nine tails;
Ol an bôbel en Porthîa ha Marghas Jowan	All the people in St Ives and Marazion
Nerva na wôr dh 'ê gensenjy.	could never get hold of him.]

The song is a riddle, and although Tonkin thought it was about a ray, it is probably about an octopus. In 1704 a local man named William Allen who was one of Tonkin's informants gave him a proverb – the theme of which is a cynical view of marriage:

Kensa blethan, byrla a baye,	[First year, hug and kiss,
Nessa blethan, lull a laye,	Second year, billing and cooing,
Tridgya blethan hanna drubba,	Third year, coming to blows,
Peswarra blethan, mol a Dew war ef reeg dry hy uppa	Fourth year, the curse of God on who brought her here.]

Tonkin was also aware of the work of Edward Chirgwin, who in the same period offered him a Cornish-language version of the popular folk song, commonly known as 'Strawberry Leaves'.

From *Delkiow Sevi* [*Strawberry Leaves*] by Edward Chirgwin.

Pelea era why moaz, moz, fettow, teag,
    Gen agaz bedgeth gwin, ha agaz blew mellyn?
Mi a moaz tha'n venton, sarra wheag,
    Rag delkiow sevi gwra muzi teag.

Pea ve moaz gen a why, moz, fettow, teag,
    Gen agaz bedgeth gwin, ha agaz blew mellyn?
Greuh mena why, sarra wheag,
    Rag delkiow sevi gwra muzi teag.

[Where are you going pretty fair maid,
    With your white face and your yellow hair?
I'm going to the well, sweet sir,
    for strawberry leaves make maids fair.

Shall I go with you pretty fair maid,
    With your white face and your yellow hair?
Do what you want, sweet sir,
    for strawberry leaves make maids fair.]

● The Bolster Bank, St Agnes

SW 705494 to SW 716500. *Follow the B3277 into St Agnes. Turn left into Goonvrea Road, just beneath St Agnes Beacon. The bank runs to the north of Goonvrea Farm.*

Archaeologists are still unsure about the date of this ambitious defensive bank, which has come to be associated with the local folklore of the Bolster giant. It may well date from the fifth or sixth century CE. Elsewhere though, these structures to date to the Late Bronze Age.

● Saint Agnes and the Bolster Giant, St Agnes

SW 698496. *Chapel Porth may be reached by taking a minor road west from St Agnes. The stained rock is on the right-hand side of the cove.*

The giant Bolster became infatuated with a beautiful woman by the name of Saint Agnes. He followed her incessantly, always declaiming his love for her. However, Bolster was already married. The saint became annoyed at the giant, and so she explained to him that she would accept the giant's love if he would fill a hole in the cliffs at Chapel Porth with his blood. He reached out his arm and cut it with a knife. Out poured his blood but there seemed no opportunity to quench the flow. Soon, the giant became faint and then died soon after. Apparently, the saint was aware that the hole in the cliffs carried on to the sea, and that his blood flowed to the ocean. The cliffs here are still marked by the red stain of the giant's blood. Bolster Day is a community promenade play which re-enacts the battle between the giant and St Agnes. It is played on the cliffs close to Rescue Point and near the ruined chapel – which was probably dedicated to Saint Agnes.

● The Meadery, St Agnes

SW 719506. *Follow the B3277 into St Agnes. The Meadery is on the left-hand side.*

Meaderies are specific Celtic-themed restaurants in Cornwall, often decorated with pseudo Celtic lettering and steeped in Celtic knotwork and Arthuriana. They sell food which is generally eaten without cutlery insinuating early Medieval dining. Mead is a grape and honey-based drink which was popular in the Medieval period, and is said to work as a aphrodisiac – hence why it is often called 'the honeymoon drink'. The first meadery opened in 1965, in a converted cinema in Newlyn. Others are found at Redruth, Falmouth and Penzance.

● *Bewnans Ke* [*The Life of St Kea*], Old St Kea Church, near Truro

SW 543417. *Follow the A39 from Truro to Penryn. At Kea Primary school, turn left and follow the road to Churchtown Farm.*

Old Church, Kea is dedicated to St Ke. The saint has long-held connections to this area and his life has been dramatised. *Bewnans Ke* [*The Life of St Kea*] is an epic verse drama written in Middle Cornish. The present manuscript of the play dates from the late sixteenth century but is probably a copy of several earlier versions. It is held in the National Library of Wales. The manuscript only came to light in 2000 in the papers of the late Welsh scholar J.C. Caerwyn Williams. The play was the first 'new' traditional Cornish language manuscript to be discovered since the *Tregear Homilies* in 1948, and the fact that it contains substantial Arthuriana material made it an exciting discovery. The cultural geography of the play locates in firmly in the parish of Kea near Truro, on the River Fal. Several place-names in the drama connect directly with the area. However, in no way is the play parochial. It deals with both pan-British and pan-European events.

The play can be divided into two sections equating to two days of performance. The first day deals with the life of Saint Kelodocus [or Ke], while the second day deals with Arthuriana matter, closely related to material in Geoffrey of Monmouth's *The History of the Kings of Britain*, titled *The Book of the Acts of King Arthur*. There are some missing pages to the manuscript but the drama follows very closely the later transcription of *The Life of St Ke* written by Albert Le Grand, the seventeenth-century Breton hagiographer.

The life of Saint Ke has many expected elements of a Saint's life: the travel from Brittany and arrival in Cornwall, his striking of a rock from which a holy well flows, and his founding of chapel. While in the forest of Gudrun [Goodern is a present-day farm in the parish] Kea encounters a tyrant named Teudar. Teudar views Kea an interloper and tries to torture him. Kea meanwhile, tries to develop the settlement; the ploughman having a pair of stags pulling his plough:

In rag, Kyrnyk ha Kella!	[Forward, Kyrnyk and Kella!
In hanow Du uhella,	In the name of the highest God,
gonethough heb bysmeras.	plough without reproach.
Me a lever, ru'm besow!	I say, by my ring!
neffra ny'n gevyth esow	never will he be in want
a venna Du e weras.	whom God wishes to help.]

There is then an extended comic sequence with a witch called Oubra who through her charms, gets Teudar stuck in a bath. The implication is that Kea remains focused on making the local environment a better place, but having achieved this, he will now need to move onto wider British matters.

Part two of the drama is a complex merging of narratives which it would be impossible to explore in full detail here. However, the second day opens with Cador, the Duke of Cornwall, leading a discussion between leaders and bishops over the future of Britain. Arthur enters and we learn that he has refused to pay tribute to the Roman Emperor Lucius. Seven Kings are also received: Orkney, Norway, Dacia, Iceland, Gotland, Krakow and Castile. Legates arrive from Rome hoping to persuade Arthur to pay but he refuses. A trap is posited, with Mordred's indication of failure a prediction of future events. While Arthur is in France dealing with Lucius, Guinivere is left alone, with Modred [Mordred] in charge. They begin an affair. News of this reaches Arthur, while Modred enlists a Saxon named Cheldric to assist his forces. Cornish colour is offered when a message is blessed with Saint Cleer and Saint Ia. The fate of Britain ends disastrously however with Modred's rise to power. The solution appears to be that Kea operates as a peacemaker between Arthur and Modred, while Guinevere is persuaded to join a nunnery. Although a less than satisfactory ending for a modern audience, for the Late Medieval audience, this resolution would be spiritually and morally correct.

Bewnans Ke has not yet been performed in the modern era. In its blending of hagiography and Arthuriana, it is a highly innovative drama, and fully asserts the Arthurian connection with Cornwall. Kea parish is not far away from the Collegiate Church of Glasney at Penryn, and there may well have been a connection between that institution and the play's production here. In the parish is a village, close to Kea, known as Playing Place.

● Cross Shaft, Old Kea Church, near Truro

SW 844 416. *The cross shaft is located close to the tower of Old Kea Church.*

The shaft is undecorated aside from a band at the bottom. Its considerable size and shape however, suggests important dedication – perhaps to Saint Kea.

● Playing Place, near Truro

SW 814419. *The village is on the A39 from Truro to Penryn. It is located in the field to the east of Old Coach Road.*

For many years scholars puzzled over the text which might have been performed at Playing Place. This question was answered in 2000 when the drama *Bewnans Ke* was rediscovered. This is the most likely place for performance of this Middle Cornish play. The Tithe map names this field 'Plain Place'. Some observers believe that there were in fact two plain-in-gwarrys at the location, and that an older round may have once existed further to the north. If this were the case, then it may fit the dramaturgy of *Bewnans Ke*, since the play consists of two days – and it would be convenient to set events (one hagiographical, one Arthurian) in two different spaces.

● Feock, near Falmouth

SW 826385. *Feock is located at the end of the B3289 off the A39.*

It is alleged that around 1645, the Vicar of Feock and Chaplain to Pendennis Castle, one William Jackman, regularly conducted Holy Communion in Cornish because his older parishioners did not understand English.

Churchyard Cross, Feock

SW 825384. *The cross sits on the south side of the churchyard.*

This is a highly unusual and superbly crafted cross, with a somewhat strange figure. It is presumably Christ, but his legs are missing.

Round Wood Cliff Castle, Cowlands, near Feock

SW 837404. *The castle is located in a wood accessed on the minor road from Penlewey to Cowlands. It lies opposite the famous Tolcarne Cottage.*

The site here is a multivallate enclosure fort and looking over the confluence of the Truro and Fal Rivers, is well placed for trade. The site is from the Iron Age. The archaeologist Barry Cunliffe interprets such locations as a type of Iron-Age livestock market.

St Piran's Well and Church, Perranworthal, near Penryn

SW 779388. *From the A39 travelling in the direction of Penryn, turn right into the village of Perranworthal. Follow the road around to the north-west, where you will find the church. The well is situated next to the church.*

This is another dedication to Cornwall's patron saint, Saint Piran. The well water here is rich in iron and was deemed to be good for curing sickly children. It is interesting to note that the tidal reach of this stretch is long. For any arriving or departing saint, travelling by sea, It would have facilitated travel up Restronguet Creek to the present location of Perran wharf.

Cross outside mylor church old drawing. This illustration of 'Mylor Old Church – South Porch' reproduces a pencil drawing of unknown origin and shows the church before the 1870 restoration. The cross is shown head downwards, supporting the bulging south wall.

Lady Holy Well, Kennal Vale, near Ponsanooth

SW 750376. *The well is reached walking in a south-westerly direction along the Vale. In summer, the well is quite hidden by undergrowth, but is found to the north west of Roches Wood.*

For Medieval Celtic Cornwall, the Marian cult was significant and there are many wells across the territory devoted to St Mary. For Christians, she is the mother of Jesus, but there is plenty of evidence to suggest that she is just a variant of the Goddess Mother figure. Mary appears as a significant figure in both the Passion and Resurrection sections of the *Ordinalia* cycle, performed not too far away from Kennal Vale at Penryn. Two additional Marys feature in the *Ordinalia*: Mary Magdalene and Mary, mother of Joseph and James.

Churchyard Cross, Mylor

SW 820352. *Mylor is found north-east of Falmouth. The cross is in the south side of the churchyard.*

This is an unusually designed cross with two projections at the neck. Concentric circles decorate the cross shaft.

Churchyard Cross, Mylor.

Aerial view over Feock, centre, with Truro far distant.

● Mary Penrose, Matthew Arnold and Celtic Literature, Penryn

SW 787346. *The Parish Church of St Gluvias can be found on a minor road off the B3292 on the western side of Penryn.*

Matthew Arnold (1822-1888) was a British poet and cultural critic who famously wrote one of the first pieces of modern literary criticism on Celtic Literature: *On the Study of Celtic Literature* (1867), which has had a lengthy influence on the field. Although the volume is somewhat critical, arguing that the Celts seem too passionate to run their own affairs, the work does put Celtic literature on a par with other classical literature across Europe, and demonstrates its on-going impact and reception. Arnold was the son of the historian Thomas Arnold (1795-1842), who had married Mary Penrose, the daughter of the Reverend John Penrose of Penryn (1753-1829). Supposedly, Arnold had become interested in his Celtic heritage through his mother. The Penrose family were baptised at the Parish Church of St Gluvias.

● Glasney Collegiate Church of St Thomas the Martyr and the Virgin Mary, Glasney, Penryn

SW786342. *The location is a field in the lower part of the town. Drive past College Terrace, and then into College Hill. This leads to College Ope. A memorial stone and piece of masonry mark the site.*

The collegiate church of Glasney in Penryn, was founded in 1265 by Walter Bronescombe, Bishop of Exeter, and during the Late Medieval period it was a centre of church and literary life not only in Cornwall but throughout western Europe. According to legend, Bronescombe had a vision in which St Thomas the Martyr (Thomas à Becket) told him to build a church in the woods of Glasney at Polsethow. There he would find a hollow willow tree, its trunk containing a bee's nest. Its founding would fulfil the Old Cornish prophecy: *In Polsethow ywhylyr anethow* [In Polsethow shall be seen marvels (or dwellings)].

The church grew rapidly, and had 13 secular canons, one of whom was appointed provost. It received the tithes of fourteen parishes around the river Fal estuary, and grew into a great seat of learning. It may well be that the College co-ordinated literary and dramatic production in the individual parishes. Figures such as Master John Pascoe who obtained a prebend at Glasney in 1463 were crucial figures in this world of literary production.

The church was a sizeable structure covering the whole of the present field and extending beyond its reaches as well. Crediton church in Devon, has a very similar layout. The college, of course, included many other structures as well. It was clearly useful to be at the head of Carrick Roads, having good transportation links in and out. Its location in south Cornwall meant that links to Brittany were easily maintained.

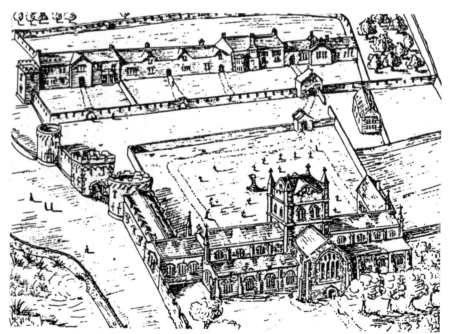

The layout of Glasney College, from a print c.1580.

Very little of the College remains at this site, though probably much of its stonework and features were used in other buildings around the town. However, an archaeological dig in 2005 revealed survivals of the walls. Many observers feel that had the College not been destroyed in the dissolution of the monasteries instigated by Henry VIII, it would have evolved into a native Cornish university. It is perhaps fitting that the present Combined Universities of Cornwall is to be found not too far away – at Tremough, near Penryn.

The first section of Origo Mundi.

● *The Ordinalia*, Penryn

SW786342. *The Ordinalia was most likely to have been written in this vicinity.*

The *Ordinalia* is the conventional title of a Middle Cornish dramatic trilogy written sometime at the middle or end of the fourteenth century and composed of the following three plays: *Ordinale de Origine Mundi* (*Origio Mundi* [The Beginning of the World]), Passio Domini Nostri Jhesu Christi (*Passio Christi* [Christ's Passion]) and *Ordinale de Resurrexione Domini* (*Resurrexio Domini* [The Resurrection of the Lord]). *Ordinalia* is the plural of the Latin *ordinale*, meaning prompt or service book, effectively 'script'. The language of the plays is Middle Cornish with around eight different metrical forms used. French, English and Latin are also incorporated. The place-names of the plays, which combine a biblical land-scape with a Cornish one, include many from the Penryn area and indicate probably authorship at Glasney College.

Like other Cornish plays from this period, the *Ordinalia* seems to have been staged over three days in the open-air amphitheatres known as plain-an-gwarry or playing places. Staging and production techniques are indicated by diagrams in the manuscript which shows circles with the characters' names on their peripheries. The *Ordinalia* is a highly unified work showing the fall and redemption of humanity. Many of its themes are derived from apocryphal sources, the most important of which is the Holy Rood. It follows the history of the cross, and begins with three seeds from the tree of life being placed in the mouth of the dead Adam by Seth who is in search of the oil of mercy. The trilogy is also highly comic in places with earthy humour.

Origo Mundi begins with the creation of the world, Adam and Eve, Cain and Abel, Seth, Noah and Abraham and Isaac. In one memorable sequence, Adam names the animals of the world and it is perhaps fitting that in a maritime culture like Cornwall, the creatures of the ocean are given emphasis:

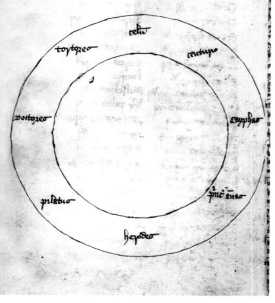

Plan for the staging of Passio Christi. *Bodleian Library*

yt'hanwaf bugh ha tarow	[I shall name cow and bull,
ha margh yw best hep parow	and horse that is a beast without equals
the vap den rag ymweres	to give assistance to mankind;
gaver yweges karow	goat, hind, deer,
daves war ver lavarow	sheep in a few words
hy hanow da kemeres…	its name to take…
…y rof hynwyn the'n puskes	…I shall give names to the fishes,
porpus sowmens syllyes	porpoise, salmon, eels,
oll thy'm gustyth y a vyth	all of them will be subject to me,
lenesow ha barfusy	ling and cod,
pysk ragof ny wra skvsy	not a fish shall evade me
mar corthyaf dev yn perfyth	if I worship God perfectly.]

These sections form individual set pieces, followed by Moses' discovery of the three rods which will combine together to form the Rood. After a love affair with Bathsheba, a remorseful King David writes his psalms and vows to place the rods in a temple. He dies before its completion and the construction of the temple is finished by Solomon. Comically, the rood, now used as beam, fits nowhere in the structure. The first play concludes with the prophet Maximilla; her clothing catches fire from the rood causing her to prophecy Jesus Christ, and she is duly executed.

Passio Christi opens with the temptation of Christ in the desert. This is followed by Psalm Sunday, the Hebrew Children, the miracles of Christ, and events leading to the Crucifixion. The Crucifixion itself is both brutal and comic, with the torturers delighting in their task. An incompetent Blacksmith is asked to make the nails for the cross, but assisted by the Smith's wife, eventually an executioner has to do the job:

me a nyth auel guas da	[I will blow like a good fellow;
nynsus den vyth yn pow-ma	There is not any man in this country
a whytho guel	Who blows better.
ny won gof yn ol kernow	I know not a smith in Cornwall
a whytho gans mygenow	Who can blow with the bellows,
certan byth wel	Certainly any better.]

The link between Adam and Christ is made by the finding of the Rood being used as a bridge at Cedron. Longinus, the blind Roman soldier, Mary, Joseph of Arimathea, and Nicodemus conclude the second day. Joseph of Arimathea would appear to be a significant character for the Cornish because of the Phoenician tin trade completed with Cornwall, and popular legend that Christ travelled to Cornwall with him. In Cornish folklore, Phoenicians, Jews and Saracens were used interchangeably and hence why Joseph might have been seen as a Phoenician.

Resurrexio Domini neatly follows on from the Passion, with the release from prison of Nicodemus and Joseph of Arimathea, the Resurrection of Christ, and (disguised as a gardener) his encounter with his mother, the harrowing of Hell, and the three Marys. Meanwhile, the protracted disbelief of Thomas contrasts with the faith of Mary Magdalene. Thomas' centrality fits because Glasney College is dedicated to his namesake. A sub-plot to *Resurrexio Domini* is the death of Pilate, which provides the producers of the play with several opportunities for comedy and special effects, as Pilate's corpse is rejected by the earth and the river Tiber. Eventually his body is carried off by the devils, while the play concludes with the Ascension.

Some observers have commented that, alongside the textual evidence, the transition made between *Origo Mundi* and *Passio Christi* indicates a lost 'nativity' or a play looking a Christ's childhood, which would have been destroyed during the Reformation. We should temper this with the notion that Christmas was a less important festival than Easter for many centuries. *Gwreans an Bys* [*The Creacion [sic] of the World*] from Helston, shows several similarities to *Origo Mundi*, while the *Pascan Agan Arluth* (found at Sancreed) is a poetic mirror of *Passio Christi*. Major revivals of the trilogy occurred in 1969 at Perran Round, near Perranporth and in 2004 at St Just-in-Penwith.

● An Garrack Ruen, Carrick Roads, Falmouth

SW 834316. *The rock is best viewed from the coastal road around Pendennis Point.*

In the first play of the *Ordinalia – Origo Mundi* [*The Beginning of the World*] King Solmon rewards the mason building his temple with the following:

dew vody tha ough yu guyr	[Two good bodies ye are truly,
ha rag bos agas wheyl tek	And because your work is fair
my a re thyugh plu vuthek	I will give you the parish of Budock,
ha'n garrak-rue gans hy thyr	And the Carrack Ruan with its land]

Budock is a sizeable estate to the west of Falmouth and would be a considerable reward. At first sight, Solomon issuing reward of the *Carrack Ruan* (sometimes called the Black Rock) and all its land, may seem something of a joke. The rock is after all, a small island in the middle of Carrick Roads. However, up until the nineteenth century this rock was used to collect tax off shipping vessels to use the harbour, so in fact, Solomon's gift was generous because the rock would have given the mason much wealth. This is another example of the way Celtic and Biblical landscape are fused in the *Ordinalia*.

● Institute of Cornish Studies, Tremough Campus, Penryn

SW 773353. *The Institute is located in the Peter Lanyon building. A prior phone call is recommended.*

The Institute of Cornish Studies is a Cornish and Celtic research institution in Cornwall, affiliated with the University of Exeter. Originally, it was located at Pool (first at Trevenson House, later at the Trevithick Building of Cornwall College), then moved for a short while at Hayne Corfe in Truro, and is now based in the Peter Lanyon building of the Tremough Campus. It was founded in 1970 with Professor Charles Thomas as the first director. From 1991, the Institute was lead by Professor Philip Payton. The Institute offers both graduate and post-graduate courses in Celtic Studies. The Institute produces a respected journal: *Cornish Studies*, which contains much Celtic Studies-related material.

● Prayer Book Rebellion Memorial, Penryn

SW 788343. *The memorial is found at a junction at the bottom of the town close to Quay Harbour.*

The so-called Prayer Book Rebellion was a popular revolt in Cornwall and the west of England in 1549. In that year the Book of Common Prayer was introduced, presenting the theology of the English Reformation. This move was unpopular in areas of Britain that were still firmly Catholic and it led to much anger and anxiety in Cornwall. The response to the rebellion was swift and harsh from the government of the young Edward VI. Edward Seymour, the 1st Duke of Somerset, leading an army of partly of German and Italian mercenaries, was sent to suppress the rebels. The West Cornish in particular reacted very badly to the introduction of English into church services. The eighth article of the Demands of the Western Rebels states: 'and so we the Cornyshe men (whereof certen of us understand no Englysh) utterly refuse thys new English'. They also observed that they would 'not receyue [receive] the new seruyce [service] because it is but lyke a Christmas game'. Traditional religious processions, pilgrimages and services were banned, many of them rooted in the Celtic church. Commissioners were sent out to remove all traces of Catholicism.

   Led by rebels such as Henry Bray, Humphrey Arundell and John Winslade a series of battles took place across Devon: at Plymouth, Crediton, Exeter, Fenny Bridges, Woodbury Common, Clyst St Mary, Sampford Courtney and at Clyst Heath (where 900 of the rebels were bound and gagged, and later killed in ten minutes). Proposals to translate the new Prayer Book into Cornish were also suppressed. Around 5,500 people lost their lives in the rebellion and under the auspices of Sir Anthony Kingston, mercenary forces then moved through Devon and Cornwall, executing many others before the rebellion was finally wiped out. The event is now regarded as a turning point in the history of Celtic Cornwall. In 2007, the then Bishop of Truro, the Rt Reverend Bill Ind, was reported to have said that the suppression had been 'an enormous mistake'. The memorial in Penryn has the following inscription:

Hemm a govha an an koll a Gollji Glasnedh ha n mernansa vilyow a wlask aroryon Gernewek yn unn dhefendyaa ga fydh, yeth ha devosow keltek.

[This commemoratwes the loss of Glasney College and the death of thousands of Cornish patriots in defence of their faith, language and Celtic customs.]

1549-1999
Kernow Arta
[Cornwall Forever]

● Calidnack Enclosure, near Mawnan Smith

SW 782293. *Travelling trom Mabe Burnthous to Mawnan Smith, first head to the centre of the village, then turn north to Bareppa. The enclosure is up a lane. Permission must be sought to visit.*

This Iron Age enclosure looks over the valley leading to Maenporth Beach. A modern house is located in the middle of it.

● Warin Penhalluryk. Wendron Parish church. Wendron

SW 679311. *Wendron is found three miles north of Helston on the B3297.*

The church is of interest here, not least for its porch, but also a brass dedicated to Warin Penhalluryk, who was one time rector of St. Just-in-Penwith, Wendron and Stithians. Dying in 1535, he was obviously a Cornish speaker, and preached to Cornish-speaking congregations in those communities.

● Lychgate and adjoining walls, Wendron Parish church, Wendron

SW 679311. *The lychgate opens onto the main B3297 road to Redruth.*

This late eighteenth-century lychgate (a temporary shelter for a coffin during funerary processions) seems to encapsulate the organic building traditions of Celtic Cornwall. It is made of granite ashlar walls, with a scantle slate roof. There are also granite coped gable ends and the room over it is approached by a flight of stone steps from the churchyard. Two stone benches are found on either side of the central coffin rest.

● Gilbert Hunter Doble, Wendron Parish Church, Wendron

SW 679311. *Doble's grave is close to the church.*

Gilbert Hunter Doble (1880-1945) was born in Penzance, and attended Exeter College, Oxford. Displaying Anglo-Catholic tendencies early on in his career, he was first barred from working in Cornwall, but was eventually appointed curate in the parish of Redruth – serving there until 1925. He then spent another twenty years at Wendron, becoming an honorary canon at Truro cathedral in 1935. Doble displayed a fascination with the lives of the saints in Brythonic Britain – specialising in Cornwall, but also devoted considerable energy to Brittany and Wales too. His five volume work on the saints of Cornwall was the standard hagiographical reference for the twentieth century. In 1928, he was made a bard of the Cornish Gorseth, taking the bard name *Gwas Gwendon* [Servant of Wendron]. Doble was also responsible for organising the first modern performance of *Bewnans Meriasek* [The Life of Meriasek] in 1924. His grave is found in the churchyard here.

● Early Tin Stamping, Poldark Mine, Wendron

SW 682316. *The complex is signposted on the B3297.*

Poldark Mine is named so to capitalise upon the successful set of Anglo-Cornish mining-themed novels written by Winston Graham (1908-2003). Earlier mining practice in the area was conducted under the auspices of Wheal Roots and Balcoath. Archaeological evidence has shown that on the site are found examples of early tin stamping. This was where depressions were made in the granite bedrock, and then crushed by hand-wielded mortar stones. This practice was taking place in Celtic Cornwall probably between 2000BCE and 1200CE. More mechanised stamping only began to be introduced in the twelfth century. The first recorded tin stamping mill was also found here in Wendron, erected in 1483, when John Trenere held a lease for its development. This is an important example of industrial Celticity in Cornwall. Poldark Mine is part of the United Nations Educational, Scientific and Cultural Organization (UNESCO) World Heritage Site of the Cornwall and Devon Mining Landscape.

● Wendron Crosses, in and around Wendron

SW 678310, SW 679310, SW 701291, SW 669322

Inside the church is the cross head of Boderwennack, originally found on the Boderwennack Estate (SW 678310). By the western door of the church at Wendron, is the so-called Belfrey Cross (SW 678310) and near the south porch is a four-holed churchyard cross (SW 679310). In the cemetery opposite the church is the mutilated Mayhay Vean Cross (SW 679310) which once stood at the nearby crossroads. At Polglase Hill (SW 701291) is Meruny Cross (probably originally Merthr Euny). Bodilly Cross is in the hamlet of Bodilly Veor (SW 669322).

● Merthr Euny Well, Merther Euny, near Helston

SW 704295. *Travelling in south-westerly direction from Penryn to Helston, just after Manhay turn right to Merther Euny.*

From his work in Lelant, Redruth and Sancreed, St Euny eventually moved to the parish of Wendron, where he was martyred. Hence, the name here: Merther [martyr]. The well feeds a muddy pool, so access is difficult. Close by is a small ruined chapel. This was known as Sancti Euny in 1337 but was abandoned after the Reformation. Recent excavations at the site have suggested that it was once a fortified settlement, with conversion to Christian community coming by the eighth century.

● Merthr Euny Cross, Merther Euny, near Helston

SW 703293. *The cross is not far from the well and is on private land.*

Close to the well can be found Merther Euny Cross, probably marking the site of Euny's martyrdom. We know that in 1886 human bones and oak coffins were discovered close to the monument during the stone's re-erection. This iconic cross is crudely made but is covered in rich decoration. The shaft is carved with incised circles and lines.

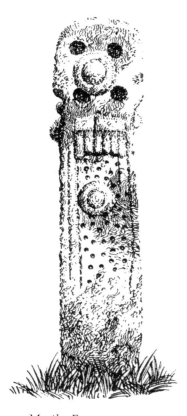

Merthr Euny cross.

Far left: Merthr Euny Well.

Left: Merthr Euny cross.

● Crosses, Constantine

SW 720315, SW 729304.

Several interesting crosses may be found in and around Constantine. Many are not accessible to the public (being on private land) but Trevease Cross, near Trevease Farm is accessible (SW 720315). This is found two and a half miles north west of Constantine churchtown. This cross is unusual since it has an additional bar. Trewardreva Cross is on the roadside close to Trewardreva Mill (SW 729304).

● Pisky Hall Fogou, near Constantine

SW 728300. *This is located in a field opposite Trewwardreva House, on the B3291.*

The fogou here is from the Iron Age / Romano-British period. Over time it has come to be associated with more modern folklore in the form of Cornish piskies.

● Mawgan Cross, Mawgan-in-Meneage, near Helston

SW 707249. *The cross is found in the middle of the village.*

This is an inscribed stone, probably a cross shaft, though without the head *in situ*. On it is carved CNEGUMI FILI GENAIVS [Cnegumus, son of Genaius]. These would appear to be Celtic names from the eighth to eleventh centuries.

● Caervallack hill fort, Mawgan-in-Meneage, near Helston

SW 726246. *From the B3293 from Helston, locate Mawgan-in-Meneage. The hill fort is found between Mawgan-in-Meneage and St Martin-in-Meneage, close to the hamlet of Gear.*

This is a circular Iron Age hill fort, with an extended area to the east of the central fort with two embankments sloping to the road. Close by is the settlement known as Gear Camp (SW 721248). This is large enclosed area having connections to the fort here.

● Ancient Court, Helston

SW 660274. *Helston is found on the A394.*

The Cornish language name for Helston is *Hellys* or *Henlys* which translates to 'ancient court', and may demonstrate Helston's long-term connections with the Stannary parliament and courts. The 'ton' of the name was probably added later to denote a Saxon manor, Heliston. It is one of the five Stannary towns of Cornwall (the other four being Lostwithiel, Bodmin, Liskeard and Truro). The name Coinage-hall Street indicates is previous function (coinage being one of the Stannary processes, where a tax was levied on dressed tin). The town was granted its charter in 1201 and was originally a thriving port. However, the River Cober silted up and over the years the town's function as a harbour declined. Helston is also famous for being the birthplace of the Celtic boxing legend, Bob 'Ruby Robert' Fitzsimmons (1863-1917), the first triple world boxing champion. His birthplace is found on Wendron Street and is marked by a blue plaque (SW 663274).

● Helston Folk Museum, Helston

SW 661275. *The Museum is located in the middle of the town, close to the Guildhall.*

Founded in 1949, the museum's collection reflects both the social, cultural and industrial history of the town and The Lizard peninsula. Many of the exhibits demonstrate early Celtic practices in farming, fishing and mining which have survived into the modern era. Helston also has an Antiquarian and Arcane Society which meets regularly in the nearby Guildhall to discuss Celtic, Pagan and esoteric aspects of Cornwall's past.

The blacksmith shop Helston where World Boxing Champion Bob Fitzsimmons is said to have been apprenticed as a farrier.

● *Gwreans an Bys [The Creacion [sic] of the World]* **by William Jordan, Helston**

SW 658277. *Helston is found on the A394. The church is close to the centre of the town.*

Gwreans an Bys [*The Creacion* [sic] *of the World*] is a biblical drama written in Cornish and was probably designed for outdoor performance in or near Helston. The church-going public of Helston would have known of it at the end of the sixteenth century. It is likely to be the surviving part of a longer work, similar to the *Ordinalia*. The play may well be linked to long-term festival activity there. A colophon reveals that the text was written by William Jordan and dated 1611, but this is probably just a transcription, with the actual text being written much earlier. The incorporation of the Rood legend (relating to the origin and growth of Christ's cross) and Adam's consignment to limbo indicate a Catholic work, while the likely presence of the story of the Virgin in any second play would have contributed to the rest of the cycle's destruction and loss at the time of the Reformation.

There are marked similarities to the first play in the *Ordinalia* – namely *Origo Mundi* [*The Beginning of the World*] – either formulaic or borrowed, *but Gwreans an Bys* contains additional sequences. For example, Lamech, a descendant of Cain, the author of moral deterioration and the first polygamist –

an apparently poor-sighted huntsman, meets his infamous forebear and kills him by accident. Additionally, the play contains the rebellion of Lucifer and the unusual character of Death, who offers a homiletic speech:

First page of the manuscript of
The Creacion of the World.
Bodleian Library

me yw cannas dew ankow	[I am the envoy of God, Death,
omma dretha appoyntys	appointed by Him here.
rag terry gormenadow	For breaking commandments
tha adam gans dew ornys	ordained to Adam by God
ef a verve hay ayshew	he and his progeny shall die.
yn della ythew poyntyes	Thus it is ordained
tha vyns a vewa in byes	to all things that may live in the world.]

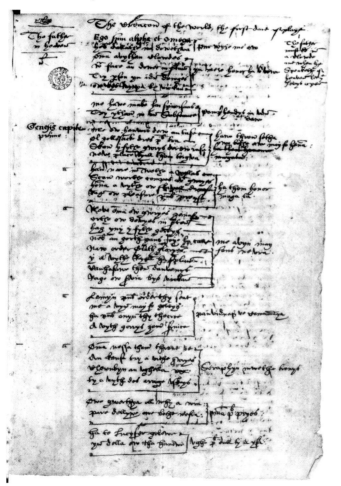

Death as a character may have some pan-Brythonic similarities to the Breton figure of *Ankou* – who features in much folklore and literature there.

In many ways, the play is more structurally and linguistically sophisticated than *Origo Mundi*. The 7-syllable line is not strictly followed in the text, but 8-syllable lines would become 7-syllable in actual speech if the elision of the vowels is recognised. The play also has various notations about the use of the 'conveyor', which may refer to an early dramatic effect, signified by the remains at Piran Round. The manuscript is held at the Bodleian Library, Oxford.

Kent and Saunders have recently argued that, though common to many dramas across Europe, the specific subtitle here – 'with Noye's Flood' may have had special significance for the industrial Celts of Cornwall. In many Cornish mining communities it was believed that their mineral wealth was given to them by the redistribution of the earth's resources in the aftermath of God's cleansing of the world through the Flood. This is especially the case in Helston which was a Stannary town. Its hinterland is surrounded by mining developments which have been in place since the Early Medieval period. Interestingly, no plain-an-gwarry location has come to light. This is somewhat strange considering the Celtic dramatic tradition found in the town with *Gwreans an Bys* and *Hal an tow*.

● The Murder of William Body, Helston

SW 659274. *The centre of Helston is marked by the Guildhall.*

In 1548, William Body was in charge of organising the destruction of all instruments of Catholicism in Cornwall. This involved the destruction of Rood screens, icons, statues of saints, carvings and possibly several Cornish language texts. The desecration he completed led to his murder in Helston on 5th April. This was completed by William Kylter and Pascoe Trevian. Immediate retribution followed in the aftermath of Body's murder: twenty-eight Cornishmen were executed at Launceston Castle, while Martin Geoffrey – a priest from St Keverne, near to Helston, was taken to London. He was executed there with his head impaled on a staff upon London Bridge.

● Furry Dance or the Flora, Helston

SW 660270. *Traffic through the town is closed on the day of the Flora. Additional car parks are provided.*

Many Cornish towns have so-called *Furrys* – which are processional dances, rooted in Celtic ritual and celebration. The most famous of these is that held in Helston every year on May 8th (or the Saturday before if May 8th falls on a Sunday or a Monday). It is a celebration of the passing of winter and arrival of spring. The Furry Dance is also known as the Flora. Music is provided by Helston Town Band, and the day commences with the first dance at 7am. Others follow including the children's dance at 10am, the midday dance and the evening dance at 5pm. The midday dance is the best known of these. Traditionally, this was when the local gentry danced and today's dancers still wear formal clothing. The music for the dance has never been written down, but according to the folklorist Margaret A. Courtney the tune was sometimes called 'John the Bone', and a traditional children's rhyme accompanied it:

> *John the Bone was walking home*
> *When he met with Sally Dover,*
> *He kissed her once,*
> *He kissed her twice*
> *And he kissed her three times over.*

Helston Flora Day c.1930

There has been a revival of processional dances in Cornwall over the past decade. Among those of interest is the so-called Snail Creep dance taking place in the mid-Cornwall village of Rescorla (the leaders of the procession hold up twigs which resemble the horns of a snail, and then the dance spirals like a snail's shell). Other furrys take place in Grampound, Boscastle and St Cleer.

● *Hal an tow*, Helston

SW 657272. *The play takes place in various locations on Floral Day.*

Hal an tow is a Mumming-style event, play and song which has existed at least from the late eighteenth-century, and evolved during the twentieth and twenty-first centuries to become a vibrant expression of Cornish Celticity. The central present-day drama conducted is the battle between St George (once a pan-British saint, and not just associated with England) and a dragon. The play may have a Celtic Medieval origin, but it may well have been invented in more modern times. The welcoming of summer clearly suggests another origin in the pagan celebration of the turn of the ritual year. The play seems to be summer version of other Mummers plays collected elsewhere in Cornwall (for example in Redruth and Mylor).

The current vision of the play has curiously attempted to integrate more Celticity – including an appearance by St Piran (often played by the Member of Parliament for St Ives, Andrew George). The song draws on wider British May themes such as Robin Hood and Little John but there is also the integration of a Spanish section – perhaps drawn from the 1595 attack on Cornwall. The title of the song (and now event) might be translated to 'woody swamp' [*Hal*], while '*tyow*' might mean 'houses'. Thus the full title would equate to 'in the moorland and in the town'. With quite a striking parallel to May Day ceremonies and song in Padstow, the opening verse and chorus are as follows:

> *Robin Hood and Little John they both are gone to Fair-O,*
> *And we will to the merry green wood to see what they do there-O,*
> *And for to chase-O, to chase the buck and doe.*
> *Hal-an-tow, jolly rumble-O,*
> *For we are up as soon as any day-O*
> *And for to fetch the Summer home, the Summer and the May-O,*
> *For Summer is acome-O and Winter is agone-O.*

● Arthuriana at Loe Pool, near Porthleven

SW 644243. *Take the B3304 from Helston to Porthleven. At Porthleven pass the harbour and take the south minor road to the area known as the Highburrow. Walk along the coastal path to the Pool and Bar.*

Loe Pool (sometimes called The Loe) [Cornish: *An Logh*] is the largest natural freshwater lake in Cornwall. The Loe was originally the estuary of the River Cober, which flows through nearby Helston. The river was separated from the sea by the growth of the shingle bank known as Loe Bar, which is thought to have formed in the thirteenth century. The mysterious nature of Loe Pool is probably the reason why Arthuriana has attached itself to the location. It is supposedly the lake into which Bedivere cast King Arthur's sword. An alternative location for this event is Dozmary Pool in east Cornwall. Loe Pool seems unlikely as the receptacle for Excalibur since it was formed much later than any historical narrative concerning Arthur. That has not stopped the persistence of the legend here however.

● The Halzephron Inn, Halzephron, near Helston

SW 656219. *Take the A3083 road from Helston to The Lizard, and take the right turn signposted to Gunwalloe.*

This inn here is over five hundred years old and probably had Cornish-speaking guests and landlords. It is located at Halzephron which means 'Hell Cliff' – a dramatic indication of the scenery just below the public house. Cornish language proverbs and expressions are often chalked on the beams in the main bar.

● Church of Saint Winwalloe, Gunwalloe, near Helston

SW 66042055. *Gunwalloe Cove is located three and a half miles south of Helston.*

The church here is dedicated to Saint Winwallow who is also celebrated at Towednack. The church itself was probably built in the late fourteenth or early fifteenth century but the tower is older – perhaps from the thirteenth century. This was when it was a manorial church. A number of observers have commented on the ley lines which run through the tower here. A wheel-headed wayside cross is located on the south eastern side of the churchyard. It is believed that a holy well runs under the churchyard. Celtic Christianity is hard to avoid at this site – with the church and tower being located so close to the ocean.

● The 1497 Rebellion, St Keverne

SW 792213. *St Keverne is located in the south-east of The Lizard peninsula on the B3293. The memorial plaque is found on the eastern side of the village square in the churchyard wall.*

Statues of Michael Joseph 'An Gof' and Thomas Flamank, St Keverne.

The Cornish Rebellion of 1497 was a popular uprising conducted by the people of Cornwall. Its primary cause was the response of people to the raising of war taxes by King Henry VII on the Cornish to fund monies for a campaign against Scotland, motivated by brief border skirmishes that were inspired by Perkin Warbeck's claim to the English throne. A core issue was that tin miners were angered at the scale of taxes which challenged their previous rights granted by Edward I to the Cornish Stannary Parliament which exempted the Cornish from all taxes of 10ths or 15ths of income. As a reaction to the King's demands, Michael Joseph (*An Gof* [blacksmith]) from St Keverne and a lawyer from Bodmin named Thomas Flamank incited a rebellion. They led an army of some 15,000 into Devon, on to Taunton, and then Wells (where they were joined by James Touchet, the seventh Baron Audley).

The army marched on through Salisbury and then onto Guildford. The King ordered Lord Daubeney to meet the Cornish and a battle ensued a Gill Down, outside Guildford on Wednesday 14th June 1497. After Guildford, the Cornish army moved via Barnstead and Chussex Plain to Black-heath, looking down upon the River Thomas and the City of London. In the battle of Blackheath (sometimes known as the Battle of Deptford Bridge), the Cornish faced overwhelming odds. Despite Cornish skill with archery, Henry VII's forces had mustered cavalry and artillery. Around 2,000

Memorial Plaque, St Keverne.

Cornish were slaughtered and An Gof and Flamank were both hanged, drawn and quartered. They were executed at Tyburn on 27th June 1497. An Gof is believed to have said before his execution that he would have 'a name perpetual and a fame permanent and immortal', with Flamank arguing 'Speak the truth and only then can you be free of your chains'.

An Gof and Flamank are regarded as heroes of Celtic Cornwall, symbolising resistance to English oppression as much as William Wallace in Scotland. Much literature and poetry celebrates these events; for example, the 1997 play by Jonathon Plunkett titled *A Name Perpetual*. In the same year, an organisation named *Keskerdh Kernow* [Cornwall Marches On!] was formed to oversee the quincentennial anniversary of the Rebellion, which resulted in a commemorative march tracing the original route from St Keverne to Blackheath.

Earlier, in 1966, the Cornish nationalist party, *Mebyon Kernow* erected a plaque on the outside churchyard wall of St Keverne Church to commemorate their lives. The plaque reads:

Dhe gof a Myghal Josep An Gof ha Thomas Flamank, Hembrynkysy an lu Kernewek a geskerdhas bys dhe Loundres ha godhevel ena dyalans, Metheven 1497. "Y a's tevyth hanow a bes vynytha ha bry a dhur hep merwel." Drehevys gans Mebyon Kernow 1966.

In memory of Michael Joseph, the Smith and Thomas Flamank, leaders of the Cornish host who marched to London and suffered vengeance there, June 1497. "They shall have a name perpetual and a fame permanent and immortal." Erected by Mebyon Kernow 1966.

Meanwhile, at SW 788211, on the road into St Keverne, may be found statues of Michael Joseph 'An Gof' and Thomas Flamank. The statues were erected in 1997 as part of the 500th anniversary of the Rebellion. The achievement and pain of the rebellion is no better expressed than in a work titled *An Ros Du* [*Blackheath*] by the poet Tim Saunders (b.1952). On Blackheath in south London, to this day, may still be found the mounds that contain the bodies of the Cornish dead. Although distant from St Keverne, it is a powerful reminder of the fate of Cornish Celticity of this period.

An Ros Dhu [*Blackheath*] by Tim Saunders

Pyu a bew an beth y'n ros,
hep hanow, hep men, hep fos,
deu vyl seson ow cortos?

[Whose is the grave in the heath,
without name, without stone, without wall,
waiting two thousand seasons?

Pyu a bew beth pen an hens
may can hen govow y'n gwyns?
Ruth y fu gwels arak kens.

Whose is the grave at the end of the road
where ancient memories sing in the wind?
Grass was formerly red.

Pyu a bew an beth y'n knogh?
Pan drelyr lagas dh'y logh,
Gwreth colon a vyth pondrogh.

Whose is the grave in the mound?
When eye is turned into lake,
heart's roots are cut by pain.]

Trelanvean cross.

● Trelanvean Cross, near St Keverne

SW 751195. *This is found in the corner of a field at Trelanvean Farm. It is beside a public footpath.*

The cross had fallen but was re-erected in the late nineteenth century. It is a slightly unusually-shaped wheel-headed wayside cross. Close by, at Trelan Barrow, a bronze age mirror was found – this dating from the fist century BCE. It shows signs of Celtic decoration.

● The Three Brothers of Grugwith, near St Keverne

SW 761198. *The stones can be found close to Zoar garage.*

In the final play of the *Ordinalia* – 'Resurrexio Domini [The Resurrection]', a land grant is made by Pilate to the guards who must watch over Christ's tomb. Pilate chooses some interesting places here. He mentions Donsotha which is thought to be close to St Agnes, but also Grugwith, which may be a piece of integrated local knowledge. At Grugwith is a quoit-like structure – in effect, a Bronze Age burial chamber formed by three stones (the three brothers). Is it that the author or authors of the *Ordinalia*, knew this structure and thought it might be a clever pun on the fact that the guards were looking after Christ's burial chamber too? The sequence runs as follows:

gueyteugh ol e agas fyth,
pan bostyas the pen try deyth
y tasserghy the vewnans
gobar de why agas byth
gon dansotha ha cruk heyth

[All take care on your faith,
Since he boasted at the end of 3 days
He would rise again to life;
A good reward shall be to you,
The plain of Donsotha and Grugwith.]

⬤ St Ruan's Well, Cadgwith

SW 716147. *The well is found just above the village near Bruggar Farm.*

St Ruan was known locally as St Rumon, and he is the patron saint of Ruan Major and Ruan Minor here at Cadgwith, but is also the patron saint of Ruan Lanihorne on the upper stretches of the River Fal. Ruan was also honoured in that area of the island of Britain now known as Devon, and the shrine containing his relics was to be found at the abbey in Tavistock (founded in 974, dissolved in 1539), now part of the Parish Church of St Eustachius. His feast day is August 30th. Stories say that Ruan was a sixth-century saint who came from Ireland, and he received his training at Glastonbury. According to John Whittaker in 1804, Ruan then made his way to Cornwall in order 'to court that holy solitude, and to enjoy that heavenly contemplation in our valleys and upon our shores…'. Ruan apparently had a great love of animals and he was often called 'the hairy' with one story accusing him of being a werewolf. As a test, dogs were set upon him with the hounds trained to catch wolves. However no wolf scents were found upon him so he was set free. Ironically, it is Ruan who is said to have driven all the wolves out of Cornwall. After his martyrdom his cult grew and it was Ordulph, the Ealdorman of Devon in the year 981 who ordered that his remains be transferred to Tavistock Abbey. Later, Ruan's bones may have travelled to Brittany, to the village of Locronan, but there were many saints named Ruan, Ramon or Ronan – so there may not be a connection. The well at Cadgwith is well-cared for and the granite shelves are filled with offerings. Close by, at Ruan Major, are the remains of his church (SW 703165) a touchstone to lost Medieval Celtic world.

St Ruan's Well, Cadgwith.

● Plain-an-gwarry, Ruan Minor

SW 713156. *This is found partly in the road leading from Ruan Minor to the A3083, some 100 metres from the crossroads at Treleague on the southern side of the raod.*

Various scholars – among them – Richard Polwhele, author of a *History of Cornwall* in 1803, have noted a possible plain-an-gwarry here. Polwhele claimed it was 'a round… [with a] diameter of ninety-three feet'. A local cottage still carries the name Plain-an-Gwarry, and in 1969, while digging foundations for a builders found trace of a ditch. Considering the fame of St Ruan in Cornwall and elsewhere, a verse drama once existing about his life seems quite likely.

● Chynhalls Point Cliff Castle, near Coverack

SW 785174. *Taking the coastal path south from Coverack, the fort is easily located.*

There are two Iron Age ramparts here at the neck of the promontory. A community here would have had excellent views north to Falmouth Bay and across the British Channel.

● Lankidden Cliff Castle, near Coverack

SW 755166. *Lankidden is found along the coastal path running west from Coverack, not far from Chyhalls Point.*

Looking out upon the rocks at Carack Lûz, this cliff castle is approximately the same size as the one at Chyhalls Point. Here, however, there is just one single rampart as part of Iron Age defences.

● Lys Ardh and Predannack, The Lizard

SW 701115. *The Lizard is found at the southern end of the A3083.*

Lizard Point is the most southerly tip of the British mainland, and it is located in the parish of Landewednack – which translates to 'church site of Winnoc [Winwalo]'. The name Lizard is probably derived from Lys Ardh – meaning 'high court'. There are some suggestions that this site was well known by some classical writers. The Lizard may once have been known as Predannack [British headland]. This may therefore be one of the oldest place-names not only in Cornwall, but also in the islands of Britain. We know that the Britons were known as the Pretani. The name is still remembered in the nearby airfield known as Predannack. However, this material may be pure invention. The airfield was a misspelling of Pednannack. Tredannack lies close by.

Predannack cross.

● Predannack Cross, The Lizard

SW 670170. *This cross is found on the footpath running from Predannack Manor to Mullion.*

This is a fine example of a taller wayside cross. The field nearby is known as *Gwell Crouse* [Cross Field].

● Celtic Heath, The Lizard

SW 737213. *Stop at one of the parking places on the B3294 close to the former sire of Goonhilly satellite earth station. A number of footpaths cross the heath.*

Perhaps because of the distinctive geology of The Lizard peninsula (composed of exposed ophiolite), a distinctive kind of Cornish heath grows on the Downs of the area. The heath [*Erica vagans*] is found nowhere else in Britain. The heath has obviously influenced the down-land culture of the surrounds. Goonhilly means 'hunting downs'. Although now being re-shaped to accommodate new technologies, Goonhilly satellite earth station once drew on the Celto-Arthurian heritage of Cornwall by naming its satellite dishes: Uther, Arthur, Merlin, Tristan, Lancelot and Geraint. Some of the structures have been taken down and there are plans to develop a science park at the location.

● James Dryden Hosken, Goonhilly, The Lizard

SW 737213. *From this point there is a good walk to the south-west heading toward Penhale.*

The ancient down lands of Goonhilly form the background to many of the poems by the Anglo-Cornish poet James Dryden Hosken (1861-1953). Born in Helston, Hosken had an interest in ancient Celtic Cornwall and was one of the first of those barded at the Cornish Gorseth of 1928. The Phran of the poem *Phran of Goonhilly* (1928) seems nothing to do with Saint Piran. Hosken has spent much of the late twentieth century being unappreciated as poet, but his work is starting to be reappraised in Cornish Literary studies.

From *Phran of Goonhilly* by James Dryden Hosken

The magic sea on either hand
Hath cast a spell upon the land,
  Controlling change and nature;
Traditions gray and vanished things
Take shape in casual visitings,
Fair ladies, knights and Cornish kings,
  And many a dwarfish creature.

Midway the down a cromlech stands,
Reared long ago by giant hands
  As told in antique story;
And some have gone on pilgrimage
To see the place where Phran the sage
Wore out his life from youth to age,
  Within that cromlech hoary.

● Kynance Gate round house settlement, near Kynance Cove

SW 688139. *Travelling from Helston to Lizard on the A3083, turn right and cross Carn Goon to the National Trust car park. The round house settlement is situated approximately half a mile up the valley from Kynance Cove.*

There are two main sites here – both initially occupied in the Bronze Age period, but later used in the Iron Age. The southern group is enclosed by a wall, while the northern group are more separated.

View over Kynance Cove looking towards the Kynance Gate round house settlement site.

● Halligye Fogou, Garras, near Trelowarren

SW 713239. *The fogou is located close to Garras, on the B3293. Walk up the hill across the field. The fogou is managed by 'English' Heritage.*

This is the largest of all the surviving Cornish fogous. It is an Iron Age construction and is actually T-shaped in layout.

● Chytodden Cross, near Godolphin

SW 609312. *This is found close to the north porch of St John the Baptist church at Godolphin.*

This is a Latin wayside cross and is roughly constructed.

● St Breaca Church, Breage, near Helston

SW 618284. *Breage is found on the A394.* The church is in the middle of the village.

Breaca or Breage, also known as Briac, is the dedication of this church. A life of her once existed and was seen by the antiquarian John Leland, who noted a few details about her life. According to Leland, Breaca was born in the region of Lagonia and Ultonia in Ireland, perhaps referring to modern-day Leinster and Ulster. She became a nun at an oratory founded by Saint Brigid of Kildare, and then around 460 travelled to Cornwall with a company of other Irish saints – among them Germoe, Senanus (Sithney), Mavuanus (Mawnan), Elwen, Crowan, Helenas and Tecla. Settling at Revyer on the River Hayle, some were killed by the tyrant Teudar. Apparently, Breaca travelled south visiting the hill at Pencaire and establishing a church at Trenewith. Breaca's feast day was traditionally May 1st, and then later, June 4th. Locally it is thought that while Germoe was a King, Breaca was a midwife.

The present church was built of granite in the fifteenth century and is famous for its five surviving Medieval wall paintings. Four saints are portrayed: Ambrose, Christopher, Corentien and Hilary and there is also an image of Christ and the Trades - similar to that found in St Just-in-Penwith. The Christopher image contains an image of a mermaid, probably to represent the dual nature of Christ. Situated behind the altar in the Godolphin Chapel is the Trewavas cross head or reliquary. The stone features the crucifixion and the figures of Mary and St John.

St Germoe's Chair (see opposite).

● Churchyard Cross, St Beaca Church, Breage, near Helston

SW 618284. *This is situated close to the south porch of the church.*

The cross here is a four-holed churchyard cross. So it is said, this cross was formed from sand and the blood of fallen warriors who fought in a local battle. West of the church may be found Trevena Cross (SW 612284).

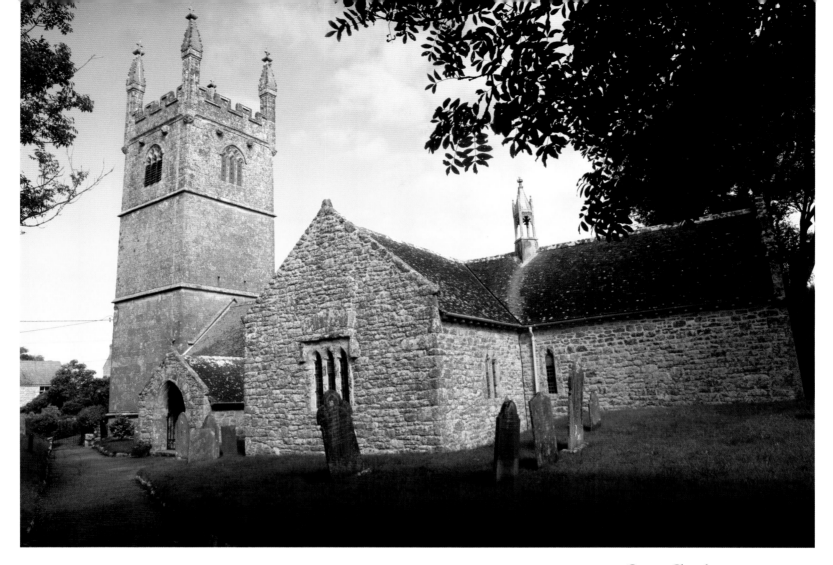

Germoe Church.

● St Germoe's Well, Chair and Plain-an-Gwarry, Germoe, near Helston

SW 584294. *Take the A394 from Helston to Penzance. Turn right at Germoe Crossroads. The church and well are at the north end of the village.*

St Germoe's Well still exists, though it is housed in an unattractive stone base covered with a grill. Like the nearby Saint Breage, Saint Germoe is said to be one of the saints who crossed from Ireland. In the Medieval period he was known as King Germoechus. In north east of the churchyard is a some-what quirky building known as Germoe's Chair. The double-arched building which contains a stone bench or chair dates from the fifteenth century – and was perhaps a shrine to Germoe. It is believed there may well have been a plain-an-gwarry close to the church at Tresowes Green. This fits with other knowledge we have of the location. In 1586 some players from Germoe were paid to put on a play in St Ives. Germoe is located twelve miles away from St Ives so the piece must have been good enough to show in a large town. The play could well have celebrated the life of King Germoechus.

Pencare hill fort near Germoe

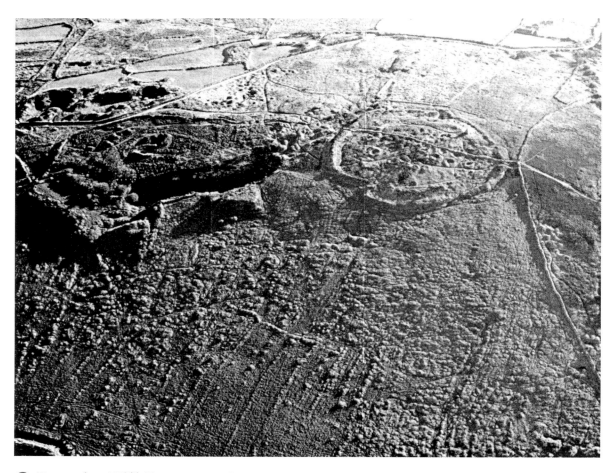

● Pencaire Hill Fort, near Germoe

SW 599300. *On the A394, travelling from Helston to Penzance, turn right at Aston and then follow the footpath up Tregonning Hill.*

Although partially destroyed by quarrying, the walls of this Iron Age hill fort are still impressive. Several roundhouses would probably be located inside the fort. The eastern area of the fort is characterised by an ancient set of field systems, in which are found two other rounds – one to the north east and another to the east.

● Bernard Walke, St Hilary Church, St Hilary, near Goldsithney

SW 551312. *St Hilary Church is found off the B3280 at the eastern end of Goldsithney.*

Bernard Walke is an important figure with the Celto-Cornish revival of the early twentieth century. Walke was born in Wiltshire, but came to Cornwall after being ordained into the Church of England, first at St

Ives, and then at Polruan. However, in 1912, he was offered the position of Vicar of St Hilary, in West Cornwall, and was involved with the church and parish there until his death in 1940. His ministry itself lasted for twenty years. At St Hilary, his tenure there was notable for two reasons. First of all, 'Ber' Walke (known there as 'Passon [Parson] Walke') tried to bring his fiercely independent parishioners back to the faith of their pre-Reformation forefathers. He had a strong sense of ritual, drama and art, connected to his Anglo-Catholic sensibilities. This activity ensured a good deal of anxiety amongst certain observers, and in 1932, the church was broken into by extremist Protestant agitators of Kensitite persuasion.

The second reason for Walke's fame is related to the first. In the 1920s and 1930s, Walke wrote a series of dramas, which explored a Celto-Catholic Cornish experience, beginning in December 1926, with a radio broadcast version of a Christmas-themed play titled *Bethlehem*. With the success of *Bethlehem*, Walke wrote a series of plays; some of which were staged in the church; with a number also broadcasted by the BBC.

In some respects, Walke fits into a tradition of ecclesiastical eccentrics which goes back to figures such as the poet Robert Stephen Hawker, who also embraced Anglo-Catholicism (fully committing to Catholicism on his death bed), but in other senses, Walke was extremely progressive in understanding the power of liturgical drama. We also note that he knew very well indeed the connections between place and performance in St Hilary, and had a deep knowledge of the purpose of ritual, community and landscape in theatre. In a 1939 anthology of his plays, Walke explains his influences:

> In the Parish of St Hilary, within sight of the Church, there is a field called 'Plain-an-Gwarry'— the Field of the Play. Here, in the Middle Ages, from a farm wagon or rough staging, the men and boys of the parish paraded and gestured in scenes from the Old and the New Testament representing man's fall from grace and God's redeeming love in the death and resurrection of His Son. It was the thought of this field, still known to the people as 'Plain-an-gwarry', that led me to write these plays for St. Hilary.

Walke's other plays include *The Little Ass*, a 'Passion play' called *The Upper Chamber*, *The Eve of All Souls* and *The Stranger at St Hilary*. These works were completed in a close fusion of Biblical and Cornish landscape, which is redolent in the paintings of Walke's wife, Annie Walke, and also with the other artists whom he commissioned to decorate the church; painters now established amongst the finest in modern Cornish art: Ernest Proctor, Harold Harvey, Norman Garstin, Harold Knight, Alathea Garstin, and Gladys Hynes. Very often, such paintings also looked at the lives of Cornish saints; Walke was keen to imitate the surviving colour and energy of the churches where pictures and images had survived - for example, at nearby Breage, and at St Just-in-Penwith.

● Plain-an-gwary, near St Hilary

SW 553313. *This is found in the hamlet called Plain-an-Gwarry at Gear Lane. Plain-an-Gwarry may be reached by footpath from St Hilary Church.*

There is considerable evidence for theatre space near to St Hilary; the plain-an-gwarry lying just off Gear Lane. Gear is Cornish for 'Hillfort' or 'Round' and the playing place may well have been an adaptation of that original earthwork. If this is the case, then Walke's writing at the start of the twentieth century shows considerable correlation with what may well have occurred there some four or five hundred years before.

Aerial view over Perranuthnoe towards, where legend has it, the Trevelyans escaped the Lyonesse flood by riding a white horse

● Crosses, St Hilary

SW 550312.

Trevabyn Cross stands on the right hand side of the path that leads to the south porch of St Hilary Church. On the opposite side is Trewhella Cross, which is mutilated.

● The Trevelyan Horse, Perranuthnoe

SW 540293. *Perranuthnoe is located just south of the A394 between Marazion and Germoe.*

Horses are often significant creatures in Celtic mythology and it is therefore not surprising that one of the ancestors of the Trevelyans (or Trevilians) escaped the Lyonesse flood, by riding on a horse and landing at Perranuthnoe – probably on Perran Sands. Trevelyan is derived from a place in Cornwall or Lyonesse meaning 'village of Elian'. The Trevelyan coat of arms has upon it a horse rising from the sea. Perranuthnoe seems to take its name from the church which is dedicated to Saint Piran, and the name of the Manor – Uthno. The Vivians of Trelowarren also have a coat of arms relating to the same or similar legend.

Mid Cornwall

● 'The Land of the Saints', Truro Cathedral, Truro

SW 824448. Truro Cathedral is found in the middle of the city. 'The Land of the Saints' painting is located on the northern side of the nave.

Cornwall had its own Bishop at St Germans until the latter part of the tenth century. The Cornish Diocese was then held jointly with the Devon Diocese at Crediton and then in 1050 at Exeter. Effectively the Cornish Diocese ceased to be a separate entity. Over 800 years later, in 1877, the Cornish Diocese was re-established at Truro, its first Bishop being Edward White Benson (1829-1896). This was to be marked by the building of a new cathedral. Construction of the cathedral at Truro began in 1880 on the site of the 16th century parish church (St Mary the Virgin), with the building consecrated in 1887. The central tower was added in 1905 with the two western towers completed in 1910. The cathedral was designed by John Loughborough Pearson (1817-1897) who gave it a Gothic 'early British' style along with Breton and French influences. Despite its Anglicanism, much of Cornwall's Celtic Christian heritage is embedded in the cathedral – best seen in a painting titled 'The Land of the Saints' (1980) by the artist John Miller (1931-2002). The spectacular painting shows beams of heavenly light shining on major saint-linked locations across Cornwall.

Truro Cathedral under construction.

Truro Cathedral.

● Bardic Chair, Truro Cathedral, Truro

SW 824448. The Bardic Chair is usually found on the southern side of the nave, except on the first Saturday of September when it is used in the Gorsedd ceremony.

The Bardic Chair held in Truro Cathedral is a recognisable symbol of modern Celtic identity in Cornwall, though some observers might argue that it is 'anglified' by being located in this building. Nevertheless, designed by the bard Leslie Libby, the chair was first used at the 1983 Gorsedh and is an incredible piece of craftsmanship. The name of every Grand Bard since 1928 is inscribed on the chair, and there are iconic images of Celtic Cornwall also carved into the wood. On it is the Cornish inscription *An Gwyr Erbyn an Bys* which means 'The Truth against the World'. The website of the Cornish Gorsedd offers viewers the chance to look at other bardic symbols and regalia form the ceremony. These include the Awen. This translates to 'Muse or Inspiration' and is derived from the three shafts of light of the rising sun. It represents the three concepts of Love, Justice and Truth. The Grand Bard's crown, made of beaten copper and designed by Francis Cargeeg also bears the Awen symbols along with a motif of oak leaves.

Other regalia include the Grand Bard's plastron (which includes Celtic knotwork and a fifteen bezant shield), the sword-bearer's plastron (holding an image of the sword and the Awen) and the chaplain's breastplate (a Celtic cross with the Awen). Gorsedd Marshalls carry staves made of hard wood with repouseé heads bearing the Awen symbol. Another important part of the annual ceremony is the Horn or *Corn Gwlas*. This is a genuine buffalo horn with copper knotwork added by Francis Cargeeg in 1940. A new sword has recently been made for the Joining of the Swords ceremony, a symbol of the uniting of the three Brythonic Celtic nations – Cornwall, Wales and Brittany. The handle of this sword is made of wood from St Columb (the first Grand Bard, Henry Jenner, coming from the town) and the blade bears the inscription '*Lymm own lown heb own a boon*', the Cornish for 'sharp my blade without fear of pain' – taken from a poem by Tim Saunders called 'Bardh an Werin'.

● Plain-an-gwarry, Truro

SW 823450. This is on the site of the Courts of Justice, just above the car park for the Courts.

The playing place here was observed by John Leland in his *Itinerary* written in 1540, and its location seems to indicate multi-purpose use. Leland describes it as a 'castelle a quarter mile by west out of Truro… used for a shooting and playing place'. This is a high spot in the city and would have had commanding views of the river and surrounding countryside before the urbanisation of Truro. Saint Kenwyn (or Keyne) being close, it might be that a possible life was performed here. Clearly, this was originally a twelfth-century motte-style castle that was re-used for leisure purposes.

● St Piran's Cross flag, Truro

SW 813446. The flag can be seen outside 'County' Hall and elsewhere across Cornwall.

For a number of years, the St Piran's Cross flag was only flown by Cornish nationalists. However, the cross has now come to signify Cornish identity and is flown and worn by thousands of Cornish people at home and abroad. The flag's origins need further investigation. Some believe it to be modern invention; others argue for a longer heritage. Kernow and St Piran's flag car stickers may be observed both in and outside Cornwall. Davies Gilbert mentions the flag in 1838 but evidence before this is harder to find. Michael Drayton mentions a different flag flown at Agincourt – the symbol of two Cornish wrestlers.

● Bishop's Wood Hill Fort, Idles, near Truro

SW 829487. *Bishop's Wood is located close to Idles off the B3284 running north out of Truro. At the car park, first cross St Clement Woods then enter Bishop's Wood.*

Although located in the middle of woodland, this oval fort is still noticeable. It is probably from the early Iron Age period, and has three entrances.

● Sunnyside Corner Well, near Truro

SW 846433. *This is located on the minor road south from Truro to Malpas.*

In 1755 there was a well here which would cure 'all disorders'. A spring can be found half-way up the lane, close to Sunnyside House, which indicates its former existence.

● Ignioc Inscribed Stone, St Clement churchyard, St Clement, near Truro

SW 851439. *The church is found by taking the minor road south east from Truro.*

The inscription reads: VITALI FILI TORRICI [Vitalis, son of Torricus] and this is then repeated in Irish ogham script. The stone is dated between the fifth to seventh centuries. Another inscription just below the cross head, says IGNIOC. This is a personal name now lending its name to the stone.

● Helena Charles, St Clement, near Truro

SW 852438. *Helena Charles' house (Condurrow House) in Cornwall is found at St Clement. It is located a short distance along from the car park.*

Helena Charles (1911-1997) was a Cornish humanitarian, Celtic cultural activist and poet. In January 1951, she became the first leader of the Cornish political party *Mebyon Kernow*, and then led party for the first four years of its existence. In 1950 she organised a performance of *Bewnans Meriasek* for the Celtic Congress which was meeting in Cornwall. This drama was then entered in the 1951 Festival of Britain. With her husband Guy Sanders, Charles could often be seen punting in a gondola on the Tresillian River, an interest that may have led her to work for the welfare of feral cats in Venice. Condurrow House is highly decorated with modern ornate Celtic-style triscals sculpted by Sanders.

St Celements church Truro.

● Tristan and Yseult at Malpas, near Truro

SW 846427. *Malpas is south east of Truro, at the confluence of the Fal and Tresillian Rivers.*

In most versions of *Tristan and Yseult*, the lovers end up at Malpas [*Malpas* being Norman French for 'bad step']. In Beroul's version, the lovers agree to meet there with Yseult reminding Tristan of 'all the pain and all the anguish' she had borne through her retainer Perinis. The poet writes:

> *"Tell him that knows the marsh well,*
> *At the end of the plank-bridge at Malpas:*
> *There I soiled my clothes a little,*
> *On the mound, at the end of the plank-bridge,*
> *and a little this side of the Lande Blanche."*

Clearly a plank-bridge assisted the crossing of the tidal estuary at this point, although we might expect Yseult's clothes to be soiled as at low tide, the river is very muddy indeed. The information about the Lande Blanche has intrigued scholars. The location is vague, but the Lande Blanche [white heath] has been viewed as both the southern side of the river (towards Old Kea), as well as it being a possible reference to the china clay-bearing land around mid-Cornwall to the east. This would mean a crossing to St Michael Penkevil. For the former location, we know that the Manor of Blancheland was located west of Truro, and was administered from Nansvallen (SW 812434). This would indicate a location east of the Truro river.

At Malpas, Yseult advises Tristan to dress as a leper, carrying a cup for alms. In some versions Mark's men try to pursue them across the estuary, but they are drowned by the incoming tide. In other versions, Arthur offers a solution here – or sometimes a test of Yseult's loyalty to Mark.

● Churchyard Cross and other crosses, St Allen

SW 822506. *St Allen is found approximately four miles north of Truro, accessed from the A39. The cross is by the south porch of the church.*

This six foot tall cross is an impressive feature in the churchyard here. It is a wheel-headed cross with projections at the neck. A range of smaller crosses can also be found around St Allen churchyard. There is a two foot tall wayside cross in the south east side (SW 822505) and Trefronick Cross (found at the farmhouse at Trefronick) is also mounted in the south east (SW 822506). A gothic-style Latin cross is found inside the church (SW 822506). There is also an impressive cross close by at Zelah (SW 817518) – known locally at Trevalsa Cross.

● St Piran, Perranporth

SW 753548. *The beach at Perranporth is very accessible. There is a car park close by.*

Piran's origins are generally thought to have been Irish and he is often conflated with the history of St Ciaran. The legend usually attached to him suggest that in Ireland he performed many miracles and invoked the jealousy of the Irish Kings who took him to the top of a cliff, chained him to a millstone and threw him into the sea. Expecting him to drown, he actually floated on the millstone while those watching instantly converted to Christianity. Travelling south, the saint eventually made landfall in Cornwall at this beach; the day he arrived being March 5th. He was found with the millstone – which may have been an altar stone, or perhaps even ballast for a coracle-type boat.

Piran moved inland, building a cell, and his first converts are always described as being three animals: a fox, a badger and a bear. On cooking his meal, one day he noticed that a stream of white metal ran from the rock that he was heating. This was tin, and Piran then showed local people how to extract and use the metal (hence his role as the Patron Saint of Tinners, and the flag of St Piran being both the tin in black rock, and the light of Christianity in the dark). Supposedly, Piran lived to be 200 years old and remained very youthful, with Nicholas Rocarrock in his *The Lives of the Saints*, observing that he had 'no loss of teeth, not having any defect in his teeth or eyes'. Other legends about him appear to cross and fade through the centuries. Roscarrock also notes that Piran became 'the chapalyne of King Arthur who made him the 8th Archbishop of York' but this may just be the wilful conjoining of two important legendary figures.

During the Medieval period we know that the chapel containing the relics of St Piran was one of the great places of pilgrimage (along with the Holy Trinity Chapel at St Day and St Michael's Mount). By the late thirteenth century, his bones, staff and bells were still preserved and carried to different places across Cornwall for veneration; hence perhaps, the wide variety of other dedications found across Cornwall.

Opinions on the origins of St Piran's Day vary greatly. Some observers trace a longer heritage, though it is known that March 5th was especially celebrated in and around the Perranporth district, and was popularly known as 'Perrantide' – with special allowances given for this festive period. The patron saint of Cornwall status of St Piran has risen and developed through the twentieth century. Many towns, villages, schools and institutions now celebrate the Day with calls by several people to make the day a public holiday in Cornwall.

Of late, one of the most spectacular celebrations of the saint's life is seen on St Piran's Day when the town's surf life-saving club bring ashore a statue of St Piran carrying it from the waves into the town. St Piran's origins are very old, but this has not stopped the saint being reprocessed as a contemporary Celtic icon. Indeed, Skinners Brewey in Truro (a company well-known for their innovative Celtic and folkloric branding) have configured St Piran and his millstone as Cornwall's first surfer on their bottles of 'St Piran's Ale'.

St Piran's Oratory, Penhale Sands, near Perranporth

SW 767564. *Pathways lead across the dunes marked by white stone, and the Oratory is relatively easy to find. A commemorative stone marks the spot.*

This is also known as the 'lost church' and it presently lies beneath a concrete shelter under the dunes placed there in 1910. The site was however, excavated in 1835 and this gave much insight into the building. It had a stone bench facing the altar and three carved heads were discovered now held at the Royal Institution of Cornwall in Truro. These are probably St Piran himself, and perhaps his mother, while the third head is of a mythical beast (maybe one of the animals he first converted). It is generally accepted that these were positioned above the door. This building was dated to around the eighth century, though of course, the site may well have had an earlier origin. Nearby was found another cell in which were the remains of mussel and limpet shells, and some fragments of pottery. We know that Celtic missionaries often carried with them a portable altar stone (often called *lecc*) on their travels, and maybe this was viewed by some observers as the famed millstone. The St Piran's Trust is an organisation who are keen to open up the oratory to the public.

● St Piran's Church and Cross, Penhale Sands, near Perranporth

SW 772565. *The church is a short distance from the oratory. The cross lies close to the ruined church.*

This is St Piran's second church which was the parish church until 1805. Like the oratory, this church was abandoned because of the encroaching sand. The walls of it still remain. This church was constructed in the twelfth century initially, and then was rebuilt in 1462. It would have coped with numerous pilgrims. The monument has a St Andrew's-style cross with projections at the neck. The cross shaft is decorated with punch dots. Offerings are often left at this cross, and in spring it is usually surrounded by daffodils. It is beautifully covered with lichen and moss. The cross is thought to be one of the most ancient crosses in Cornwall. In a charter from 960 during the reign of King Edgar, it was known as 'Cristes-mace'.

St Piran's cross.

● Lowender Perran Festival, Perranporth

SW 756545. *The Ponsmere Hotel is located the head of the beach.*

This is Cornwall's major Celtic festival, and it is generally held in and around the Ponsmere Hotel in the town. The festival began in 1978 and aims to celebrate Cornwall's distinctive musical heritage and demonstrate pan-Celtic links with Brittany, Ireland, the Isle of Man, Scotland and Wales, though it has also occasionally welcomed Galician performers. The festival generally takes place in the middle of October and a wide variety of events are on offer. As well as performances, sessions and *troyls* [*ceilidh*-style called dances], there are stalls (the 'Celtic Market'), parades, storytelling, workshops, poetry and fringe events. Most of the musicians and groups associated with traditional Cetlic-inspired music in Cornwall have performed there. Occasionally, the festival also holds conference and seminar sessions on Celtic identity in Cornwall. Recent innovations attached to the festival include a colourful obby oss and the integration of more *noze looan*-style dance events. The festival has many links with other large Celtic festivals, such as the one found at Lorient in Brittany.

● St Piran's Day Play and pilgrimage, Perranporth

SW 769551. *The pilgrimage and play begin near the Perran Sands Holiday Park at Tollgate.*

On the closest Sunday to St Piran's day, many people arrived at the dunes near Perranporth to walk across them to the saint's cross and chapel. This event has grown in magnitude over recent years and now features a promenade-style performance about the saint's life. A host of local people use the natural environment of the dunes as a 'playing place'. In some years, local children have symbolised tin flowing from the rock, using silver coloured streamers.

● Piran Round plain-an-gwarry, Rose, near Perranporth

SW 779544. *The round is found at Rose, approximately one mile along the B3295 from Goonhavern to Perranporth.*

Piran Round is the best surviving example of a plain-an-gwarry and has good claim to be the oldest theatre space in continual use in Britain. The earthwork is in good condition with two entrances and two massive banks of equal height. It is 130 feet in diameter and provides excellent acoustics for those performing. The layout of the Round compares well with what we know about the staging of drama in Late Medieval Cornwall (from plans in the manuscripts of the *Ordinalia* and *Bewnans Meriasek*). Most observers agree that raised stations marked the starting point of a character's performance, and that audience participation was a combination of some static bobservers sitting on the banks, with others following the action. An ancient pathway runs through the site – probably part of the pilgrim route to the chapels in the north.

In the centre of the Round is a curious depression which has been called both the Devil's Spoon and the Devil's Frying Pan. It seems that this was an Medieval dramaturgical special effect, and that for example, actors could crawl through the tunnel section, which could be hidden, and then appear out of the ground, if a framework of twigs and grass covered the structure. This might, for example work with God created Adam and Eve from clay. Others have speculated that it would allow devils to appear – hence its name. Local tradition says that if you run around the frying pan seven times, when you put your ear to the ground in the middle of it, you can hear the devil frying.

Piran Round.

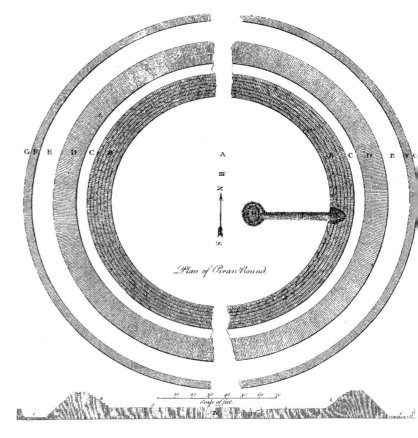

Plan of Piran Round.

Above left: The arrival of the dove during Noah and the Ark sequence, from the 1969 production of Ordinalia.
Courtesy of University of Bristol Theatre Collection

Above right: Plan of Perran Round, Borlase, Natural History of Cornwall, plate xxix.

The size and dimensions of Perran Round certainly make it an important celebratory space, and this would appear to fit the significance of St Piran. There was likely to be a large-scale Piran-themed drama, since the theatre space is only a short distance from the oratory. Indeed, in 1971, following a revival of the *Ordinalia* at the Round in 1969, a play by Donald R. Rawe, *The Trials of St Piran*, was performed here. Since then, numerous other sections of the mystery plays, and other theatre has taken place here. In the past, the Round has been used for Methodist open air services as well as local wrestling competitions. The 1970, 1985 and 1992 Cornish Gorsethow also took place here.

● St Piran's Church and Oratory Cross, Lamborne, near Goonhavern

SW 770520. *This is found on the main A3075 from Goonhavern to Redruth.*

Part of the original church in Penhale Sands dunes were used in the construction of this church, which is now the parish church of Perranzabuloe. The Oratory cross is found on the south side of the church-yard. This cross once stood on the concrete shelter over the original oratory, and perhaps was located beneath the covering at one point in time.

● Caer Dane Hill Fort near Perranzabuloe

SW 778522. *The hill fort is found up a lane from the A3075 at Perranzabuloe heading toward Ventongimps.*

This is an Iron Age oval hill fort, now very overgrown. It has commanding views of the valley to the north east.

● Caer Kief Enclosure, Carn Kief, near Goonhavern

SW 783525. *Access is not easy here. You must walk along a track heading south east from the A3075 at Perranwell.*

This round enclosure is located in square plot of woodland. It is thought to be from the Iron Age, though was less likely to have been a fortification. It lies opposite Caer Dane.

● John Tregear's Homilies, St Newlyn East

SW 828564. *St Newlyn East is best accessed via the old A30 road through Summercourt. The church is in the middle of the village.*

John Tregear was one of the few Cornish-speaking priests known to have made translations of Christian works for his Cornish-speaking congregation. Tregear was a Priest associated with the parish church at St Newlyn East (dedicated to St Newlina), but had connections with Glasney College at Penryn. His translation of these *Homilies* (twelve of which originated with Edward Bonner, the Catholic Bishop of London under Mary Tudor) remains one of the most important texts of Cornish literature, giving us an understanding of the language during this phase.

Their translation was completed sometime between 1550 and 1560. The text argues that the true Catholic church derives its authority through succession from the apostles, back to Christ himself. Its purpose was to reinforce the conviction of many Cornish people at this time that the Protestant church created by the Reformation was an inherently false church.

At times, Tregear seems uncertain how to represent mutations in writing indicating the immutable nature of written text compared to the fluidity of the spoken word. The translator appears to be compromising between deference to the form of the authoritative source text and making its inner meaning accessible to the target audience. The example below, from *Homily 13*, describes the mystery of the sacrament of the altar, and we see the author at work trying to construct a rhyme:

An bara ha]n gwyn dir goir Dew ew trylis the corf ha gois chris[t]
Bara han gwyn dir geir Dew ew gwris corf ha [gois Christ]
Bara ha gwyn dir gyrryow Dew, Corf ha gois Christ gwrie a thew.

[The bread and the wine, through the word of God, are changed into the body and blood of
  Christ.
The bread and the wine, though the word of God, is made the body and blood of Christ.
The bread and the wine, through the words of God, the body and blood of Christ are made]

The Tregear manuscript was a late discovery (1949), and its importance relies on two factors: firstly, that it is only prose text from this period, and because its language requires writers and readers of Cornish to redefine the boundaries between the Medieval and early modern phases of the language. New light on John Tregear was offered by D. H. Frost in 2007, who argued that ecclesiastical writing in Cornish was undertaken in the nearby parishes of mid- and West Cornwall, rather than always at Glasney College itself. Trerice - associated with the important Catholic Arundell family – lies only a short distance north.

⬤ John Trevisa, St Enoder Church and plain-an gwarry, St Enoder

SX 893569. *St Enoder Church lies close to the Kingsley Village shopping complex at Fraddon on the A30.*

John Trevisa (c.1342-c.1402) was born in the parish of St Enoder in mid-Cornwall, probably hailing from Trevessa or Trevuzza [SW 898587]. As a child, Trevisa would have worshipped at St Enoder. He was an important writer, translator and Cornish speaker. He may have initially had contact with Glasney College at Penryn, but was educated at Exeter College, Oxford from 1363 onwards. In 1373 he opposed the appointment of a new Provost – Thomas Carlisle, which sealed his reputation as something of a militant cleric. Around 1374 he was appointed vicar of Berkeley in Gloucestershire and later became a canon of Westbury-on-Trym.

Trevisa's major contribution to wider British culture was to complete an English-language translation of Ranulf Higden's *Polychronicon* from its original Latin. Ironically, as part of the translation he notes two Cornishmen (named Johan Cornwall and Richard Pencrych), probably Cornish speakers, defending English against the dominance of French. Trevisa was a contemporary of John Wyclif at Oxford and there are controversial but learned suggestions by some observers that in his attempts to popularise the teachings of the church, Trevisa may well have contributed to dramatised versions of the gospel – perhaps the *Ordinalia* itself. Given Trevisa's abilities, perhaps he may have authored a dramatic work for this location.

A plain-an-gwarry (SW 892566) exists nearby on the south side of the old A30, opposite the road which leads to St Enoder. A Church Terrier of 1601 identifies a 'playne place or Fayre Park' which may also have been known as Penhale Round.

⬤ Surfing, Newquay

SW 785620. *Fistral Beach is on the western side of Newquay.*

Surfing is now regarded as the premier contemporary Celtic sport. Fistral Beach at Newquay is probably Cornwall's surfing epicentre and is where many international competitions are held. Inter-Celtic competitions are also held. Surfing has inevitably been influenced by the twentieth-century Celtic Revival and many surf boards are manufactured with neo-Celtic designs and lettering. One of the most famous board manufacturers, *Down the Line* based at Hayle, manufactures boards with Celtic knotwork copied from Cornwall's Celtic crosses. The company also decorate boards with St Piran's Flags. Surfing has reinvigorated an age-old Celtic connection with the ocean.

Newquay's beaches, from Towan Beach (nearest to the harbour) around to Watergate Bay, are among the best in Europe for surfing.

● Celto-pop culture, Newquay

SW 805618. *Walk around the main shopping streets of Newquay above Towan Beach.*

The Celtic Revival has had a strong influence on the design of and lettering found on clothing, necklaces, brooches, posters, music and many aspects of popular culture for young people. A walk around the shops, bars and restaurants of Newquay will demonstrate this influence and fusion. Often, Celtic knotwork has been combined with old neo-tribal designs from other cultures, such as those from North American and the Maori culture of New Zealand. Tattooing is also an important area of modern Celtic self-identification with the tattoo premises at Wesley Yard in the town the most famous. One of the most prolific clothing companies is that of *Hager vor surf* [Ugly Sea Surf]. This culture proves the on-going importance of Celtic Heritage in contemporary Cornwall.

● Huer's Hut and Horn, Newquay

SW 808624. *The huer's hut is found on the eastern side of Town Head, close to the Atlantic Hotel. It looks over Towan Beach.*

The huer was the man paid to look out for shoals of pilchards at sea, and would warn fisherman of the town by shouting the Cornish word 'Hevva!' [Shoal!] and by blowing the huer's horn. The Horn is now contained in the Newquay Museum which is presently located at nearby Dairyland Farm Park (SW863582) and maintained by Newquay Old Cornwall Society. On hearing the horn and the cry, the seine boats would put to sea. Sometimes the huer would hold furze or gorse bushes (because of their bright yellow flowers) in his hands to direct the boats to the fish. The small white washed building here is of uncertain age and some estimates suggest a fourteenth century origin.

● Trevelgue Cliff Castle, Porth, Newquay

SW 825631. *Park at Porth and take the footpath west past the putting green towards Porth Island and Trevelgue Head.*

The area has had a long period of occupation from the third century BCE to the sixth century. The barrows show its Bronze Age history, but the many lines of defence on the neck of the Head show it was an important Iron Age site too. Inevitably, the break in the Headland also helped its defence, with the people able to remain on the island in event of an attack.

● Griffin's Point Cliff Castle, Mawgan Porth

SW 842664. *Mawgan Porth is found on the B3276 from Newquay to Padstow. The castle is easily reached along the coastal footpath running south from Mawgan Porth.*

This is an Iron Age cliff castle, with three defensive ramparts on the northern side of the site.

● Settlements, Mawgan Porth

SW 852673. *The settlement is in the centre of the village, close to a holiday park.*

Three groups of buildings can be found here, and they were probably occupied sometime between 850 and 1050. With the protection of the valley, but also easy access to the ocean, this was a convenient location.

● Holywell Bay Well, Holywell Bay, near Newquay

SW 764602. *The well is to be found at the south-western corner of Kelsey Head. It is only accessible at high tide.*

This spectacular well is to be found in a cave. It is composed of a series of calcareous basins, often know as 'rimstone' pools. The well has healing qualities and a local tradition exists of bathing sickly children initially in the lower pools, then progressively passing them towards the upper pools, finally to immersion at the well's source at the upper end of the cave. According to some traditions, this well is also dedicated to St Cubert (Cuthbert).

● Kelsey Head Cliff Castle, near Holywell

SW 765608. *Park at Holywell, north west of the A3075. Walk north on the coastal path to Kelsey Head.*

The remains of an Iron Age rampart and ditch are found here. The site looks over the Chick rock. Several earlier Bronze Age round barrows (or burial mounds) are also found on this headland.

● Penhale Point Cliff Castle, near Holywell

SW 758521. *Park at Holywell. Walk south on the coastal footpath to Penhale Point.*

At the neck of the point are several Iron Age ramparts. The site looks over Holywell Bay to the north.

● St Cubert's Well, Trevorrick Valley, Holywell

SW 773588. *The well is found across the sand dunes beside a pool close to the golf course.*

Cubert is most likely to be the Gwbert of Dyfed in west Wales, whose origins around Cardigan appear to have a connection with this area. The village to the south east of the Well bears his name. Another story however, related that in 995 the body of St Cubert was being taken to Ireland, when after a storm, he and his followers were washed up here. They took this as a sign of God's intent, with his relics perhaps touching the basin-formed well on the beach and them building another well at this location in the valley. Water from the well feeds the pool nearby. The well site was restored by Newquay Old Cornwall Society in 1936 and a plaque upon it reads '*Ewnys gans Cowethas Kernow Goth Towan-Blystry*' [Put in order by Newquay Old Cornwall Society]. It also reads 'May God refresh thee with the water of life'.

● Inscribed Stone, Cubert

SW 786577. *The stone is built into the wall of the church tower.*

This looks to be a memorial stone dedicated to a powerful local chieftain or king. The Latin inscription reads CONETOCI FILI TEGERNOMALI [Conetocus, son of Tegernomalus]. These names are Brythonic and the stone is thought to be from the fifth to seventh centuries.

● Cubert Round, Cubert

SW 796574. *The road to Cubert from the A3075 bisects this site.*

Some observers have viewed this as a settlement but it is more likely to have been a plain-an-gwarry. On the 1696 *Lanhydrock Atlas*, the field just north is known as the 'playings'. Cubert was a significant saint so it is a possibility be that a drama was devoted to him and performed here.

● Our Lady of the Nance Well, Colan, near Newquay

SW 870604. *From the A392 turn into the hamlet of Mountjoy. The well is north-east of Mountjoy Farm.*

This Marian-themed well is so named so because it is in the valley [Cornish: *nance*]. Its original dedication however, may well have been to Saint Colan, now the name of the village directly north of the well. Colan's name is associated with Llangollan in Clwyd and Langolan in Brittany. A Late Medieval *Life* exists in Welsh, but it seems to have been fused with other lives. The waters at Colan were reputedly used for baptism, healing eyes, and for prediction. Richard Carew, visiting the site, in the late sixteenth century, was however, more disparaging of its powers: 'Upon Palm Sunday, these idle-headed seekers resorted thither with a palme cross in one hand and an offring in the other; the offring fell to the priest's share, the crosse they threw in the well; which if it swamme the party should outlive that yeere; if it sunk a short ensuing death was boded, and not altogether untruely, while a foolish conceyt of this halsenin might sooner help onwards.' The modern Carew was sceptical of such Celto-Catholic superstition.

● St Pedyr's Well, near St Columb Minor

SW 859624. *This well is located just off the A3059 from Newquay to St Columb Major. A footpath runs across Treloy Farm to Trebarber. The well is located in a small copse.*

This is probably dedicated to Saint Peter who was martyred by the Roman Emperor Nero around 64CE. The water here was used for the treatment of sick people up until the seventeenth century, but then was abandoned. Despite this the wellhouse is in reasonable condition with a pitched roof and Gothic door arch. The water flows into an oblong basin.

● Hurling, St Columb Major

SW 913637. St Columb Major is located close to the A39 between Newquay and Wadebridge.

Hurling is an outdoor team sport of probably Celtic origin played only in Cornwall. St Columb is the most famous venue where it takes place, though it was traditionally played in other towns and villages as well – notably St Ives, Bodmin, Helston and Probus. The sport is mentioned by the historian John Norden who visited Cornwall around 1584. He notes that it was 'dangerous' and that there was 'hurling to goales, and hurling to the countrye'. In his *Archaeologia Britannia*, collected in 1700, Edward Lhuyd notes an old saying in the Cornish language which goes, '*hyrlian yw gwaré nyi* [Hurling is our sport]'. The game is in essence a game of mob football, perhaps with similarities to Irish hurling and the game of cnapan, found in south-western Wales in the nineteenth century.

At St Columb Major the games are played on Shrove Tuesday and on the second Saturday following, a generally rougher and more aggressive version is held. The game involves a physical battle on the streets between the 'townsmen' and the 'countrymen' of the parish with local shops and houses protecting their windows from damage. This starts with a throw up at 4.30pm followed by a large scrum. The ball is thrown to the crowd at the Market Square and the players' objective is to possess the silver ball in any way possible. Sometimes the play is stopped to allow spectators to touch the ball for fertility or for younger players to participate. Team affiliation is thus less relevant. After about an hour the ball is then hurled towards the two goals which are set about two miles apart at either end of the town. The winner of the ball is then carried on the shoulders of his team mates back to the town to the strains of the 'Hurling Song'. At 8pm the winner calls up the ball again. This is followed by the ball being immersed in gallon jugs of beer. The traditional ball in St Columb had the inscription 'St Columb Major and Minor, do your best. In one of your parishes I must rest' though the modern played ball has upon it 'Town and Country do your best'. A pub in the town is called 'The Silver Ball'.

The hurling ball and crowds in the Market Square St Columb Major.

● Crosses, St Columb Major

SW 913636, SW 912636, SW 909 606

At SW 913636 there is an impressive four-holed cross supported by a short section of shaft. Knots decorate the cross bars. This cross has been used as the model for many of the modern memorials crosses produced in Cornwall in the nineteenth, twentieth and twenty-first centuries. It stands on the east side of the churchyard. Close by is an inscribed cross slab (SW 912636). Built into the recess of a garden wall at SW 909 606 is a small Latin cross.

● Cornish Wrestling, St Columb Major

SW 912635. The Red Lion Public House is found in the middle of St Columb Major. The plaque dedicated to James Polkinghorne is on the northern end of the building.

Cornish wrestling is part of a wider tradition of wrestling that has taken place for centuries in both Britain and Brittany. The earliest written evidence is found in a 1627 poem by Michael Drayton (1563-1631), called the *Battaile of Agincourt*, which explains how at the battle of Agincourt, Henry V was accompanied into battle by Cornishmen holding a banner on which were two Cornish wrestlers. There is also the folkloric origin story that the Trojan refugee Corineus (the mythical founder of Cornwall) wrestled a giant named Gogmagog on Plymouth Hoe. It is known that Cornish and Breton wrestlers have been taking part in inter-Celtic matches since the fifteenth century.

Wrestling in Cornu-English dialect is known as *wrasslin'* and the referee is named the 'stickler'. In Cornish wrasslin', both contestants wear tough jackets to allow them to gain a better grip on their opponent. Holding below the waist is forbidden. The objective is to make your opponent land on his back as flat as possible.

On The Red Lion public house is a plaque dedicated to the memory of one of the greatest ever Cornish wrestlers. This was James Polkinghorne who was born in St Keverne in 1788, but who spent much of his life in St Columb Major, where he ran The Red Lion. In 1826 he competed in a match against the Devon champion, Abraham Cann of Colebrooke. The match took place at Devonport, in Plymouth and some ten thousand people attended. While Cann fought in the Devon style, Polkinghorne used the Cornish 'hug' method. Despite both battling well, the contest was a declared a draw. The plaque reads, 'Cornwall County Wrestling. St.Columb Wrestling Committee. Centenary 1826-1926: To the memory of James Polkinghorne of St Columb in commemoration of his famous encounter with Abraham Cann, Champion of Devon, for the Championship of the West of England 1826'.

Cornish wrasslin' has a small but dedicated following. Exemplar contests are held at the Royal Cornwall Show in June every year, and often before the Cornish Gorsedd ceremony. Wrasslin' also spread acround the world to wherever the Conrish migrated – South Africa, South Australia, and California. The sport is often associated with the Cornish language adage: *Gwary wheag ew gwarry teag* ['Sweet Play is handsome play'].

● Lost Play or Poem of St Columba, St Columb Major

SW 913637. *The church of St Columba the Virgin is located in the middle of the town.*

It is perhaps not surprising to observe a significant amount of theatrical activity in St Columb Major. A potential drama of St Columba, is mentioned by Nicholas Roscarrock (c.1550-1634), where he talks about 'an olde Cornish Rhyme (possibly a verse drama?) containing her Legend, translated by one Mr Williams, a Phis[it]ion there, but howe authentick it is I dare not say'.

In St Columb Major it is the 1580s and 1590s where we find most evidence of theatre at work. The Churchwardens' Accounts of St Columba the Virgin carry a range of information. In 1584, there is mention of the following items: 'coates for dancers, a ffryer's coate, 24 dansinge belles, a streamers of red moccado and [boc] locram, and 6 yards of white woollen clothe'. This certainly makes for some kind of spectacle within the town. By 1587 the dancers' coats, appear specifically to be for Morris work, since 'morrishe coates' are then listed. These entries in the so-called *St Columb Green Book* continue into the 1590s, although in 1594, we learn of 'Rychard beard owethe to be payd at our ladye day in lent x.s. of Robyn hoodes monyes', and that 'Robert calwaye owethe for ye same'. The Morris coats continued to be mentioned in later accounts, from 1595 to 1597. It would appear then, that some kind of performance took place in St Columb Major which involved a Morris/guizing-styled interpretation of Robin Hood.

A plain-an-gwarry may also be found at St Columb Major at SW 911636. The location is not far from the church in the middle of the town. It was at the site now covered by Halveor Close, opposite a building called 'Lanherne'. The Church Terrier of 1727 records that there was a playing meadow in this location. Presumably, this was connected to the 'rhyme' or play recorded by Nicholas Roscarrock.

Henry Jenner, the so-called 'father' of the Celtic revival in Cornwall was born in St Columb in 1848.

● Michael Tregury, St Wenn, near St Columb Major

SW 968646. *St Wenn is best reached by following the B3274 from Roche. Turn left past Tregonetha down a minor road to the village.*

Michael of Tregury—or just Michael Tregury—is a spectacular example of Cornu-Celtic academic and religious success. Tregury was born in the mid-Cornwall parish of St Wenn, and educated at Exeter College, Oxford. Certainly, he would have been a Cornish speaker and writer, though became a distinguished scholar and cleric, becoming first chaplain to Henry VI, then rector of the University of Caen in 1440, before eventually becoming the Archbishop of Dublin in the years 1450-1471. This was a quite meteoric rise, but perhaps his earliest written work again may have been dramatic. St Wenna (d.18th October 544) was a Cornish saint and Queen, who may have made good subject-matter.

● Chapel or St Mary Magdelene Well, Rosenannon, near St Columb Major

SW 958664. *On the B3272 turn into Rosenannon. The well remains are close to Hill Farm, north of the village.*

A clear stream of water comes from the back of the rock where the wellhouse was originally built. A few crystalline rocks may still be observed which may well have been part of this structure. A chapel dedicated to St Mary Magdelene was close by. These were partially destroyed during the Civil War.

● Lanherne Cross and other crosses, St Mawgan in Pydar

SX 872659. *St Mawgan in Pydar is to the north west of St Columb Major is a located off the A3059.*

No better Celtic cross defines Celtic Cornwall than Lanherne Cross. It is a spectacular four holed memorial cross found in the grounds of Lanherne convent, close to the public chapel. It is decorated with intricate knotwork patterning and the cross head has a Christ figure. Two inscriptions are found on the cross. The first is in Hiberno-Saxon characters and translates to 'The Blessed Eid and Imah'. A second is found at the base of the shaft which reads 'Ruhol'. Close by is St Mawgan churchyard, and on the south western side of the churchyard is found a gothic Lantern cross (SW 872659). Within the Lantern are four images: the Annunciation, the Virgin Mary, bishop one and bishop two. The cross dates from the fifteenth century. A wayside cross can also be seen outside the chancel wall (SW 872659) and the so-called wheel-headed Bodrean Cross is close by (SW 872659).

Lanherne, originally home of the Arundell's, now a convent where the cross stands in the garden.

● Castle-an-dinas Hill fort, near St Columb Major

SW 946624. *From the A39, take a minor road past Tregatillin Holiday Park and Tresaddern. Turn north up a track to Castle Downs. Parking is available.*

This is the remains of a spectacular Iron Age hill fort, though there were probably many eras of its construction. Huge earth ramparts dominate the surrounding landscape. It has excellent views of the surrounding countryside and to the north-east in the direction of Tintagel. There is a large inner bank, surrounded by several outer defences. Inside the fort can be found a pool, a well and two Bronze Age barrows. Considering the size and location of the hill fort here, it is not surprising that the complex has come to be associated with King Arthur. Several accounts refer to the castle as a seat of Arthur, with many alluding to perhaps a summer or battle residence here, with a winter, or more long-term residence at Tintagel. The historian William Hals (1655-c.1737), who draws on Geoffrey of Monmouth, but adds important local knowledge, asserts that a deciding battle take place here between Arthur and his traitorous nephew Mordred. Castle-an-dinas looks straight over the western end of the Goss Moor, over Demeliock and the hill fort at St Dennis. Interestingly, the writer John Trevisa was born not far from this location, at St Endor, and perhaps this is why he wrote a now lost book titled *The Book of the Acts of King Arthur*.

● St Dennis Church and Field Systems, St Dennis

SW 951583. *St Dennis lies on the B3279 between Nanpean and Indian Queens.*

Saint Dennis (or St Denis) was celebrated in the Medieval period. Dennis was regarded as one of the seven champions of Christendom and he completed many adventures. There was also an earlier third century Denis (or Dionysus) who was a missionary and martyr, and to whom this church is dedicated. The name here however, is much likely to be derived from the Cornish *Dinas* [castle] and it is clear that the church enclosure was once a hill fort. Remains of ramparts can be traced on the north and north east sides. As Hals notes it was Mordred's armies who faced Arthur's forces at Castle-an-dinas, then to fight at an area known as Demeliock. This would fit as Demeliock lies between the two locations. Thus can be seen the layering of names and history across the ages. The field systems around the churchyard were enclosed in the Iron Age.

St Dennis church.

● Churchyard Cross, St Dennis Church, St Dennis

SW 950582. *The cross strands on the south side of the churchyard.*

This cross is *in situ* in the middle of what was originally an Iron Age hill fort. The monument is incised with decoration and one of the symbols appears to be either a holy chalice or is hour-glassed shaped.

● Demellick Farm, St Dennis

SW 944595. *The farm lies just over the old railway bridge on the road between St Dennis and Indian Queens,*

Demellick or Demeliock [*Dun Maeloc*] probably translates to Maeloc's fort – and this may refer directly to the hill fort in which the church of St Dennis is located. Demeiloc is mentioned in Geoffrey of Monmouth's *The History of the Kings of Britain*. In Hals' account, it seems this location is where Morded's forces gather.

● Saint Austell's Longstone, Roche

SW 986601. *The longstone is found in the middle of Roche, at Holmleigh Crescent on the road to St Dennis.*

The longstone is actually a Bronze Age menhir, but it has come to be associated with the story of Saint Austell. The story is recounted in the *Popular Romances of the West of England*, by Robert Hunt. The saint was returning to his cell on St Austell Downs (now Hensbarrow Downs) but the Devil was watching him. For fun, the Devil worked his spell and the sky became black and the air windy. The saint's hat was swept over the Downs and so Austell ran after it, with the Devil enjoying the sport. The saint's long staff impeded his progress so he stuck it into the ground and planned to return to it later. He stumbled on, but later, neither the hat nor the staff could be found. Resolved to find them in the morning, the saint returned to his cell and slept. By the morning though, the Devil had turned both the staff and the hat to stone. Austell's Hat was apparently removed in 1798 by a regiment of soldiers who were camped near it. They felt the stone was a harbinger of evil because the camp was always waterlogged, and so they destroyed it. The longstone stood *in situ* for many years, but was relocated to Roche in the 1970s, from its original site on Hensbarrow Down at SW 984561, as this location was to be used for the expansion of china clay workings.

● St Gundred's Well, Roche

SW 985617. *The well is located directly north of the village, on the northern side of the A30, close to Victoria.*

St Gundred's Well was an important pilgrimage site during the Medieval period. It once had a statue of the saint on top of the roof of the well. Saint Gundred may well be the same saint as Gonand. The well was known for being a good cure for eye diseases, with M. and L. Quiller Couch noting that it was particularly effective 'on Holy Thursday and the two following Thursdays before sunrise…' after 'the offering of a pin, sometimes bent, before being thrown in the water'.

Churchyard cross at St Dennis.

St Gundred's Well, Roche.

St Gundred's Well.

● Chapel of St Michael, Roche Rock, Roche

SW 991596. *The chapel is reached on the B3374 near the centre of the village.*

This spectacular chapel is located on an outcrop of quartz and tourmaline. The present chapel was built around 1409 though it is probable that the site was of spiritual significance for centuries before that. The two-storey chapel is only accessible by a metal ladder attached to the side of the Rock. Care is advised. The location is associated with the numerous tellings of the narrative of Tristan and Yseult. Supposedly, the lovers took refuge here from Yseult's angry husband King Mark. This fits geographically with the narrative as it lies directly south from Tintagel. In Beroul's version, the lovers are met by a hermit called Ogrin, who advises them to repent. Ogrin is very old and wise man who spoke to them about Holy scripture. The Rock is located in the middle of the china-clay mining district, the propensity of white clay in the area perhaps making it the site of the 'White Heath' in several of the narratives.

Other stories have persisted at the site: another hermit is thought to have lived here, as was a leper, and the location is also associated with the 'Faustian' narrative of Jan Tregeagle, an unscrupulous lawyer and landowner who makes a deal with the devil. A link to the nearby holy well is found in some accounts of St Gundred who is said to have been the devoted daughter of her leprosy-afflicted father who lived in the cell on top of the rock. In this way we can see how the Celtic narratives of Cornwall merge and conflate. Recent archaeological studies have discovered a ring of wells around the Rock, suggesting a wider sacred purpose for the location. Roche Rock was one of the places chosen

Left: The Chapel of St Michael, Roche Rock.

Below: Roche Rock.

for one of the earliest modern Cornish Gorsedd ceremonies in 1933. A painting of the ceremony exists. This was by Herbert Truman and is part of the collection of the Royal Institution of Cornwall.

⬤ Tremodrett, near Roche

SX 004612. *The site is found heading in a north-easterly direction from the village of Roche, passing the Sewage Works and under the railway line.*

On the eastern edge of Roche is Tremodrett Farm. Tremodrett translates to Mordred's Farm. Given the historical accounts of the conflict between Arthur and his nephew Mordred (not least in the nearby location of Castle-an-Dinas) there is a tantalising link here. Modred is also a significant character in the second day of the play of *Bewnans Ke*, once performed in Kea Parish, near Truro. However, the Mordred here may simply be the name of a later occupier or owner.

⬤ Plain-an-gwarry, Innis Downs, near Lanivet

SX 031627. *This is located around 200 metres south of the present double roundabouts on the west side of the road to St Austell.*

An R. Thomas, writing in *Statistics of Cornwall* (1852) notes 'an oval earthwork' about an acre in size at this location, and in 1964 Charles Thomas found that 'the ditches [of this Late Neolithic henge site] during the Middle Ages were cleaned of silt and an entrance made on the southern side'. This could mean that the earthwork were altered to perhaps form a plain-an-gwarry. The remaining bank is quite steep compared to other plain-an-gwarrys but this site has been an important crossroads for centuries so it may have been a suitable theatre space. The fifteenth-century St Benet's Abbey (a former Benedictine monastery) may be connected with the site. On maps, the monument is described as a 'henge'. This is because the ditch is found on the inside.

⬤ Lanivet Church, Lanivet

SX 039644. *The church is found on the south eastern side of the village. The church is not always open but a contact number is provided outside.*

The church here offers a useful insight into Medieval Celtic Cornwall. There are two significant wall paintings: the first is known locally as 'the whale' but it is, in fact, a painting of the harrowing of Hell, with Adam and Eve walking out of the jaws of Hell – a sequence depicted in the surviving Creation play of the *Ordinalia*. The second is an image of 'Our Blessed Lord', which appears to show the wounds of Christ – another image of visualised theatricality from the Medieval period.

⬤ Churchyard Crosses, Lanivet

SX 039642. *The crosses are located on the south and eastern sides of the churchyard.*

This first cross on the southern side is perhaps the most spectacular cross to be found in mid Cornwall. The cross head is slightly damaged but features a wheel-head design. All four sides of the cross are

Lanivet churchyard cross.

divided into panels many of which are punch decorated. Intriguingly, there is one panel which shows a strange figure of a man with a tail which may show an earlier Pagan influence. The second cross is close by on the eastern side of the church and the cross shaft is heavily ornamented with knots and plaitwork. Knots also decorate the limbs of the cross head.

● Crosses, Lanivet

SX 046633, SX 059633, SX 061629, SX 055641, SX 0205650, SX 073588, SX 027639, SX 035646.

A range of crosses maybe found around the area. South east of the village at SX 046633 is Reperry wayside Cross, while just south of the A30 Bodmin bypass is St Ingunger Cross (SX 059633). There was apparently once at holy well dedicated to St Ingunger but this has not survived. It may be reached by a minor road between Lanivet and Lanhydrock. At the hamlet of Fenton Pits is another wayside cross (SX 061629). Another may be found about a mile east of Lanivet (SX 055641). This is called Treliggan Cross. It was used as gatepost in the farm of the same name. At Tremore can also be found a small wayside cross (SX 0205650). This is to found to the north east of Lanivet. The ambition of cross-building and carving in the parish can also be seen at the following locations: SX 073588 (Trethew Cross), SX 027639 (Woodley Cross) and SX 035646 (Lamorrick Cross).

● Lesquite Cross, near Lanivet

SX 665626. *This cross is found on the entrance drive to Lesquite Farm, close to Fenton Pits.*

A tall, spectacular cross, it has its origins in this parish, but at one time was located near St Breward.

● St Bernard's Well, Nanpean, near St Austell

SW 963558. *This spring is located close to the ground of Nanpean Football Club on the B3279.*

At one point, this Well was well known and had a baptistry built next to it. The baptistry was probably destroyed because of china clay mining. The spring water is now enclosed in a conduit and comes out near some cottages. The well water here was known to have 'medicinal properties'.

● St Stephen's or Foxhole Beacon, Foxhole, near St Stephen-in-Brannel

SW 960546. *On the B3276, at Foxhole Post Office, turn left towards Goonabarn. The Beacon is on the left.*

St Stephen's, or Foxhole Beacon has had limited excavation but it is known to have been a Neolithic tor enclosure. This can be seen from nearby Watch Hill. On Watch Hill there are Bronze Age cairns (ritual monuments, sometimes of a funerary nature). Local house names recall a King Pippin who once lived there. The local place-names Carpalla and Carloggas seem to incorporate the word *Ker* [round settlement], so could refer to an Iron Age or Medieval settlement, or to the Neolithic tor enclosure. The hill was once used as a beacon to celebrate midsummer.

● The Charter Endorsement, St Stephen-in-Brannel

SW945534. *The church is located in the middle of the village just off the A3058.*

At St Stephen-in-Brannel we learn of the oldest surviving secular text of length, written in Cornish. Usually dated around 1380-1400, the so-called *Charter Endorsement* was discovered by Henry Jenner in 1877 on a land charter originally from the parish of St Stephen-in-Brannel in mid-Cornwall. The text contains forty-one lines of Middle Cornish rhymed strophic verse jotted down on the back of a charter (this dated to 1340). The initial section appears to be some kind of speech in which the speaker is offering marriage to a girl, who is praised and would seem to make a good wife. She is also described as being very beautiful, though she is clearly quite young. This first part also makes reference to a bridge on the River Tamar, and how there is none like her on this side of it:

Lemen yz torn my as re	[Now into your hand I shall give her
ha war an greyz my an te	and on the Faith I swear it
nag usy par	that there is not the like
an barz ma ze pons tamar	on this side of the Tamar bridge
my ad pes worty byz da	I ask you: to her be good,
ag ol ze voz hy a wra	and all your will she will do
rag flog yw ha gensy doz	for she is a child and it is wise
ha gaffy ze gafus hy boz	to get consent from her and me.
kenes mes zymmo ymmyug	Although I am ashamed, kiss,
eug alema ha fystynyug	go from here and hurry.]

In the second part of the text is more difficult to draw meaning from. Here, it would seem there is perhaps another speaker, and now a woman is being told how to 'manage' a man. While control of this man would seem to be her objective, we also learn that the man himself is both gracious and considerate. Some observers have viewed the fragment as part of a larger lost play, while others have seen the piece as a wedding speech, the lines casually written on the back of a discarded charter. If the text presented was a secular drama, then St Stephen-in-Brannel was fairly unique. This does seem a slim possibility, but the *Endorsement* at least proves that a poetic/dramatic impetus could be could be found there around 1380-1400.

● Plain-an-gwarry. St Stephen-in-Brannel

SW 944534. *The plain-an-gwarry was located on the site of the former Primary School, now community buildings. It lies just north of the church.*

In the nineteenth century, this location was used for wrestling competitions, though we know that in 1658 it was recorded as 'playing green'. Its proximity to the church makes it a likely location for drama, if the multi-use pattern across Cornwall is extended to here.

● Godfrey of Cornwall, St Stephen-in-Brannel

SW 944534. *From the site of the 'playing green', there is a good view back to the church.*

Godfrey of Cornwall, who was alive in 1320, was born, in St Stephen-in-Brannel, and was educated at Oxford and Paris, at which latter place he became Reader in Divinity. Godfrey would have spoken and written in Cornish – and he is a potential playwright. He eventually joined the Carmelites and wrote in defence of that Order. William of Cornwall, Abbot of Newenham in 1272, is believed to have been his brother. From lowly origins in Cornwall, he seems to have had a pan-European influence. Of course, it is hard to think of Godfrey without thinking of the *Charter Endorsement*. He is a bit early to be its creator, since the *Endorsement* is usually dated around 1380 but is closer to the Charter itself (from 1340).

● Resugga Hill Fort, St Stephen-in-Brannel

SW 940510. *From the centre of the village, travel south on a minor road past Brannel School. The fort is on the eastern side of the road.*

This is a little known, but impressive Iron Age structure on land above the Fal Valley. It is round-shaped with a single rampart, although another separate rampart is found to the north west. It may have had connections to the fort at Golden.

● The Church of St Probus and St Grace, Probus

SW 899477. *Probus is just off the main A390 from St Austell to Truro. The church is in the middle of the village.*

Probus is similar to St Buryan in that it was made a collegiate church by King Athelstan in 926, having a dean and four prebendaries. Prior to this, the church was a classic *Lann*-type 'holy enclosure' – marked still by the present delineation of the churchyard. St Probus and St Grace were early British saints, whose images are carved into the tip of a Lantern-style cross (built as a war memorial) at the front of the church. It is believed that Probus was a West British chieftain, and that when it came to him erecting his first church he prayed to St Grace for assistance. This she gave, but upon its consecration he made no mention of her. A mysterious voice was then heard saying 'St Probus and Grace, not the first but the last' From thereon, the early church was dedicated to both.

Two skulls of a man and a woman were found buried in the chancel wall when the church was being restored in 1851, and their concealment would note their importance – especially during the Reformation. It is thus assumed by some that they are the relics of the saints – and they are presently stored in an aumbry in the north wall of the sanctuary. Permission to view them can be granted by the church warden.

The church tower is the tallest in Cornwall and it is made of 'porcelain' stone, (a very white stone) mined nearby at St Stephen-in-Brannel. Now encrusted with moss and lichen, when it was constructed around 1530, it would have been like a white beacon in the middle of the landscape. Wooden and colourfully painted statues would probably have been found in the several large niches seen in the lower third of the tower. A small and brightly coloured fragment remains from this era

The Church of St Probus and St Grace, Probus.

and is held in the church. At the bottom of the tower, on the northern side, may be observed a delicate carving of a hound chasing a fox. According to tradition, Nicholas Carminow who was involved in the building of the tower represents the fox. Several holy wells may be seen around the edge of the church, which in the eighteenth century were turned into village water pumps.

● Hurling, Probus

SW 899477. *The north porch of the church can be observed from the Square, with the Hawkins Arms a short distance away.*

Although nearby St Columb is recognised as the centre of contemporary Hurling in Cornwall, Probus also had a long tradition of hurling which continued into the early part of the twentieth century. The expansive parish of Probus allowed for a wide-ranging game in the 'town' and in the 'country', although it seems that regular contests were held here between the men of the village and anyone else from Cornwall who wished to try their chances. It was traditionally played on the 16th July each year. The ball at Probus was kept at the Hawkins Arms public house in the village, and was thrown up from the porch at the northern side of the church. The two goals are both located exactly half a mile away from the church, one at Helland Turn (SW 899488), then the other at Lower Trestrayle Farm (SW 904464). The hurling goal at Helland Turn was *in situ* until it was stolen in the 1990s. The whereabouts of the one at Lower Trestrayle is not known.

● Venton Glidder Well, near Probus

SW 902494. *The well is located on the farm at Venton Glidder, south of the Penzance-Paddington railway line. The well is accessible, but ask for permission to view.*

The dedication here is obviously to St Clether, a saint also associated with the well of that name on Bodmin Moor. Clether is said to have been one of the sons of the legendary children of Brychan from Wales who first entered south-west Britain at Hartland Point. Descending steps lead down to the well, although it is presently blocked by a grill. The water here is said to be 'pure and clear' though no healing properties are noted.

● Venton Perran, near Probus

SW 867468. *The well is just off the A390 at Tresillain, close to Tregeagle Farm.*

This well, dedicated to St Piran, is in a somewhat ruinous state and is only accessed through a usually muddy field. There is some indication that this well was located on a very rich mineral vein, and that there was a mine close by in the nineteenth century. The mining connection therefore might have helped give its dedication since Piran is the patron saint of tinners.

Holy Well, Venton Glidder.

● Gweal an Chapel Cross, Tresillian

SW 871465. *The cross is located at bend in the road on the A390 in front of the Mission Church at Tresillian.*

At Trefcelst, now Tregellas, once stood a small chapel, which had on it a cross. The chapel was there in 1517, and this cross is from it. It was moved to its present site in 1863 when it was moved from *gweal an chapel* [chapel field].

● Golden Manor and Chapel, near Probus

SW 922468. *From the crossroads near Trewithen follow the minor road to Tregony. Golden is located on the left.*

Golden Manor is not actually a manor, but more properly a barton. In Cornish, it was once known as Trewygran. The house here was the one time seat of the Wolvedon family, and later Francis Tregian. The Tregians were a Catholic family who hid the recusant priest Barnstaple-born Cuthbert Mayne during the Reformation. Mayne, who refused to conform to the English establishment's view of worship was caught and executed in 1577, only a few years after the Prayer Book Rebellion. Tregian was not executed but as was the case during this period, he lost all his lands and property. Tregian's story is usually told on religious lines, but for him, his religion was very much bound up in their Celtic identity. Tregian is ironically now known for his important contribution to musical history - collecting and arranging the Fitzwilliam Virginal Book, the most important source for early English keyboard music.

Mayne and he were not the only Catholics to suffer in this period: the hagiographer Nicholas Roscarrock – originally from St Endellion – was also racked in the Tower of London in 1581. Mayne was canonized in 1970. Local legend tells of a 'priest's hole' in the house at one time, and even of a tunnel running from Golden to the churchyard at Probus. Opposite the house at Golden can be seen a Medieval chapel (now used as a barn).

● Golden Hill Fort, near Probus

SW 924469. *The fort is found just past the manor and chapel at Golden.*

This is an impressive Iron Age site overlooking the River Fal. It may also have had Roman occupation, and it is speculated that this was once the famous Voliba listed by Ptolomy (90-168CE).

● Carvossa Enclosure, Trewithen, near Probus

SW 919483. *This enclosure is found just south of the A390, and is reached down a lane. A quick climb over a wall locates the northern bank.*

This was a Romano-British settlement, with a mixture of native and Roman pottery from Britain and elsewhere in the empire. Enclosures and forts such as this one straddle the banks of the River Fal from Tregony to St Stephen-in-Brannel, giving evidence of the river's strategic and trading importance. It may have profited from tin and iron production in exchange for Roman goods.

The cross from Gweal an Chapel.

Site plan Carvossa near Probus.

CARVOSSA

A = Excavation of main defences
B = Footings of rampart found
C = Section of main ditch and rampart
D = Site of rectangular enclosure and ditch
E = Excavation of main entrance with a
    road flanked by large post holes

The stone cross at Great Trelowthas.

● Plain-an-gwarry, near Probus

SW 915481. *This is found in the northern corner of Sorn Field just to the north of Trewithen Farm.*

Evidence about a round here is rather limited. However, Richard Polwhele quoting Tonkin, suggests 'a round for Cornish games'. In 1824, Hitches and Drew note a 'theatre of games' at Sorn Field.

● Trelowthas Cross, near Probus

SW 885466. *The cross is found just off the A390 between Trewithen and Tresillian. The cross is located on a public right of way.*

Originally round-headed, this cross was found in the 1940s by a member of Probus Old Cornwall Society called William Moyle. It was covering a well at Trelowthas.

● St Just-in-Roseland Church, St Just-in-Roseland, near Truro

SW 848356. *The church is located six miles south of Truro on the Roseland peninsula, accessed on the A3078.*

This thirteenth-century church perches on the edge of a tidal creek beside Carrick Roads, and for many people, says much about the link between Celtic Christianity and place. The church is dedicated to St Just – who also appears in Penwith. The churchyard is planted with semitropical shrubs and trees, and contains a number of finely carved nineteenth and twentieth century Celtic crosses.

● St Ruan's Well, Ruan Lanihorne, near Truro

SW 894421. *The well is in the middle of a field close to the church, with a distinctive arched roof.*

St Ruan was known locally as St Rumon, and he is the patron saint of Ruan Lanihorne on the upper stretches of the River Fal but is also the patron saint of Ruan Major and Ruan Minor at Cadgwith. The location of the well here is supposedly a short distance from where St Ruan was originally laid to rest. In the transept of St Ruan Lanihorne church is an impressive ancient stone figure of the saint.

● St Mawe's Well, St Mawes

SW 847332. *The well is found up a hill close to the Victory Inn.*

Now enclosed by a wooden door, embossed with a relief image of him, St Mawe arrived in Cornwall from South Wales. Romantically described by L. and M. Quiller Couch, 'he settled at a point of the seashore here, then all solitary in itself, and merely a long sloping descent of rock to the water, with a broad leafy heath at the back of it… There he lived as a hermit.' So it is said, he made himself a chair out of rock just above the well, where he could sit and meditate. Later he travelled to St Malo in Brittany, where he is commemorated at Ill Maudez and Lanmodez. After his death more pilgrims came to visit his well and chair, and during the Reformation his chair was said to have been relocated to the churchyard to avoid destruction. Nineteenth-century accounts of it exist, though it may well have been just a piece of modern fancy to support the legend. Either way, the chair no longer exists in the churchyard.

The church of St-Just-in-Roseland.

The Holy Well St Mawes.

● Veryan Castle, near Veryan

SW 909388. *The castle is located to the south west of the village, down a minor road.*

Known locally as 'Ringaround' this site has been heavily ploughed but is in a significant location overlooking the valley. It is Iron Age. Close by is Carne Beacon – a Bronze Age barrow (SW 913387) .

● Dingerien Castle Hill Fort, near Gerrans

SW 882376. *The fort is found on the eastern side of the A3078 between Ruan High Lanes and Gerrans.*

Given the local place-name Gerrans and the elements of this location (Din or Dyn – meaning 'castle' and Gerien, meaning 'Gerent', it is hard to not connect this Iron Age fort with King Gerent, the dark age King of Dumonia. However, we know that whilst Gerent was an important ruler, the dedication of the church here is to Saint Gerent, who was somewhat earlier and who may be traced back through Saint Erbyn, Just, Selevan and Cuby. It appears this fort was also named after the saint and not the King.

● Gerrans Cross, Gerrans churchyard, Gerrans

SW 872 351. *The cross is easy to spot on the south side of the churchyard.*

This tall cross is one of the few crosses found on the Roseland peninsula. The crosses on the cross head are only lightly carved but can just be seen.

● St Cuby's Well, Tregony

SW 928450. *The well is located down a lane on the south-eastern side of the village on the road to Goviley Major.*

Saint Cuby is associated with Duloe in south east Cornwall, but he may have been born at Tregony. The well at Tregony is rather neglected with no basin or surviving wellhouse. How people travelled to Tregony may be explained by the fact that until it was silted up in the nineteenth century, it was accessible as a port. Indeed, further up the Fal, the Iron Age / Romano-British hill fort at Golden was reached in the same way.

● Inscribed Stone, Tregony

SW 927453. *Tregony is on the B3287. The stone is on Cuby Church in the south-western corner.*

The stone reads NONITTA ERCILINI RIGATI TRIS FILI ERCILINI [Nonitta, Ercilinus, Rigatus, the three children of Ercilinus]. It is likely to have been carved in the late sixth or early seventh centuries.

The church of St Gerrans c.1904

● Crosses, Grampound

SW 936482, SW 944484, SW 955473.

Market Cross is found in the middle of the village outside of St Naunter's or St Nun's Chapel (SW 936482). The cross is from the fifteenth century but the cross head has been missing since before 1858. Nancor Cross (so-called because it was located at Nancor Farm) lies on an small embankment above the A390 road from St Austell to Truro (SW 944484). There is a tiny crucifix figure carved upon it. Fair Cross, meanwhile, lies on a minor road to Grampound close to the B3287 Tregony to St Austell Road (SW 955473). It is a Latin style boundary cross.

● The Forest of Moresk, Pencoose, near Truro

SW 965465. *Pencoose is located on a minor road off the B3287 St Austell to Tregony road.*

In their various journeying from King Mark's castle, in the Béroul version of the narrative, Tristan and Yseult spend considerable time hiding in the forest of Moresk – sometimes called Morois. Moresk is now an electoral ward in Truro, but it has been suggested that the forest stretched much further to the east, and might have included the hill fort of Pencoose near Grampound. This part of mid Cornwall would have been much more wooded than in the present era, and would indeed fit this sequence of the narrative where Beroul writes:

> They were in the forest of Moresk;
> that night they lay on a hill.
> Now Tristan is safe
> as if he were in a castle with a wall.

In the forest of Moresk, it is Tristan who demonstrates his skills as an archer shooting a deer for food. He is accompanied on his hunting mission with his friend Governal. In the Forest of Moresk, Tristan and Governal also start to deal with the evil barons, laying various traps for them there.

● St Mewan Well, near St Austell

SX 995519. *The well lies close to the village of Trewoon. Follow the minor roads to Bosithow and find the well in a field next to Glebe Farm.*

Mewan and Austell were great friends, and Mewan is best remembered at Saint Méen in eastern Brittany. He originally came from Gwent in South Wales and was a relative of Saint Sampson. Little remains of his wellhouse here, except the stone door jam which can be found in the field wall. The remains of the well are surrounded by boulders. Close by is the church of St Mewan.

● Menacuddle Well, St Austell

SX 013535. *The well is found down a sharp left hand turn on the B3274 leading north from the town toward Penwithick.*

The well at Menacuddle

Menacuddle Well c.1890

Menacuddle Well.

It would be hard to find a more beautiful well site in Cornwall than Menacuddle. A variety of suggestions are offered for the translation of Menacuddle. Some suggest it means 'hillside with a thicket'. Others posit that it is derived from *mean-a-coedl* meaning the 'hawk's stone' and another possible interpretation lies in *mena* [meaning 'sanctuary'] aligned with the saint's name [Cuddle, or Guidel]. Very little is known about St Guidel, but this was clearly a significant religious site in the Late Medieval period. Commenting in 1827, the local writer Samuel Drewe observed that 'Weakly children were carried thither to be bathed, ulcers have also been washed in its sacred water, and people, in seasons of sickness, have been recommended by the neighbouring matrons to drink of its salubrious waters'. Nestled into the wall of the road, the wellhouse is a gothic moss-covered structure, surrounded by a grove of ancient trees and rhododendron bushes. Inside the well house may be found the channels through which the healing waters can flow. The location gives a strong feel of what it would be like to come to the well in the Late Medieval period. The well was restored in 1921 by Sir Charles Graves Sawles in memory of his son who was killed in the First World War. To the south of the well is a small stone chair, known by local children as the 'druid's chair'.

● Bagpiper Gargoyle, St Austell Church, St Austell

SX 014525. *The church is located in the middle of the town. Binoculars are advised to see the gargoyle. He is found on the outside above the west door.*

Viewed high on the magnificent church tower here is a carved gargoyle, playing a set of bagpipes.

Bagpipes were a common piece of Celtic instrumentation in Cornwall. The gargoyle's hair is standing on end, and his cheeks are full of air.

● Treverbyn Cross, St Austell

SX 016524. *The cross is found in the south eastern side of the churchyard.*

This cross once stood on the nearby Treverbyn Estate but was erected here in 1879.

● Castle Gotha, near St Austell

SX 028496. *On the coastal road from St Austell to Pentewan, the Castle can be found close to Lobb's Shop and is reached by a footpath.*

Traces remain here of a single rampart. The site is most likely originally an Iron Age one, though occupation would have lasted into the Roman period.

Bagpiper gargoyle, St Austell church.

Looking inland to Castle Gotha Farm (centre). The curved single rampart of the castle can be seen in the hedge-line just north of the farm itself.

● Towan Well, near Lobb's Shop, St Austell

SX 015489. *The well is best found by taking the coastal road from St Austell to Pentewan. At Lobb's Shop, turn right toward East and West Towan. The well is not far from West Towan at Towan Farm.*

This well is rarely spoken of but was known by Thomas Quiller Couch in 1882. He described it as a 'stately well, built of shaped and shapely granite slabs'. On the end wall is a pedestal, once intended for a statue of the saint. Some observers feel the dedication might be to Saint Tovinianus, a friend of Saint Sampson and Saint Mewan. This would fit since the church of St Mewan is a only few miles away. The well was restored by St Austell Old Cornwall Society in 1937.

Towan Well near Lobb's shop.

● Black Head Cliff Castle, near St Austell

SX 039479. *Parking is found at Trenarren. Walk east towards the coastal path.*

At the neck of the promontory are found three embankments built for defence at this Iron Age fort. A climb to the top of the mound gives excellent views of surrounding St Austell Bay. The Trenarren residence of the Anglo-Cornish poet and historian, A(lfred) L(eslie) Rowse (1903-1997) looks down upon Black Head. The promontory inspired a number of his poems and works. Close to the cliff castle, a monolith commemorates his life.

● Brass Well, near Mevagissey

SX 009457. *The well is located at Treleaven Farm, close to the recreation ground in the village.*

The well has been much changed over the years, but in 1730 was reputed to have had 'curative powers'. A series of steps once led down to the well, but it is now constructed of plain stone.

● Cornish at St Ewe, near Mevagissey

SX 977461. *St Ewe lies close to the Lost Gardens of Heligan, on the road to Gorran off the B3273.*

In the dispositions of the Bishop's Consistory Court at Exeter from 1595, we learn that a girl from St Ewe testified that two of the witnesses in a case had been speaking together. They had used both English and Cornish, suggesting that Cornish was being spoken quite late in this part of Cornwall. This fits, since St Ewe is an isolated community.

● Crosses, St Ewe, near Mevagissey

SW 978460, SW 984457, SW 999464

In the middle of the village, close to the Parish Church is a mutilated large Market Cross positioned on blocks of Pentewan Stone (SW 978460). At a nearby road junction (SW 984457) leading to Gorran, is Corran Cross (named after the nearby farm). In the grounds of Heligan Manor is another spectacular cross named Bokiddick Cross which was moved here from Lanivet (SW 999464). A cross base with

The Market Cross, St Ewe.

the inscription LARATECUS FECIT CRUCEM + O PRO ANIMA SUA [Luratecus erected this cross for the good of his soul] lies between Polgooth and St Ewe at SW 989478. This is an intriguing survival and it is a pity the cross is missing.

● The 'Hack and Cast', The Dodman, near Gorran

SX 001399. *There is a car park at Penare, close to Gorran. A public footpath leads to the structure and the coastal path.*

The 'Hack and Cast' is the name usually applied on the defensive structures found at the neck of the Dodman cliff castle. These Iron Age ramparts once formed a line from one side of the point to the other. The name of the Dodman is could be derived from the Cornish for a bank or dyke of this kind: *tomen*. However, it may have an English language origin: the Deadman.

● The Biscovey Stone, St Mary's Church, St Blazey Gate

SX 058535. *The church is to the east of St Austell on the A390.The stone is located on the south side of the churchyard.*

This is a mysterious inscribed cross shaft here which has upon it the words ALRORON or CILRO-RAN and ULLICI FILIUS. Translated this reads as 'the stone of Alroron [or Cilroran], son of Ullicus'. The lettering is of insular Celtic script and the names could be Celtic.

● Prideaux Castle Hill Fort, near St Blazey

SX 059556. *Prideaux Wood is located not far from the Eden Project, just off the A390 at Tywardreath Highway.*

This is an Iron Age hill fort composed of two defensive ramparts and a third outer ring of defence. It has commanding views of the local area.

● St Sampson's Well and church, Golant, near Fowey

SX 121551. *Golant is found off the B3269 to Fowey. St Sampson's wellhouse is found on the side of the church.*

Sampson or Samson is a famous Celtic saint, his father was Amon of Dyfed and his mother, Anna of Gwent (a well is found devoted to her at Whitstone in North Cornwall). Aged five, Samson was sent to be schooled at the monastery of Saint Illtud at Llwnilltud Fawr, not far from Cardiff. Illtud has a reputation as being 'of all the Britons, the most learned in the Scriptures'. Initially Samson travelled to Ireland, performing healing in many communities and defeating a serpent. He then travelled to Cornwall with three companions, aiming perhaps for Brittany.

It was while crossing the Hundred of Trigg that he found people paying honour to a pagan idol with a play, dancing and singing. He converted them and defeated a further serpent in Cornwall. He also carved a cross on a pagan standing stone. From the banks of the River Fowey he then made his way to Brittany where the vast cathedral of Dol is dedicated to him. Sampson died back in Wales in

The Holy Well of St Sampson.

The Church of St Sampson, Golant.

Medieval bench ends at St Sampson's Church.

Lantwit Major in 565. There is a detailed *Life* of Sampson in Breton, with the Bretons wishing to know more about his early life. Sampson has also given his name to one of the Isles of Scilly but the derivation of that remains unclear. A Medieval bench end in the church, now part of the pulpit shows the image of a Bishop, who may well be Sampson.

Another story connects St Sampson to Tristana. It is said that Yseult presented her priceless robe to the monks here. Beroul notes that in his day, the monks still proudly displayed her gift.

● Plain-an-gwarry, Golant, near Fowey

SX 121551. *The site is at Tanhay Moor, 100 metres away to the east - from St Sampson's Church.*

A document held in Cornwall Records Office in Truro, dating from 1740 tells how an elderly woman named Susannah Mitchell swore on oath that Tanhay Moor(s) was a playing place when she was younger. The playing place must thus have still been in existence in the late seventeenth century (c.1680). By this time however, the Reformation and Puritanism had shut down any kind of performance of this kind, and the language had more or less retreated to being only spoken the area west of a line from Truro to St Agnes. Possible dramas performed there in an earlier age might be a 'Life of St Sampson' – which with his dragon-slaying powers – and ability to convert the Pagan Cornish – might have made quite a spectacle on the banks of the River Fowey. Considering the wider cross-Brythonic significance of St Sampson, a dramatic life seems a real possibility. The local legend of Tristan and Yseult might also have offered possibilities.

● Castle Dore Hill Fort and Lantyan, Golant, near Fowey

SX 103548. *This is just beside the B3269 on the eastern side of the road, travelling north to Lostwithiel from Fowey.*

This is a well-preserved Iron Age hill fort, composed of two circular ramparts. There is also an additional enclosed area to the east of the main site. Excavations here have revealed an earlier Bronze Age history but it is known that the site was occupied during the sixth century – and that a timber-built

An aerial view of Castle Dore

structure was contained inside the fort. Inevitably, the site has come to be linked with the Tristan and Yseult narrative because of the close proximity of the Tristan stone, and other observations about the cultural geography of this Celtic epic. Some observers have argued that this was the residence of Mark, though the evidence is far from compelling. The twentieth-century novelist Arthur Quiller Couch (1863-1944) began writing a novel about the site and its modern implications called *Castle Dor*. This was eventually completed by Daphne du Maurier and published in 1962.

Lantyan (SX 105574) meanwhile is identified as being the narrative's Lancien. In Beroul, this is where the love scenes in a garden at King Mark's palace take place. This site is a little to the south of Milltown Wood. However there is another possibility here, that the site a little to the north may better fit Beroul's narrative. This is now called Castle (SX 100583) and on deeds of 1395 is called 'Nantyhan Parva Castel'. It could be that Mark used either of these locations as a residence while retreating to the confines of Castle Dore when danger beckoned. Some theorists have proposed that the name Mark is actually a horse god [Margh].

● The Tristan Stone, Fowey

SX 110524. The stone is close to Four Turnings on the A3082 on the western side of Fowey.

This intriguing stone has upon it an inscription which reads: DRVSTANVS HIC IACIT CVNOMMORI FILIVS [Drustanus lies here, son of Cunomorus]. Located originally closer to the site at Castle Dore, the stone was later moved here and set on a modern plinth. The stone has been dated to the sixth century. In legend and hagiography, it is known that there was a King Quonomorius who ruled over both Dumnonia and the Breton region known as Domonee, so there could be a link. The difficulty with the stone and the narrative is that here Tristan [Drustanus] is presented as the son of Mark [Cunomorus], and in the narratives, he is generally either not a relative or a nephew. However, he may well have an affiliation to Mark which might have rendered him a 'son' as part of his retinue. The stone is also decorated with a small Tau cross at the top.

The Tristan Stone.

● Celticity and Daphne du Maurier, Menabilly, near Fowey

SX 101512. The house is not accessible but a good flavour of the territory can be gain from walking the coastal path from Menabilly Barton (SX 098508) to St Catherine's Castle at Fowey (SX119508). You can then return on the Saints Way footpath (SX 111517 to 095518)

Although hailing from London, Daphne du Maurier (1907-1989) could trace her roots back to Brittany. Living first at Bodinnick, du Maurier later moved to Menabilly House, the traditional seat of the Rashleighs. From here, she commenced many of her literary projects. Du Maurier's work has become synonymous with a historical-romantic conceptualisation of Cornwall. However, realising the changing nature of Cornwall in the middle of the twentieth-century, and perhaps even the effect of her own texts, such as *Jamaica Inn* and *Rebecca* in shaping views of the territory, du Maurier became more committed to Cornish Nationalism and joined Mebyon Kernow, the Cornish political party. Correspondence with her sister Foy demonstrates how pleased she was to be part of this organisation. Always aware of Celticity in her fiction, du Maurier's 1972 novel *Rule Britannia*, was a controversial work. The novel looks at revolutionary nationalism in Cornwall in the context of Britain leaving the

The landscape of Menabilly

European confederation and joining the United States of America. In order to put down the Celtic rebellion in Cornwall, American marines land in Par bay. Unappreciated in 1972, the novel now stands as one of du Maurier's most insightful and ambitious works. Du Maurier's final residence at Kilmarth can be seen at SX 094526.

● The Sherwood Sermons, the Rashleigh Family, Menabilly, near Fowey

SX 101512. *The house is not accessible, but an alternative walk is available around the Gribbin Head which looks back to Menabilly. From Menabilly Barton (SX 098508) walk south towards Gribbin Head and then north to Polkerris, returning to the car park via the road.*

The *Bibliotheca Cornubiensis* compiled by G.C. Boase and W.P. Courtney in 1882 is a huge list of all the books ever published about Cornwall or published by Cornish writers. The volume mentions a manuscript of some sermons preached by the Reverend Joseph Sherwood, at St Ives, Marazion and Penzance in 1680, and that they were in the care of one Jonathan Rashleigh of Menabilly. These Sermons have never been found and have therefore become something of a holy grail for scholars of Celtic Cornwall.

North East Cornwall

● St Petroc's Church, Bodmin

SX 073671. *The church is located in the middle of the town on the A389.*

Saint Petroc had a colourful and interesting life. The earliest *Life* of him states that he was the son of a Welsh King, but this was re-worked in Bodmin in the twelfth century, offering that his father was actually King Glywys of Glywysing in Pembrokeshire. Petroc initially studied in Ireland, becoming the teacher of Saint Kevin, but then began a mission to Cornwall, founding monasteries at Padstow and Bodmin. The earliest monastery was at Lanwethnioc near Padstow. Lanwethnioc had been founded by an earlier holy man, but Petroc appears to have developed it, making Padstow a later centre for Petroc's cult [Padstow means Petroc-stow (Petroc's place)]. Sometime in the ninth century, Bodmin became the centre for his veneration and his relics were moved there from Padstow. By the eleventh century, Bodmin monastery had become very wealthy, perhaps because of the fame that Petroc brought.

After thirty years of work in Cornwall, in which it is said he converted the pagan ruler of Dumnonia, King Constantine, Petroc then travelled on pilgrimage to Rome, journeying there via Brittany. From Rome, Petroc journeyed back via Devon (where there are numerous dedications to him), but there are other tales about him completing a trip to India and living there on an island in the Indian ocean. Accounts say that he died on a journey back to Lanwethioc at a house belonging to a family named Roval, which is now thought to be a farm called Treraval near Little Petherick. His name is also remembered in the place-name Trebetherick. There is a stained glass window of the saint in the church at Bodmin. The Padstow-born dramatist Donald R. Rawe (b.1930) completed a new rendering of Petroc's life in his 1970 play, *Petroc of Cornwall*.

● The Chapel of St Thomas à Becket, Bodmin

SX 073672. *The chapel is located next to St Petroc's Church.*

This is a ruin of a fourteenth-century building in Bodmin churchyard, which undoubtedly served a Cornish-speaking community. It perhaps declined due to the success of Petroc as a dedication. Close by is the so-called Berry Tower, which is the remains of the former church of the Holy Rood. We know that the Holy Rood was used as a structural device within Cornish-language drama, so this may have been integral to performance in Bodmin.

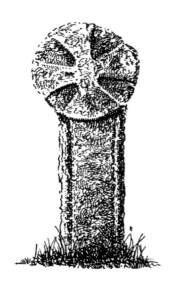

Berry Tower cross.

● Berry Tower Cross, Berry Hill, Bodmin

SX 072674. *This stands beside the Berry Tower in the cemetery.*

This wayside cross is not symmetrical and leans to one side. At one point, the cross may have been much taller.

● St Petroc's Relics, Bodmin

SX 073671. *The reliquary is held within the church.*

Petroc's relics appear to been have moved to Bodmin in the ninth century, but in 1177 they were stolen by a Breton – who took them to the Abbey of St Meen. However, through the intervention of Henry II (then controlling much of France and Brittany), they were returned eventually coming to be encased in an ivory casket. The bones were destroyed during the Reformation, but the casket survived. The reliquary was stolen and recovered in 1994.

● Manumissions on the Bodmin Gospels, Bodmin

SX 073671. *The manumissions are connected with the church at Bodmin.*

It is the custom in many countries to record legal transactions on the blank pages or margins of sacred texts. Feudal lords sometimes freed serfs as an act of piety. During the tenth-century Saxon landowners in eastern Cornwall recorded these transactions in a manuscript known now as the Bodmin Manumissions [a manumission being a certificate of freedom from serfdom or slavery]. In this text, originally written in Anglo-Saxon and Latin, most of the lords have Saxon names while most of the serfs have Cornish names. The example below shows how Celtic slaves were bought and then freed:

> *Here is made known on this book that Æilsig had bought a woman Ongy-nedhel and her son Gydhiccael for half a pound at the church door in Bodmin and paid to Æilsige the portreeve and Maccos the hundredsman four pennies for tax. Then Æilsige did as he had intended to the persons he had bought and freed them on Petrock's altar forever free of liability.*

We know that in the Early Medieval period St Petroc's bell was also carried to other locations around Cornwall in order that people might touch it and use at part of legal proceedings. Thus, in the freeing of slaves, and in his general power to witness legal transactions, Petroc clearly had considerable importance.

● Celtic Uprisings, Bodmin

SX 072669. *The public centre of Bodmin is just outside the Shire Hall.*

In 1497, the blacksmith from St Keverne, Michael Joseph, was accompanied by Bodmin lawyer Thomas Flamank (d.1497) in leading the rebellion of that year. Flamank was the eldest son of Richard

Flamank of Boscarne, by Johanna, daughter of Thomas Lucombe of Bodmin. They held the manor of nearby Nanstallon from the fourteenth century onwards. In the autumn of 1497, Perkin Warbeck (1474-1499) tried to usurp the throne from Henry VII. Warbeck was proclaimed King Richard IV in Bodmin, but Henry dealt quickly with the uprising. This did not stop the Renaissance dramatist John Ford, writing a play about his life in 1591. Here Sketon expresses the great support gained from the Cornish to Warbeck.

Save King Richard the fourth, save thee King of hearts? the Cornish blades are men of metall, have proclaimed through Bodnam [Bodmin] and the whole Countie, my sweete Prince, Monarch of England, some thousand tall, yeomen, with bow and sword alreadie vow to live and dye at the foote of King Richard.

Finally, Bodmin was also a flashpoint of the 1549 Prayer Book Rebellion. The Cornish army was formed in Bodmin. The mayor of Bodmin, one Nicholas Boyer, was hanged for his part in the rebellion.

● Bodmin Riding, Bodmin

SX 072669. *Bodmin Riding events are centred around the Shire Hall.*

The Bodmin Riding festival probably has its origins in the return of Saint Petroc's relics to the town sometime after 1177. The relics were clearly paraded around Bodmin and celebratory events took place alongside this. It also appears that the event took place on the Sunday and Monday after 7th July (St Thomas Becket's Day) – so there was a clearly a link to the Chapel. We know that as well as the relics, two large garlands were taken around the town. It was certainly occurring in 1469 and continued in some form into the early nineteenth century.

The customs of beating the bounds, and hurling are also enacted in the town – every five years. These were also probably related to the Riding ceremony. Other riding-style events have been recorded in Looe, and Lostwithiel. Bodmin Riding was revived in 1974 and now forms part of the town's Heritage and Riding Festival, which has been transformed into a community arts and cultural celebration.

● Duke of Cornwall's Light Infantry Museum, Bodmin

SX 076663. *The museum is located on the south-eastern edge of the town, on the B3268.*

The Duke of Cornwall's Light Infantry regimental museum offers an insight into this now defunct regiment. The glorious history of Cornwall's own Celtic regiment is offered from 1702 onwards, including their achievement at Lucknow in India and their endeavours in the First and Second World Wars. A scan through the collection will demonstrate the proud Celto-Cornish ideology of the regiment.

● Holy Wells, Bodmin

SX 075670, SX 065673, SX 070672, SX 057675.

The most famous holy well to be found in the vicinity of Bodmin is that of St Guron's Well, with its well-house located in the grounds of St Petroc's Church (SX 075670). The water of the well must travel through

St Guron's Well.

the churchyard, because just to the west of the church is a small trough into which flows the spring. It pours out of the mouth of two gargoyles. According to Richard Carew, writing in 1594, the journey of the waters through the churchyard 'breedeth therefore little cause of marvaile that every general infection is here first admitted and last excluded'.

A headless figure of St Guron is to be found carved into the wellhouse. St Guran is probably the same saint as St Wron who was a hermit living at Bodmin, who looked after St Petroc when he arrived in the location – eventually to found a larger Christian community there. St Wron then travelled to the south coast, there becoming associated with Gorran near Mevagissey. Gorran has its own plain-an-gwarry for parish theatre (SW996423), and presumably this dramatised the life of St Wron in some capacity. Another well, whose saintly connections have been lost is found close by at SX 065673. This is Cock's Well. Bree Shute Well (SX 070672) is less well known – but specialised in eye cures.

Scarlet's Well, meanwhile, was formerly a famous well site lying somewhat neglected just below the site of Bodmin Gaol (SX 057675) to the north west of the town. It is named after a prominent fourteenth-century Bodmin family and, in the time of Richard Carew, it was well known: 'You see it represent many colours like a the rainbow, which (in my conceit) argueth a running through some mineral vein, and therewithal possessing of some virtue'. The temperature of the water here is constant – winter or summer, at 53 degrees Fahrenheit. Bodmin was clearly a significant Celtic site in ancient, Early Medieval and Late Medieval Cornwall, and these wells reflect its significance.

● Celtic Drama, Bodmin

SX 073671. *Such drama would probably have been enacted close to the church.*

Given Bodmin's connections to St Petroc it is perhaps not surprising to see theatrical activity taking place there in the late fifteenth century. The St Petroc's Church Building accounts for 1470-1 shows receipts for 'the players yn the church hay William Mason and Iis fellowes v s.' Clearly a continuity of performance took place here, since the General Receivers accounts of 1494-5 also make reference to payment to 'Wyllyam Capynter for syluer and the making of [a] Garnement and for colours ocupyed for dyademys & crownys & such oder (longyng to Cor…) Christi game and for tynfoyle that Iohn Wythyall had of Rafe Stayner'. The energy put into the costuming and design clearly shows a drama of some significance here.

In 1505-6 we also see reference made to a Robin Hood play in October's accounts from the Berry Tower Building. This tower, was built between 1501 and 1504 and part of the chantry church of the Holy Rood. There were three guilds operating in Bodmin: the New, the Holy Rood and the St Christopher, who look to have organised the performances.

More detailed expenditure comes in the General Receivers Accounts of October 1509-10, where we learn about the 'showe of Corporis Christi'. Cloth for the manufacture of the costume of Jesus, is mentioned, as other garments and linen. Here then, we see that a Corpus Christi drama based around the life of Jesus was enacted in Bodmin in the opening decades of the sixteenth century. It seems that at Bodmin, in previous times, the Corpus Christi drama was produced by a combination of both civic and church leadership. This is noted in 1539 when St Petroc's Inventory of Church Goods lists Jesus's 'cotte of purple scarenett' as well as in 1566 '4 tormenteris cotes' and 'toe develes cotes'. A distinctive 'crowne of black' (probably connected with the devils) is also mentioned here. Purple was an expensive colour during this period as it was imported from either the Low Countries or the Mediterranean.

● Halgavor Moor, Bodmin

SX 075653. *This is located close to the B3268 running south out of Bodmin. The moor can be reached by a footpath.*

Carew, gathering material in the latter decades of the sixteenth century, mentions the para-theatrical activity which took place at Halgavor ['Goat's Moor']. This is where boxing and wrestling matches took place, and perhaps the same place was used for performances as well. According to Carew, this is where the demeaning local expression 'He shall be presented in Halgavor Court' arose. The one problem with this theory is that the site is described by Carew as being a quagmire, so it would seem unlikely to have theatrical use.

● Castle Carnyke Hill Fort, Bodmin

SX 086658. *The fort is located quite close to the A30. Follow a minor road north west which runs close to the fort.*

Now divided into four quarter fields, this is a huge Iron Age fort with commanding views of the surrounding countryside. There was possibly an inner rampart at one stage but this has now been ploughed out. Its impact on the local Iron Age culture of the period is similar to present-day Bodmin.

● Carminnow Cross, Bodmin

SX 088656. *This is located in the middle of a roundabout close to Bodmin, just off the A30.*

Carminnow Cross probably stands as one of the most recognisable crosses in Cornwall. Originally buried in a ditch, it has been moved several times to accommodate changes in the road system, and was moved to this site in 1975. The cross has five bosses and is decorated by tiny indentations.

● Churchyard Cross and Holy Well, Lanhydrock, near Bodmin

SW 085 636. *Lanhydrock is easily accessed off the A30. The cross is in the parish churchyard at the House.*

The fifteenth-century church is dedicated to Saint Hydrock. This cross is of an unusual but intriguing design. The cross head is without the ring of stone that normally surrounds it suggesting that it was removed at one point. The cross shaft is engraved with spiral decoration. A Treffry Cross may also be found on the estate at SX 085634. A holy well is also located close to the cross, behind the gardener's house. It is thought to be dedicated to St Petroc by some sources.

● Pencarrow Rings Hill Fort, Pencarrow, near Bodmin

SX 040700. *From Mount Charles, take the B3266 north. The drive to Pencarrow House bisects the site.*

Most visitors to Pencarrow House do not realise that they are passing through an Iron Age hill fort on their drive into the estate. The fort consists of an outer defence to the west composed of a single bank, followed by inner and outer lines of defence. The circle of the inner defence is quite small – only some

50 metres across. Pencarrow is usually translated to 'Stag's Head' but an alternative maybe that it means 'Head of the line of Forts'. This may fit, considering the number of hill forts in the vicinity.

● The Prior's Cross, Washaway, near Bodmin

SX 037696. *This cross is found at Washaway on the A389, Bodmin to Wadebridge road.*

This is an impressive cross, which is been so-called because of its affiliation with Bodmin Priory. The cross is marked by a *fleur-de-lys* symbol, which was a symbol of the Priory.

● The Three-Holed Cross, near Wadebridge

SX 011736. *This is mid-way along the A39 from Wadebridge to Camelford, where the road turns to Chapel Amble.*

This cross take its name from the fact that three holes of the cross head are finished, but a fourth is not. Similar to the cross on Penhale Sands dedicated to St Piran, the head here is a St Andrew's Cross.

● Penwine Cross, St Mabyn

SX 0607. *This cross is located east of St Mabyn on the B3266 Bodmin to Camelford road.*

Located close to a prehistoric longstone, the Penwine Cross is of the wayside type and holds a *fleur-de-lys* design connecting it to Bodmin Priory.

● Penhargard Castle Hill Fort, near Bodmin

SX 058699. *Follow a minor road north to Helland. Just west of Penhargard, the fort may be located. It stands in woodland.*

The fort is located on the edge of a steep slope to the west. Built during the Iron Age, there are three lines of defence before the entrance at the south west. There are two terraces within the main fort enclosure.

● St James' Well, near St Breward

SX 091 769. *The well is to be found at the bottom of the valley, under the quarry and opposite Hengar Wood.*

Located close to the River Camel, St James' Well is almost hidden by vegetation but it was once famed for its cures for painful eyes and 'other infirmities'. Two Medieval chapels once existed here: one dedicated to St James; the other to St Michael. The well is now dry.

St James' Well, St Breward.

● King Arthur's Hall, St Breward

SX 130777. *From St Breward take the various footpaths east towards King Arthur's Downs. The Hall is easily located there.*

This site probably has little to do with King Arthur. Local folklore has connected the great military leader with the 20 by 40 metre-sized low structure. Over 50 stones mark the surrounds, but these are encased within an embankment. The structure may be Iron Age, but it could also be much earlier – perhaps Neolithic.

● Middle Moor Cross, near St Breward

SX 125793. *The cross is situated close to Campendown Farm, a little to the north of St Breward.*

This is a quite crudely designed wayside cross, but it seems to suit its moorland location. According to local folklore, when the cross heard the bells of St Breward church ring, it turned around and around until it fell down.

● St Michael's Holy Well and Celtic Cross, Michaelstow Church

SX 081788. *Michaelstow may be reached by turning left off the B3266 from Bodmin to Camelford.*

The devotion here is to the warrior angel St Michael (as at St Michael's Mount). A baptistry probably once covered this site, but it is now somewhat ruined. The well is to be found near the south porch of the churchyard. The tall four holed Medieval churchyard cross is found in the south-western side. A further cross may be found at Trevinning Cross (SX 073774). Two other crosses were originally at Trevenning, but these are now on private ground.

● Helsbury Castle Hill Fort, near Michaelstow

SX 083796. *The fort may be located south of Camelford, on the road to Treveighan.*

The road here follows the northern ramparts of the fort, which is oval-shaped and still in relatively complete condition. Built in the Iron Age, the entrance is located to the east of the fort. Here may be found an additional enclosure. In the middle of the fort are found the ruins of the so-called St Syth's Chapel.

● Tresinney Cross, near Advent Church, Tresinney

SX 105812. *Advent is accessed via the B3266 from Bodmin to Camelford. Before Valley Truckle turn right to Tresinney. The cross is just south of Advent Church.*

This is a very tall, and therefore unusual wayside cross, marking an ancient track across Bodmin Moor.

Middle Moor cross.

Quoit at Edward Prynn's residence.

● Edward Prynn, St Merryn

SX 896734. *Travelling from Newquay to Padstow on the B3276, Edward Prynn's residence is to be found at Tresallyn Cross, reached by turning left just before Treveglos.*

Edward Prynn was born in 1936 in nearby St Merryn, and worked for much of his life as a quarryman. In an experiment in 1982 at his residence – now called 'Seven Sisters' - he initially constructed a stone circle, followed by a quoit, a fogou and other re-imagined 'Celtic' landscape structures. The last monument added to the collection was for the 1999 solar eclipse. In direct contrast to the Anglican and Christian leanings of the Cornish Gorsedd, Prynn formed a druid sect, in which he was Arch-druid. Interestingly, Prynn sees no conflict of interest with his working-class Methodist background. Although dismissed by some observers as an eccentric, in fact, his eclectic mysticism denotes the layeredness of Celtic spirituality in Cornwall. Prynn often conducts ritual at his property and on *logan* [rocking] stones on Bodmin Moor. His advice in constructing stone circles and Celtic monuments has been sought in America and Australia.

The Seven Sisters standing stones.

● Saint Cadoc's Well, near St Merryn

SW 885749. *Just before the turning to Trevone, take a minor road north west and find St Cadoc's Farm. The remains of the baptistry are on the plantation side of the farm.*

There is no church devoted to him on the shores here – near to Harlyn Bay, but Cadoc is a very significant Welsh saint. It is therefore logical that we find dedications to him in North Cornwall. He was the founder of the great monastery at Llancarfan in Powys. So it is said, he went on a pilgrimage to

St Michael's Mount, where he met his aunt, Saint Keyne. The well site was located close to the farm. There is now no sign of the well, but the foundations of the baptistry can still be seen in the somewhat muddy ground. The water was reputed to cure 'belly bowels, worms and pestilential infection'. It was clearly a major place of devotion during the Medieval period.

● St Petroc, Padstow

SW 918755. *Padstow is located at the end of the A389. It is also reached from Newquay on the B3276.*

As we know from Bodmin, Padstow is derived from Petroc-stowe. Petroc was the Welsh-born saint who landed at nearby Trebetherick, and who helped develop the monastery at Lanwethinoc. According to the Anglo-Saxon Chronicle, the area was raided by the Vikings in 981 and such raids might have been what persuaded the monks here to move further inland to Bodmin. There remains a church of St Petroc in the town, but there are others at Bodmin and Little Petherick. Padstow was one of the major departure points for Cornish emigrants in the mid-nineteeth century, mainly taking passengers to Canada. Petroc-stowe faces an interesting phase in its development. Although resolutely committed to its Celtic heritage, the town is now very popular (not least caused by the success of local chef Rick Stein) and this has put a strain on insider Celtic, and outsider non-Celtic relations.

● Enys Tregarthen, Padstow

SW 918755. *Tregarthen would have known the harbour at Padstow very well indeed.*

A writer very interested in the Celtic traditions of Cornwall was the author and folklorist Enys Tregarthen (1851-1923). Tregarthen was born in Padstow as Nellie Sloggett, but wrote under the pen-names of Tregarthen and Nellie Cornwall. The editor Elizabeth Yates prepared her folkloric material for publication during in 1995. Tregarthen's expertise was in the field of pixies and fairy customs of Cornwall.

● Obby Oss, Padstow

SW 918755. *The streets of Padstow are packed on May Day. Early arrival is essential.*

Held annually on May Day (1st May), which in Cornwall dates back to the Celtic festival of Beltane, the Obby Oss festival celebrates the coming of summer. The origins of the festival are lost in history, but it is widely thought that it has a pagan origin. Indeed, Obby Osses were known of in Celtic Cornwall as early as 1504, the date of the Camborne play, *Bewnans Meriasek* [*The Life of Meriasek*]. Notably, it is the pagan King Teudar who makes an analogy to them:

Re appolyn ov du splan	[By Apollo, my bright god,
kyns dyberth oy warth mas ran	Before separating only some will laugh
my a pe dhen hebyhors	I will pay to the hobby horse,
hay cowetha	And her comrades.

Padstow Hobby Hoss c.1920s.

The full complexities of the festival at Padstow cannot easily be summarised in a volume of this kind, but festivities begin at midnight with the singing of the Night Song and by the morning the town is decorated with greenery and a maypole. The climax of the day is when two groups of dancers lead around two osses known as the 'Old' and the 'Blue Ribbon' osses. Backed by drumming and accordions, each oss is lead by a 'teaser'. The osses are adorned with a mask and black-framed cape under which they sometimes catch young maidens. Meanwhile the singers and musicians play the 'Day Song'. Each oss has a stable: the 'Old' oss belongs to the Golden Lion Inn, while the Blue Ribbon oss is aligned to the Institute. Sometime in the late afternoon, the osses meet at the maypole and dance together. The Padstow-born writer and cultural historian Donald R. Rawe has completed an extensive study of Padstow's Obby Oss and May Day traditions. Other hobby horse traditions are found at Minehead in Somerset, and a so-called Mast Horse named Penglaz is found in Penzance. The Obby Oss of Padstow inspired a memorable sequence in the 1973 film *The Wicker Man* in which Police Sergeant Howie is sent to the remote Hebredian Summerisle to investigate a Celtic neo-pagan cult. The novel on which the film was based (*Ritual* by David Pinner [1967]) had Cornwall as its setting.

Padstow May Day Night Song

Unite and unite and let us all unite,　　　　*I warn you young men everyone,*
For summer is acome unto day,　　　　　　*For summer is acome unto day*
And whither we are going we will all unite,　*To go to the green-wood and fetch your May home,*
In the merry morning of May.　　　　　　*In the merry morning of May.*

● Mummer's Day, Padstow

SW 918755 *The festival can be seen on the streets of Padstow on Boxing Day and New Years's Day every year.*

In effect, Mummer's Day is the winter version of the Obby Oss festivities. It takes place on Boxing Day and New Year's Day, and is, in effect, a celebration of mid-winter and the end of the shortest day. Traditionally, members of the community blacked-up (a tradition that is found elsewhere in Cornwall and in wider Britain), and covered their faces in coal dust. The idea of this was to disguise their identity in guising-type (disguising) activities. The event was known for a number of years as 'Darkie Days' but this has now been dropped. Often, members of Padstow adorn their faces with the black and white of St Piran's flag. No Mummers' Play is enacted (as is the case at Penzance) but, as an expression of local Celtic identity, despite change, the festival looks to continue long into the future.

● Cornish Kilts and Tartans, Padstow

SX 917756. *The shop was located close to the harbour, on Market Street, near to Stein's fish and chip shop.*

Cornish National Tartan.

One of the first shops in Cornwall to sell Cornish Kilts and tartans was that owned by local folklorist and historian, Donald R. Rawe. The shop was called 'Donald Rawe: Men's Wear of Padstow' and operated in the 1970s. Rawe devised a St Piran Cornish Dress tartan. As many people now know, kilts and tartans are not an exclusively Scottish tradition, and even so, many tartans from Scotland are classic examples of 'the invention of tradition' and actually have a more modern pedigree. We know however that the Celtic peoples of Britain often wore a garment known as a *bracca* or *braccahae* (a chequered tunic) and the Cornish word *brythen* means 'striped' or 'chequered'. The Celto-Cornish cultural activist L.C. Duncombe Jewell argued that bench-end carvings often represented images of Cornish men wearing a kilt-like garment, although possibly this was just the standard Medieval tunic that was worn across Europe. Even so, Duncombe Jewell developed his theory into practice by wearing a woad-coloured blue kilt at the 1903 Celtic Congress in Caernarvon.

It was however, in 1963 that modern kilt and tartan production in Cornwall began properly. The most famous tartan is that created by Ernest E. Morton Nance, the nephew of Robert Morton Nance. This has come to be known as the Cornish National tartan. Like most tartans it is characterised by symbolism in its weave and design. The red of the tartan is for the beak and legs of the chough, the blue is for the sea surrounding Cornwall, the black and gold (yellow) represent the colours of the ancient Cornish kings (also seen in contemporary rugby jerseys), while the white and black represent St Piran's flag. The tartan has been remarkably successful and is worn by many Cornish people to display their Celticity. Many Cornish men now get married wearing a kilt in the National tartan.

Other tartans have been developed including Cornish National Day tartan and a Rosevear tartan (both by Rawe), a Hunting tartan (designed by Sandra Redwood in 1984), a St Piran Cornish Flag tartan (designed by A. Armstrong Evans), a Curnow tartan (designed by Howard Curnow), a Christopher family tartan and a Pengelly tartan. Although seen as 'old school' by some Celtic activists in Cornwall and merely a performance of Celicity, fusionist culture has reinterpreted the tradition allowing Doc Martins boots and surfing t-shirts to be worn in combination with kilts. Cornish tartan kilts and accessories can be purchased all over Cornwall, though there is now a Cornish Tartan Centre in St Austell.

● Kelly Rounds Hill Fort, near Wadebridge

SX 019736. *On the A39 from Wadebridge to Camelford, park at Three Holes Cross. The fort is a short walk along a lane.*

In several texts, one of King Arthur's homesteads is called *Kelliwic*. Given the name and location of this Round, it might be a possible candidate. The fort is from the Iron Age, and it is best preserved on the northern side. On the southern side however, the ramparts have been almost ploughed out. Although the hill fort was developed in the Iron Age, the archaeological evidence has shown that the site was originally occupied much earlier in the tenth century BCE. Another suggestion for the location of *Kelliwic* is Callington.

● The Jesus Well, near Rock

SW 938764. *From Wadebridge, take the B3314 north, and turn left into Rock. In Rock, turn right along the lane to the Golf Course. Follow the signs to the well.*

Some legends ascribed the origins of this well to the visit Joseph of Arimathea and the child Christ made to Cornwall and that, while on the north coast, the ship's company needed water and so they went inland to find this well. Alternative stories argue that an early but unnamed Christian saint was crossing this area of sand and became thirsty. He struck the sand with his staff and water flowed. Ruined at the end of the nineteenth century, it was repaired and re-roofed in 1952. Traditionally, saying the litany to the holy name of Jesus would guarantee a cure from skin disease. Located on the well may be found a plaque of Delabole slate with the following inscription: 'Jesus Well, Jesus saith unto her Give Me to Drink - *Timor Domini Fons Vitae* [Fear of the Lord, Spring of Life]'.

The Jesus Well, near Rock.

St Enodoc church.

St Enodoc Church, Trebetherick

SW 932773. *The church is found in the sand dunes east of Daymer Bay and Brea Hill, on the River Camel estuary.*

St Enodoc Church is a chapel of ease located south of the village of Trebetherick. The church is said to have been founded on the site of a cave, where St Enodoc lived as a hermit. We do know that Enodoc was venerated at Bodmin Priory, so he was clearly of some significance. The present church dates from the twelfth century, with additions made in the thirteenth and fifteenth centuries. However, by the middle of nineteenth century, the church was engulfed in sand and was known locally as 'sink-ininny church'. The parishioners had to enter through a hole in the roof. In 1864, the sands were finally stabilised. The tower of the church is highly distinctive: it is composed of two stages and is topped by a winding low broach spire.

John Betjeman's Grave, St Enodoc Church, Trebetherick

SW 932773. *The slate-formed gravestone is located close to the main path.*

Born in Highgate, London, John Betjeman (1906-1984) spent much of his childhood in north Cornwall. He was an authority on architecture, a regular broadcaster and poet laureate. Although known in wider Britain for his metropolitan verse, in Cornwall Betjeman was intensely interested in Cornish Celticity, celebrating the legacy of the Celtic saints and their impact on the landscape. This is seen in works such as 'Trebetherick', 'Saint Cadoc', 'Cornish Cliffs', 'Delectable Duchy', and his lengthy auto-biographical poem *Summoned by Bells* (1960). He also foresaw many of the cultural and economic changes which were affecting Cornwall in the light of mass tourism during the middle decades of the twentieth century. Although Betjeman was an outsider, he wrote about Cornish Celticity as an insider, a point which Philip Payton has demonstrated in his recent biography of the poet. Indeed, Payton labels him the 'celebrated Cornish nationalist'. Betjeman spent much of his later life at Trebetherick in Cornwall, and died there aged 77.

The Rumps Cliff Castle, near Polzeath

SW 934811. *Drive to the car park at Pentireglaze. Walk to the cliff castle from there.*

Viewed by many as one of the finest examples of a cliff castle, this is a complex Iron Age and Romano-British settlement probably constructed over a series of phases. Three ramparts are found at the neck of the headland, with the builders often making use of the natural ridges of rock. An entranceway passes through all three of the defences.

Nicholas Roscarrock, Roscarrock, near St Endellion

SW 986804. *The Roscarrock house lies half-way between Port Quin and Port Isaac and is accessed off a minor road from the B3314.*

Nicholas Roscarrock (c.1548-1634) was a Cornish Catholic hagiographer, who originated from the parish of St Endellion. He suffered great torture and imprisonment in the Tower of London for his beliefs, and afterwards set about writing a vast dictionary of the saints of Britain and Ireland titled *Lives of the Saints*. Of this volume, the section on Cornwall and Devon, in England, is very thorough since Roscarrock had intimate knowledge of many of the locations and narratives. Roscarrock's manuscript is presently kept at Cambridge University Library (MS Add. 3041). Roscarrock may be compared to his south-east Cornwall contemporary Richard Carew. Whereas Carew was Protestant, modern-looking and fully embracing of 'English' culture, Roscarrock was Catholic, folkloric and probably a Cornish speaker. These two writers express a dichotomy about Celtic Cornwall which is unresolved some four centuries later.

● King Arthur, St Endelient and the cow, St Endellion

SW 996786. *St Endellion church is just off the B3314 between St Minver and Pendogget.*

In one of the best stories in his *Lives of the Saints* collection, Roscarrock tells us about St Endelient and her life. Her chapel apparently lay to the south west of the church at a location called Trenteny (now Tretinney). She lived very austere life, drinking only the milk of one cow. Supposedly her cow strayed onto the land of the Lord of Trenteny, and he killed the animal. Her godfather was apparently King Arthur, and Arthur saw to it that the Lord of Trenteny was slain. However, it was St Endelient who miraculously revived the Lord, for which he was presumably grateful. When she knew death was coming, St Endellion entreated her friends that once dead, she should be placed on a 'sled' and that it would be tied to bullocks or calves. Wherever they dragged her body, that should be the place to build her church. This of course, happened, and the creatures dragged her to the top of the hill where the present church stands.

BROCAGNUS inscribed stone, St Endellion.

● Brocagnus Inscribed Stone, St Endellion

SW 989797. *This is found just off the B3314 between St Endellion and Port Quin. The stone is at a crossroads.*

This stone has upon it a significant inscription: BROCAGNI HIC IACIT NADOTTI [Borcagnus lies here, the son of Nadottus]. This is then repeated in Irish Ogham script. Brocagnus here correlates with the name Brychan, who was the Brecon-based father of a number of missionary saints who travelled to Cornwall. The inscription is from the sixth or seventh centuries CE. It is interesting to speculate why Brychan might be here. Was it that he was visiting his family in Cornwall and died whilst away from Wales? The cross is sometimes known as the Longcross.

● Tregeare Rounds Hill Fort, Pendoggett, near Delabole

SX 033800. *The fort is found approximately one mile north east of Pendoggett on a slope, close to the B3314.*

The fort is composed of two concentric rings of ditches and ramparts, constructed in the Iron Age. There is, however, evidence of occupation at the site since the Bronze Age.

● Inscribed Stone, St Kew, near Wadebridge

SX 021769. *The stone is found inside St Kew Church.*

This stone holds an inscription in both Latin and Ogham script. The Latin inscription just reads IVISTI [Justus], which might provide a link with the saint dedicated in St Just-in-Penwith or on the Roseland. The inscription has been dated to the sixth or seventh centuries CE.

● St Teath Cross. St Teath, near Camelford

SX 063806. *St Teath is located just off the A39 Wadebridge to Camelford road. The cross is close to the clock tower.*

This very tall cross was in pieces in during the nineteenth century but has been re-erected. The shaft of the cross has some interesting decoration.

● Roughtor Holy Well, Roughtor, Camelford

SX 147810. *The well is on the northern end of the tor and can easily be walked to from the car park on Poldue Downs.*

The complex Neolithic processional culture that occurred on Roughtor is now much better understood, as is the early Bronze Age when much of the area was cleared and farmed. The well at Roughtor was rediscovered as late as 1994, and though of primitive construction, blends well with the landscape

Roughtor Holy Well.

around it. A chapel devoted to St Michael once stood on the tor, and this seems to fit a general trend in this part of North Cornwall, with Michaelstow also having a dedication to St Michael. The continuity of communities at work here on the moor, would have meant that the Iron Age Celtic peoples of Cornwall also used the well for ritual and drinking.

● St Julitta's Well, Lanteglos, Camelford

SX 093 829. *This is found just below the Juliot's Well Holiday Park.*

The well here was known for alleviating skin complaints and is dedicated to a commonly found saint in North Cornwall – Saint Julitta, Juliot or Julian. She is most likely to be another daughter of the famous Brychan of Brecon in South Wales. Although, she seems to have been female, an image of a male Saint Julian is found in the Church of St Materiana in Tintagel. In the nineteenth century a gold circlet (or lunulae) was found at this well, which is now held in the British Museum. A copy of the lunulae is sometimes on display in the Royal Cornwall Museum, Truro.

● Castle Goff Hill Fort, near Camelford

SX 083826. *The hill fort is located just to the north west of Lanteglos, near Camelford.*

Castle Goff is a significant structure in this location. An Iron Age hill fort, it is composed of a circular inner fort with sizable earth ramparts, and an outer annexe on the western side. Unfortunately, modern field walls now dissect the site, but the ramparts and embankments are still visible.

● Slaughterbridge Stone, near Camelford

SX 109856. *Follow the B3314 from Camelford Station. The stone is located close to the bridge, although there is now a modern car park and tourist attraction at the site.*

The inscribed stone found at Slaughterbridge is one of the most interesting mis-symbols of Celtic Cornwall. Legendary and folk associations have ascribed this location as the place where King Arthur and Mordred met, for the decisive Battle of Camlan in 537. The stone is even referred to as the 'King Arthur's Stone'. Its proximity to Tintagel and to Camelford have prompted the connection to this location, as well as its being near a bridge. Geoffrey of Monmouth writes:

> *Arthur was filled with great mental anguish by the fact that Mordred has escaped him so often. Without losing a moment, he followed him to that same locality, reaching the River Camlann, where Mordred was awaiting his arrival.*

Camlann is not here however, and in a Cornish context is more likely to have been the River Kemyel in Penwith. Cam or Gam means 'crooked' and in actual fact refers to the crooked flow of the River Camel. The inscribed stone here is however, of significance to Celtic Cornwall. It has the following ogham and Latin inscription: LATINI IC IACIT FILIVS MAGARI [Latinus lies here, son of Magarus]. This dates from the sixth century and appears to commemorate an unknown Celtic chieftain. The Arthurian connection may possibly have come from a misreading of the final word as MACATRY for Arthur.

St Julitta's Well.

● The 'Arthur' or Artognou Stone, Tintagel Island, Tintagel

SX 049892. *The stone was first used as the cover of a drain on the island, but is best observed in either the Tourist Information office or the Royal Institution of Cornwall Museum at Truro.*

The so-called 'Arthur Stone' was discovered on Tintagel Island in 1998. Dated as being from the sixth century, it is inscribed with PATER COLIAVI-FICIT ARTOGNOV which has been translated alternatively as 'Artognou, father of a descendent of Coll, has had this constructed' or 'Artognou descendent of Paternus Colus, made this'. Artognou was claimed by some original observers to be either an early form of Arthur, or perhaps translates to 'Bear Knowing'. *Arto* is Brythnic for 'bear', while *gnāwo* is 'to know'. It is at least a cognate with the Old Breton name Arthnou and the Welsh Arthneu. There are lots of examples in Cornish culture of a connection between Arthur and bears. Other scholars have been very sceptical of any such connection with Arthur. As well as the lettering on the slate, there is also the remains of a Christogram, scratched into the surface. The stone is now held in the Royal Institution of Cornwall Museum (SW823448). A reproduction of it is found at the Tintagel Tourist Information Office (SX059884).

● Tintagel Island settlements, Tintagel

SW 050891. *Walk down the valley to the island. Climb the footpath and bridge to the inner courtyard.*

Tintagel Island is a multi-layered site with many phases of development. The image most associated with the island of Tintagel is the battlemented wall located in the inner courtyard. This was one end of the Great Hall built for Richard, Earl of Cornwall in about 1235. In essence, the project was a grand folly, designed to show guests his power and connection with the historical associations of the island. Tintagel Island was clearly where, in the fifth and sixth centuries, the kings or princes of Dumnonia, had their stronghold. On from the battlements are to be found some of the ruined houses from this period. In these buildings archaeology has discovered broken pieces of dishes, glass, plates and wine jars which suggest trade with Spain, North Africa and the eastern Mediterranean. Such information shows that Celtic Cornwall had links with many different communities across Western Europe, and was far from being isolated. Some have suggested that the so-called 'Iron Gate' above the Haven was where ships were anchored.

There has been some suggestion in the past that the island was a monastic site, but this has now been discounted, and the general view is that the island hosted a high status post-Roman community. On top of the island further features may be noted. These include a walled garden, which was perhaps developed for Richard of Cornwall's Countess and female community – as an icon of courtly love, or possibly for his Cornish mistress Joan. Meanwhile on the north of the island are further ruins from the fifth and sixth centuries, along with a curious tunnel. Having some similarities to the more western fogous, it may well have operated as a larder or food store, with cooling sea winds helping to preserve food in the summer. There is also a necessary well. There is a Norman chapel here dedicated to St Julitta or Juliot, now in ruins, which was excavated in Raleigh Radford's famous excavations of the island in the 1930s. Radford pioneered work on the island in this period, but more recent excavations have been completed under the lead of Charles Thomas, and Chris Morris of the University of Glasgow. It is likely that not all the secrets of Tintagel's past have yet been revealed.

Perhaps surprisingly, at various points in its history, the island has also been mined for slate, lead and silver. Attempts by the Wheal Heart and King Arthur Consols in the middle of the nineteenth century

Tintagel Island from the north.

The settlements on Tintagel Island.

were unsuccessful, but in the 1870s a mine-gallery was driven under the island. Some of the slate loading equipment can still be seen above the Haven. Again here, we see the industrial Celt at work.

On the island, at the highest point on the western side, may be found a hollow in the rock, known as King Arthur's footprint. The feature is probably an enhanced natural feature, with some observers believing that at such a place, a chieftain may have been initiated.

● Incised Pictorial Slates, around Tintagel

SX059884. *The tourist information building is located on the B3263 in the east of the village.*

In various archaeological excavations around Tintagel (both on the island and at the churchyard) a number of pictoral slates have been discovered. Incised upon them are a range of games and images.

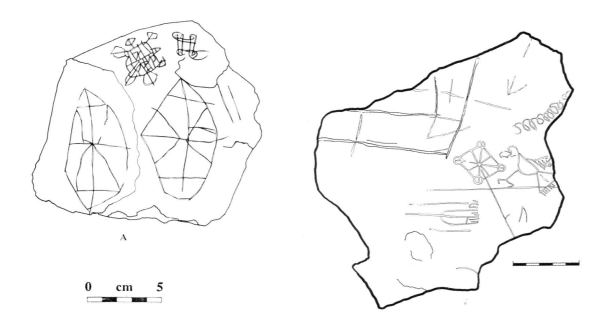

Incised pictorial slates from Tintagel. courtesy Carl Thorpe

A

0   cm   5

The games include a checker board and the board for a game widely known as Nine Men's Morris or Merrils. There is also what is thought to be a boat and its yard-arm, a stag being chased by a dog, a bird, an armed warrior and a leather-backed turtle. Difficult to date, they nonetheless give a picture of the activities and interests of post-Roman and Early Medieval Celtic Cornwall. Some copies of the images are found in the Tintagel Tourist information building.

⬤ The Church of St Materiana, Trevena, Tintagel

SX 051884. *The church is located at the end of a minor road running west of Tintagel village.*

The first church here was founded in the sixth century, and was probably a satellite church of the minster found at Boscastle. The existing church dates from the late eleventh or early twelfth century, although the tower is perhaps thirteenth century. A number of saints are featured in the stained glass windows of the church - among them St Materiana, St George and St Piran. Embedded in a side altar in the north transept of the church is an intriguing Marigold Cross. The six-armed cross encased in a triangle was found on the island and later moved here.

   The churchyard at St Materiana is also notable for the number of slate-lined raised graves: the ground being so hard and rocky here that burial in the earth was sometimes difficult. The practice seems to have begun in the Early Medieval period, but has persisted into the modern era. As excavations of the area noted in 1991, this is clearly an old burial site. In the north-east of the churchyard stands a lichen-encrusted menhir. Paul Broadhurst has recently argued that this points to the constellation of the Great Bear, which appears over Tintagel Island at the Winter Solstice. Considering some observers link the name Arthur to 'bear' this is of considerable interest.

King Arthur pulling the sword from the anvil in the stone, as depicted in the stained glass windows at King Arthur's Hall, Tintagel.

● King Arthur, Tintagel

SX 051889. *This is the imagined location of Arthur's world, both historical and mythical.*

The enigma of King Arthur continues to dominate Celtic Cornwall. The historical Arthur was clearly a chieftain who organised the wider 'British' or Brythonic Celtic resistance against Anglo-Saxon incursions into the west of the island of Britain. Arthur may have been a single man, but it may also have been a title conferred on several leaders. The various literary imaginings of Arthur have been an embellishment of this original Celtic narrative, and they have been conducted in order to suit the context of their reception. Ironically, therefore Arthur has been used by some as a symbol of England, when he in fact, was seeking to resist what become 'English' culture. Thomas Malory's version *Le Morte D'Arthur* (1485) cemented the structural aspects of the narrative, with the twelfth-century Chrétian de Troyes adapting the original Celtic narrative into courtly romance A few features stay constant within the base narrative, which hardly needs retelling here. Both the historical and mythical King Arthur have connections all across Cornwall, Wales and the south west of England.

● Geoffrey of Monmouth, Tintagel

SX052889. *The constriction is now crossed by a modern, wooden bridge.*

It is in Geoffrey of Monmouth's *The History of the Kings of Britain* (1136) that we first find reference to the name *Tintagol* [Tintagel]. It is suggested that the derivation of the name may come from the Cornish *Dun* or *Din* [Fort] combined with *tagell* [narrow or constricted place]. Thus, the name is possible 'fort at a constriction' which would fit geographically. Geoffrey of Monmouth (d.1155) was an Augustinian canon from Wales who spent much of his life living in Oxford. His History, which he claimed was based on an ancient book written in the British language, is a massive compendium of historical and mythological material, imaginatively blended into a continuous narrative. It displays the glory of the Britons from the arrival of the first refugees from Troy and culminates in the reign of Arthur. The implication of his source indicates that this was written in a Brythonic language, possibly an early form of Cornish. It is upon Geoffrey's version that subsequent versions of Arthuriana are based, with the high Medieval variants being embellished by writers of romance.

● Merlin's Cave, Tintagel

SX 052891. *The usually ascribed cave is found to the left of the Haven.*

Merlin is another figure much associated with Brythonic Britain, stretching from Scotland through Wales, to Cornwall. Merlin is seen as both a prophet and an enchanter. Under the island is found the geological feature known as Merlin's cave, though some other sources place it as on the opposite side of the Haven (SX053892). Supposedly, Merlin was the son of a Christian mother and a demon. Many stories refer to him being the individual who constructed Stonehenge as a challenge to the invading Saxons, though clearly, this is just fanciful. It was Uther Pendragon who took Merlin to be his advisor, changing him into Gorlois, so that Arthur could be conceived. In most versions, Merlin also devised the sword in the stone test to reveal that Arthur was the rightful king. Various literature is also devoted to Merlin's love of Nimue, a water nymph, and it is she who placed him (still alive) in a tomb, where he still lives.

● King Arthur's Hall or the Halls of Chivalry, Tintagel

SX 058995. *The Hall is located where the B3263 turns east in the middle of the village.*

King Arthur's Hall is an example of how the Celtic Arthurian legend has been embellished and enhanced. The Hall is a sizeable building constructed of a variety of stone from all over Cornwall. It was built in the early 1930s at the height of the Arthurian revival in Cornwall and in tandem with the wider Celto-Cornish revival of the period, by Frederick Henry Glasspoole – the maker of Birds' Custard. He intendedit to be the headquarters of an organisation called the Order of the Fellowship of the Knights of the Round Table, which would promote a reinvigorated notion of Medieval chivalry and uphold Christian values. Glasspoole's vision never quite took off, but the surviving building (added as an extension to Trevena House) is impressively decorated with a set of seventy-three stained glass windows, designed by Veronica Whall. These illustrate many aspects of the Arthurian corpus. There are also several paintings inside the Hall by William Hatherell, among them an illustration of the final battle between Arthur and Mordred. Glasspoole also collected numerous Arthurian texts from all over Europe and the Halls contain an expansive Celtic Studies library. The present Halls feature an audio-visual presentation and a shop selling much Arthuriana. Not surprisingly perhaps, the Halls also house three branches of Masonic Orders: King Arthur Lodge (founded in 1951), King Arthur Chapter (founded in 1961) and Tintagel Castle Lodge (founded in 1999).

Merlin's Cave, Tintagel.

● *The Quest of the Sangraal* by Robert Stephen Hawker, Tintagel

SX 053891. *Hawker's epic is best imagined from the Haven.*

The Quest of the Sangraal is an epic Arthurian masterpiece, written at the height of Victorian interest in such matter in 1863 by Robert Stephen Hawker. Biographical evidence has shown that the poem was written just after the death of Hawker's wife, Charlotte, whilst he was taking opium. Longfellow said, 'I have read Tennyson's 'Holy Grail' and Mr. Hawker's 'Quest,' and I think the latter poem far superior to the Laureate's.' Tennyson commented, 'Hawker has beaten me on my own ground,' and yet it was not Tennyson's - it was in fact Hawker's much-loved landscape. It is a travesty that many collections of Arthurian verse choose to ignore Hawker's epic, for it is a fine poem. Sangraal is Old French for 'Holy Grail' but it can also be read as 'royal blood'.

From *The Quest of the Sangraal* by Robert Stephen Hawker

"All gone! but not for ever: on a day
There shall arise a king from Keltic loins,
Of mystic birth and name, tender and true;
His vassals shall be noble, to a man:
Knights strong in battle till the war is won:
Then while the land is hushed on Tamar side,
So that the warder upon Carradon
Shall hear at once the river and the sea -
That king shall call a Quest: a kindling cry:
'Ho! for the Sangraal! vanished vase of God!'

A nineteenth century engraving of the Island of Tintagel.

● Tristan and Yseult by Beroul, Tintagel

SW 050891. *Beroul's version begins on the island of Tintagel.*

Evidence for a Cornish origin of the legend of Tristan and Yseult exists. The tale has developed into one of the greatest pan-European love stories ever written and it is a key narrative within Celtic Corn-wall. The story has been retold by various poets and scholars, each embellishing the legend with their own tellings, assimilating material relevant to their audience. The scholar Joseph Bédier suggested that all versions could be traced back to a probable Cornish original, so the earliest surviving texts, among them Beroul's, and that of Thomas of Britain, were probable retellings. Henry Jenner argues that the original poet was 'if not actually a Cornishman, a man well acquainted with Cornwall'. He also notes that the author took in 'real and identifiable places' and that he wrote 'when French had been added to the Celtic and English, which had for some time been concurrently spoken in Cornwall'. We know very little about Beroul himself – only that his version was composed in the middle of the twelfth century and that it was originally written in Norman French.

At the beginning of Beroul's version, Tristan arrives in Tintagel from Lyonesse with his tutor, Governal. Accepted by King Mark into his retinue, it is Tristan who accepts the challenge to fight the mighty Irish warrior, the Morholt, as a way of negating the tribute paid by Cornwall to the Irish King. Crucially, it is the blade of Tristan's sword that is lodged in the head of the dead Morholt, that provides the ignition point of the love affair with Yseult. Eventually, Tristan is challenged with the task of escorting Yseult from Ireland to Cornwall to become Mark's bride. While crossing the Celtic Sea, it is onboard their boat that the two lovers first begin to reveal their attraction to each other. Some observers have commented that the device of the love potion was actually a piece of Christian intervention in the narrative, to negate their own desire for an affair, but even so, the power of their desire is difficult to resist, so beginning their journey, which criss-crosses Celtic Cornwall and culminates in tragedy in Brittany.

New versions of Tristan and Yseult continue to be told. A film emerged in 2006, directed by Kevin Reynolds, while Kneehigh Theatre developed a comic and absurd version in 2003. Interestingly, the latter was premiered at Restormel Castle, one of the locations where the narrative was likely to have been first told.

The Sicilian coverlet (c.1400) – a quilted silk panel depicting the Tristan narrative.
Courtesy Victoria & Albert Museum

● *The Famous Tragedy of the Queen of Cornwall at Tintagel in Lyonesse* by Thomas Hardy, Tintagel

SX 053890. *View the castle from the tearooms and heritage centre at the bottom of the valley.*

Although writer Thomas Hardy (1840-1928) is most associated with Dorset, he was also intimately connected to North Cornwall. In 1870, he was sent to St. Juliot's church, near Boscastle, to commence work on its restoration. While there, he met his first wife, Emma Gifford. Emma died in 1912, and then with his second wife, Florence Dugdale, Hardy later returned to the area recalling his earlier love, and immersing himself in Arthuriana. He already had constructed his own cosmology for Celtic Cornwall - which he renamed Lyonesse or sometimes Off-Wessex, featuring in the novel *A Pair of Blue Eyes* (1873) and the short story *A Mere Interlude* (1885). Some observers have suggested that his re-telling of Tristram and Iseult - with its two Iseults - may be a psychological study of his two wives. Hardy styled his 1923 play in the form of a Mummers' drama (perhaps drawing on the well-known form in Cornwall) and has Merlin introduce the story:

I come, at your persuasive call
To raise up in this modern hall
A tragedy of dire duress
That vexed the Land of Lyonesse:-

The tale has travelled far and wide:-
Yea, that King Mark to fetch his bride,

Sent Tristram; then that he and she
Quaffed a love-potion witlessly
While homeward bound. Hence that the King
   Wedded one heart-aflame
For Tristram! He in dark despair,
Roved recklessly, and wived elsewhere
   One of his mistress' name.

Inside the original published edition of the play, Hardy completed a drawing for the frontispiece imagining the architecture of the castle from this spot.

● *Trystan hag Yseult* by A.S.D. Smith and D.H. Watkins, Tintagel

SX 052889. *View the castle from the mainland courtyard.*

A.S.D Smith (1883-1950) came from Sussex. He was a language teacher, author of popular textbooks of both Cornish and Welsh and editor of *Kernow* (1933-4), the first all Cornish periodical. Well-known for his popular *Welsh Made Easy,* he adapted similar methods for *Cornish Made Easy,* which is still in print. His 8,000 line poem on Tristan and Yseult is perhaps the most important early twentieth-century work in Cornish. The work was written while Smith was on Air Raid Warden duty during the latter part of the Second World War. The poem remained incomplete for a while. Part 18 was not completed - except as notes - and the last part, the death of Tristan is unwritten. The work was then edited by E.G. Retallack Hooper and published in 1951. The unfinished part of the story was then completed by D. H. Watkins in 1962. Watkins (1892-1969) came from the Rhondda Valley, south Wales. He taught for many years in Cornwall and finally settled here. Both Smith and Watkins follow Joseph Bédier's compilation of the various versions, *La Légende de Tristan* fairly closely. This section is from early on in the poem:

Adref an castel Tyntagel
yth esa lowarth mes a wel:
adro dhodho ke stykennow
lym ha compes avel guyow
ow tegea avallennek
ha lyes eghen frutys whek.

Y'n tyller pella a'n castel
ogas dhe'n stykennow ughel
yth esa ow tevy gwedhen:
saben vras gans lyes scoren.

[Behind the castle of Tintagel
there was a hidden garden.
About it was a palisade of stakes,
sharp and straight like spears,
enclosing an orchard
and many kinds of sweet fruits.

In the place farthest from the castle,
near these high stakes,
a tree was growing,
a great pine with many branches]

● Popular Arthuriana, Tintagel

SX 056884. *Park in the central car park and wander along the main street.*

Tintagel is actually the name now given to the village once known more properly as Trevena. The streets of Tintagel are filled with popular culture devoted to Arthuriana. These include advertising, murals, posters and lettering. A number of shops also offer various Celtic and Arthurian-inspired products. The shops *Celtic Legend, Another Green World* and *Willow Moon* are the most famous of these worth visiting for their interpretation of the myth. At nearby Boscastle, *The Mystical Place* offers Celtic and Neo-Pagan products (SX 098912).

● The Fontevrault Chapel at Trevena

SX 055995. *This is located on the road to St Matriana's church at the bottom of the valley. It has limited opening.*

This exquisite small chapel is part of the Vicarage outbuildings; its name commemorating the abbey in France which held the patronage of Tintagel during the Medieval period. The commune there is now known as the Fontevraud-l'Abbaye. It was founded by Robert of Arbrissel. Dowsers have noted strong movements in this Chapel.

● The Language of Arthur in the *Old Cornish Vocabulary*, Tintagel

SX 052887. *Walk the short distance across the cliffs from St Matriana's Church to the outer keep of the castle.*

There exists an Old Cornish-Latin thesaurus called the *Vocabularium Cornicum*, or Old Cornish Vocabulary, probably compiled by Ælfric, the abbot of Eynsham. It classifies a number of words and concepts for Cornish speakers learning Latin and was compiled around 1000. Many of the words reflect Arthurian connections, considering hunting, warfare, social structures and cultural life. If any document shows us the language and culture of the historical Arthur, then it is this one.

A page of the Old Cornish Vocabulary, *in the* Cottonian Vespasian A XIV *describing colours, birds, fish and beasts.*
British Library

From *The Old Cornish Vocabulary*, complied by Ælfric

abat - abbot
ancar - hermit
arghans - silver
arluit - lord
arludes - lady
bahet - boar
barth - entertainer
barth hirgorn - trumpeter
bleit - wolf
cadwur - warrior
caid - bondsman
caites - bondswoman
camhinsic - unjust, unrighteous
canores - singing woman
chefuidoc - powerful, almighty
cherniat - hornblower
chetua - place of assembly
chuillioc - male soothsayer
cuillioges - female soothsayer

cuntellet - congregation, assembly
curun ruy - royal crown
cusulioder - adviser
darador - doorman, porter
delc - brooch
druic - dragon
enchinethel - ogre, giant
eure - goldsmith
falhun - falcon
fiol - drinking cup
guailen ruifanaid - sceptre
guelheuin - chief
guilter - hunting dog
guirleueriat - truth-teller
gulat - country, kingdom
hebrenchiat luid - leader of army
helhiat - hunter
hudol - magician

huheldat - patriarch
huhelwur - noble
kelegel - chalice
leid - clan, tribe
liver - book
muis - table
peis - tunic
pendeuig - prince
penteilu - master of household
pobel tiogou - ordinary people
pridit - poet
ruifanes - Queen
ruy - King
steuel - dining hall
teilu - household, family
teleinor - harper
torch - wild pig
uncorn - unicorn

● Rudolph Steiner, Tintagel

SX 053891 to SX 065887. *Walk the cliffs from Tintagel Haven to Gullastern and take the footpath inland to Bossiney·*

A number of international philosophers have been inspired by Tintagel and its Arthurian associations. For example, Rudolph Steiner (1861-1925) was a Croatian-born cultural philosopher, educationalist and esoteric thinker, who spent considerable time in Tintagel and walked the cliffs there. In his attempts to deconstruct and understand further the native theology and philosophy of Western Europe, Steiner wrote a good deal on Arthuriana. He came to view Arthur as a 'Sun God' and explained that Tintagel operated as a 'centre of mystery' – ideas which have since been embellished by the writer Richard Seddon. Accordingly, Arthuriana and Celtic legend offered new insights into human consciousness. Steiner's investigations into Arthuriana, helped to formulate his foundation of the spiritual philosophy known as Anthrosophy. Steiner also wrote extensively on the symbolism of the Holy Grail and the esoteric wisdom of druidry. Steiner joins a range of visiting philosophers who also found inspiration from their time in Celtic Cornwall – Carl Jung (1875-1961) and Bertrand Russell (1872-1970)

● King Arthur's Castle Hotel, Tintagel

SX 053891. *From the B3263, follow the main road through Tintagel which bends first north east, and then north west. The hotel is at the end of the drive.*

Presently known as the Camelot Castle Hotel, the original name of this building was King Arthur's Castle Hotel. The Hotel was designed by the Cornish-born architect, Silvanus Trevail and was opened in 1899. The enterprise for the building of the hotel came from Sir Robert Harvey who hoped that the Southern Railway (its locomotive featuring many Arthurian-inspired names) would be extended from Otterham junction to Tintagel. The castellated roof of the building, as well as its general appearance has often confused many tourists arriving at the location, thinking this was Tintagel castle. The Hotel is however, testament to the wider impact of the Celtic revival in Cornwall. The decoration inside the hotel is Arthurian themed. Sadly, the railway never made it to Tintagel and so the hotel has always struggled without the mass numbers of visitors expected.

● Willapark Cliff Castle, Tintagel

SX 063896. *At Bossiney, follow the footpath to the headland.*

Narrow at the neck, this headland is defended by a single line of ramparts, now topped by a modern wall. It has a similar name to the location found at Boscastle, perhaps demonstrating their similarity and proximity.

● St Piran's Well, Trethevey, near Boscastle

SX 076892. *Travelling from Tintagel to Boscastle, the well is found up a lane just before the hamlet of Trethevey.*

St Piran is, of course, a common dedication across Cornwall and an image of him is found in the stained glass windows of the Church at St Materiana at Tintagel. The well here is somewhat neglected but we know that a chapel once stood nearby. In terms of the continuity of Celticity in Cornwall, this area is particularly strong, so it is perhaps appropriate to find Cornwall's patron saint here.

● St Nectan's Kieve, near Boscastle

SX 077885. *The Kieve is reached by walking the half-a-mile footpath from the B3263 through St Nectan's Glen.*

Saint Nectan was a male member of the Brychan family group. His connection to the north Cornwall and north Devon area is strong. Hartland Abbey reveres him and a Life of the saint has survived. It records how his chapel had a tower from which he could see the ocean. From the tower he rang a silver bell to warn sailors when there were dangerous storms. It also records how he met with his brothers and sisters at his dwelling place just after Christmas to talk with them about God's love. A mass dedicated to him has also survived, which is to be sung on Nectan's Day – June 17th: 'Guarding thy people, O Nectan, companion of the martyrs, pray to the Lord for us, now, and always…' The saint is commemorated in the spectacular waterfall and stone basin [a *kieve* in Cornish] at the head of St Nectan's Glen. After his death, two of his sisters had the falls diverted so that they could bury the saint in an oak coffin in a hollow in the rock at the location before returning the waters to their normal course again. The nineteenth-century Anglo-Cornish poet Robert Stephen Hawker was fascinated with the story and composed 'The Sisters of Glen Nectan' in memory of them. Although composed in English it nonetheless captures innate Celtic spirituality of place. Despite having a Christian association, it is with contemporary Neo-Paganism that the site has become most associated. Many offerings are left including a spectacular fallen tree, embedded with coins.

St Nectan's Nieve.

The Sisters of Glen Nectan by Robert Stephen Hawker (c.1831)

It is from Nectan's mossy steep,
The foamy waters flash and leap:
It is where shrinking wildflowers grow,
They love the nymph that dwells below.

But wherefore in this far-off dell,
The reliques of a human cell?
Where the sad stream and lonely wind
Bring man no tidings of his kind.

"Long years agone:" the old man said,
Twas told him by his grandsire dead;
"One day two ancient sisters came:
None there could tell their race or name;

"Their speech was not in Cornish phrase,
Their garb had signs of loftier days;
Slight food thye took from hands of men,
They withered slowly in that glen,

"One died - the other's sunken eye
Gushed till the fount of tears was dry;
A wild and withering thought had she,
'I shall have none to weep for me.'

"They found her silent at the last,
Bent in the shape wherein she passed:
Where her lone seat long used to stand,
Her head upon her shrivelled hand."

Did fancy given this legend birth?
The grandame's tale for winter hearth:
Or some dead bard, by Nectan's stream,
People these banks with such a dream.

We know not: but it suits the scene,
To think such wild things here have been:
What spot more meet could grief or sin
Choose, at the last to wither in?

● Rocky Valley Maze Carvings, near Boscastle

SX 073894. *The maze carvings are found next the ruined mill buildings at the top end of the valley.*

The two maze carvings in Rocky Valley have intrigued many visitors. The labyrinths carry a sense of distant mysticism. Some observers have dated them to the Bronze Age. However, it has also been argued that the carvings were merely completed in more recent times by mill workers. Their origins perhaps matter less – it is their engagement with the Celticity of space which offers meaning to those who come to look at them. Offerings and clouties are left nearby. A third maze carving – though more faded – has recently been identified at the site.

A maze carving at Rocky Valley.

● St Materiana's Well, Minster Church, Boscastle

SX 111906. *Following the B3326 from Boscastle back to Camelford. The well and church are down a lane at Trecarne Gate about Peter's Wood.*

Matriana or Materiana is a significant saint in north Cornwall, providing the dedication here as well as to her church in Tintagel. The likelihood is that the Church here was the mother church initially, with the cliff-top church at Trevena (Tintagel) an outlying chapel. Materiana may have origins in Gwent in Wales. Her feast day is the 9th April. The well seems to rise from waters underneath the church itself and gather in a stone basin.

● The Museum of Witchcraft, Boscastle

SX 098914. *The museum is located near the harbour in the village.*

Founded by neo-pagan arch-witch Cecil Williamson (1909-1999), the Museum of Witchcraft began its life on the Isle of Man in 1951, before moving to Cornwall in 1960. Just before his death, Williamson transferred ownership of the museum to Graham King. King has developed the museum with a more enlightened understanding of Pagan practice and has modernised its exhibitions and collections. The collection has grown over the years to include many examples of Cornish witchcraft – often rooted in long-forgotten Celtic ritual, folklore and practice. Information on significant Cornish witches is held there. The museum also has artefacts from the neo-pagan interest in Celtic material and is a must for anyone interested in esoteric aspects of Celtic Cornwall. The museum has a large library of esoteric and arcane books, but prior notification of interest in them is required.

Minster church nr Boscastle, the site of Materianna's well.

● Willapark Cliff Castle, Boscastle

SX 091912. *The castle is reached by taking the coastal footpath west from Boscastle harbour.*

Like the site found at Tintagel, just a single rampart defends this Iron Age cliff castle. It has excellent views of the coast to the south west and of the harbour entrance.

Boscastle and Willapark promontory fort.

● St Juliot's Well and Church, near Boscastle

SX 132912. *This is found to the right of the B3263 heading east out of Boscastle but can also be located from walking up Valency Valley from the car park in the village.*

The church here is the one famously restored and altered between 1870-72 by the novelist, poet and dramatist Thomas Hardy, when he came to Cornwall as a young architect – a visit which later inspired such Celtic-themed work as 'When I set out for Lyonesse' and 'At Castle Boterel'. Despite Hardy's Wessex roots he had an affinity for Cornwall, an area he later termed both Lyonnesse and 'Off-Wessex'. Celtic myth and legend was also to inspire his dramatic work. The well is a short distance away from the church, marked by a piece of fencing.

When I set out for Lyonnesse by Thomas Hardy

When I set out for Lyonnesse,
A hundred miles away,
The rime was on the spray,
And starlight lit my lonesomeness
When I set out for Lyonnesse
A hundred miles away.

What would bechance at Lyonnesse
While I should sojourn there
No prophet durst declare,
Nor did the wisest wizard guess
What would bechance at Lyonnesse
While I should sojourn there.

When I came back from Lyonnesse
With magic in my eyes,
All marked with mute surmise
My radiance rare and fathomless,
When I came back from Lyonnesse
With magic in my eyes!

Inside St Neot's Well, Poundstock.

● St Genny's Wells, St Genny, near Crackington Haven.

SX 149971. *The two well sites may be found close to St Genny's Church.*

The first site is to be found at the rear of the church and the hill from which the well flows. This is marked with the words 'The Holy Well of St Genny's circa 6th Cent. Restored 1927' and was probably constructed to increase awareness of its location. The actual well site is probably the nearby neglected opening, covered by a metal grill. A variety of stories are attached to the site regarding the saint. Gennys may well have been a local Celtic patron of the area. Some have suggested he was a Roman soldier who remained, or even an actor. He may also have been Genesius of Arles, who was martyred in 250CE. He declared himself a Christian after an edict from Rome forbade anyone to have such belief. It is therefore possible that in this small North Cornish village we have a dedication going back to the Christianity of the Roman Empire. If it were Genesius then he would have had a Celtic Feast Day of May 2nd.

● St Neot's Well, Poundstock

SX 204999. *Poundstock is on the A39. The well is found to the north west of the area of the village known as Bangors.*

Saint Neot is more readily associated with the village in south east Cornwall, though a tradition also exists in North Cornwall. The well site here is very beautiful with an ornate wellhouse and a chained cup to drink from.

St Neot's Well, Poundstock.

Hawker's hut.

The view from Hawker's hut.

● Ashbury Hill Fort, Week St Mary, near Poundstock

SX 228975. *This can be found one mile to the west of Week St Mary. Week St Mary is found on the minor roads leading east from Poundstock.*

This is an oval-shaped Iron Age hill fort, with two ramparts north and south, broken by two entrances. Towards the south east are two further rows of embankments broken by an entrance track.

● William de Grenville, Stowe, near Kilkhampton

SS 213113. *Stowe House is located to the east of Kilkhampton.*

An early possible scholar in Celtic Cornwall is William de Grenfild (Grenville), who was the son of Sir Theobald Grenville of Stowe in North Cornwall. Grenville became Dean of Chicester, eventually Chancellor of England when he was elected Archbishop of York in 1304. This date means that he was probably middle-aged by the time he gained this position, so he would have been born around 1260, and Cornish had already retreated beyond a line from Crackington Haven to Launceston. Therefore, although an interesting pan-British figure, he is less likely to have been a Cornish-language dramatist of any note. It was also a period before dramatic work was legitimised for the Clergy. English-language imaginings of Cornwall are more possible.

● Hawker's Hut and Morwenstow Church, Morwenstow

SS 197153. *The church is reached off the A39 through Morwenstow village. The Hut is a short walk over two fields to the cliff.*

Robert Stephen Hawker (1803-1975) was Vicar of Morwenstow. He was born in Plymouth and educated at Pembroke College, Oxford. Although operating slightly before the major Celto-Cornish Revival, Hawker was nonetheless sympathetic to the Celtic traditions, folklore and language of Cornwall. Many of his poems looked at legendary figures, witches and the spirituality of place and landscape. Known for his eccentricities, Hawker constructed a hut on the cliffs near his church. He built the hut out of timbers from shipwrecks and went there to write his poetry and gaze upon the Atlantic.

Always High-Church, and sceptical of the aims of Methodism in Cornwall, on his deathbed, Hawker converted to Catholicism. Hawker even titled some of his poems in the Cornish language. One was titled *Modryb Marya* – or Aunt Mary. This was the name Cornish people gave to Mary, mother of Jesus.

Modryb Marya - Aunt Mary by **Robert Stephen Hawker**

Now of all the trees by the king's highway,
Which do you love the best?
O! the one that is green upon Christmas Day,
The bush with the bleeding breast.
Now the holly with her drops of blood for me:
For that is our dear Aunt Mary's tree.

Its leaves are sweet with our Saviour's Name,
Tis a plant that loves the poor:
Summer and winter it shines the same,
Beside the cottage door.
O! the holly with her drops of blood for me:
For that is our kind Aunt Mary's tree.

The well of St John of the Wilderness, Morwenstow

● St Morwenna's Well, Morwenstow

SX 197155. *The well is half-way down Vicarage Cliff. Care is advised.*

Morwenna is the Celtic patron of Morwenstow. She was one of the children of Brychan from Brecon in South Wales. In the nearby church a probable wall painting of her is to be found. The Saxon king Ethelwulf apparently appointed Morwenna to be the tutor of his daughters and it is from him that she gained a plot of land to build the first church slightly inland. This is interesting piece of supposed ethnic cooperation between Brythonic and Saxon peoples. However, the story is anachronistic as they were separated by at least three centuries. The well's cliff-top site is very unusual. Holy wells attached to Celtic saints are normally found further inland.

● The Well of St John of the Wilderness, Morwenstow

SX 206154. *This well is to be found in the corner of the vicarage garden.*

Now dedicated to John the Baptist, this well would also have provided water and healing for the Christian community founded by Morwenna.

The Well of St John.

● Lundy Island, Atlantic Ocean

SS 135460. *Lundy may be reached by passenger ferries from Bideford and Ilfracombe, depending on tides.*

Lundy is almost in a perfect straight-line from St Govan's Chapel in Pembrokeshire to north Cornwall and Devon, and in particular Hartland Point. Presumably numerous travellers from Wales to Cornwall would have put in to the island to recuperate and rest from their travels, especially during stormy weather. The island is some 12 miles from the mainland coast of Devon and Cornwall, and about another 24 miles from the Welsh coast. The name Lundy is believed to come from the Norse word for 'puffin island' [Lundey]. One of the most significant Celtic sites on the island is the Beacon Hill Cemetery. The cemetery was enclosed by a curvilinear bank and ditch, still visible in the south west corner and this is comparable to the *Lann* type enclosures found in Cornwall. Four Celtic-style inscribed stones are found at the site with the following inscriptions: OPTIMI [Optimus] – a Latin, male name, RESTEVTAE – a Latin female name, either Resteuta or Resgeuta, POTTITI, - a Latin, male name, and GERNI [FIL]I TIGERNI – a Brythonic male, called Tigernus, son of Tigernus. The island was later controlled by the Knights Templar and the de Marisco family. The island was a later notorious lair of pirates. It is now famous for its distinctive wildlife.

● Warbstow Bury Hill Fort, Warbstow

SX 202908. *Take the minor road off the A395 at Hallworth to Warbstow. The fort lies to the north west of Warbstow.*

Warbstow Bury is one of Cornwall's most impressive surviving Iron Age hill forts. It is composed of two large oval shaped ramparts, with a third line of defence located in the south west corner between the inner and outer circle. In the middle of the inner set of ramparts is a Neolithic long barrow, which is known locally as King Arthur's Tomb.

● Davidstow Holy Well, near Camelford

SX 151874. *The footpath to the well is marked by a sign. It is a few metres north east of the church at Davidstow.*

This well may, of course, be devoted to Saint David, the son of Saint Nonna. Although restored in 1871, it maintains an ancient feel. Niches for statues may be found inside.

● Bagpiper Bench-end Carving, Davidstow Church, near Camelford

SX 151873. *The church is close to the A395.*

On one of the bench-ends in the church is found a female bag-piper. She is depicted as having curly hair and is playing two chanters (where the finger holes are found, to create the melody). Cornish bagpipes usually appear to have dual chanters.

Bagpiper bench end carving

● St Sidwell's Well, Jordan's Well, Laneast, Bodmin Moor

SX 229839. *Laneast is best reached by leaving the A30 on the A395 and following the signs to the hamlet. The well is located in the south east of the village.*

St Sidwell (or Sadfyl) is not a Celtic saint. An Anglo-Saxon maiden, she was murdered by Celtic-speaking peoples while walking through her father's fields near East Gate in Exeter. This was completed upon the instruction of her stepmother, who may well have been a Celt. We know that West Britons continued to live and work beside Anglo-Saxons for some time in early Exeter. The Celts, who worked as reapers, cut off her hand with a scythe and immediately a spring welled where the blood fell to the ground. Her body parts united together after three days and then she was able to walk unaided. Her shrine in Exeter was visited by 1000 and the well at Laneast might have been able to capitalise on that profit by tempting pilgrims further to the west. A relief of the saint is shown on a shopping arcade in Sidwell Street in Exeter. An image of her in stained glass also appears the Great East Window of Exeter Cathedral. Her fate may well be symbolic of early ethnic tension between Celts and Anglo-Saxons in West Britain. The church was originally dedicated to St Just.

St Sidwell's well, Laneast

● Churchyard Cross, Laneast

SX 228839. *Laneast churchyard is close to Jordan's Well.*

This is a plain but impressive cross, discovered buried in the churchyard in the 1950s. There is some evidence of decoration begun, but it was never finished.

St Clether's Well.

● St Clether's Well and Chapel, St Clether, Bodmin Moor

SX 203847. *St Clether is best reached by leaving the A30 on the A395 and following the signs to the village. The well and chapel are located in a valley north east of the village.*

Clether is most likely one of the group of saints known as the 'children of Brychan' from Brecon in South Wales. King Brychan and Queen Gladwisa had twenty-four children many of whom entered the south-west peninsula via north Cornwall and Devon (probably around Hartland Point). He is known elsewhere as Cleder, Clederi or Clederus, and was a nephew of Saint Nectan. Sometime shortly after 1894, the well and chapel were restored by the hagiographer and folklorist Reverend Sabine Baring-Gould (1834-1924). They remain in good condition with an active community still making offerings. Clether is found to the south as well: at Probus, there is well dedicated to him called Venton Glidder, and in Brittany, there is a parish called Cleder.

St Clether's Chapel.

● St Clether Cross, near St Clether

SX 205841. *This cross is found due south of the church at St Clether. It can be viewed from the road.*

This is a large, beautifully situated ancient wayside cross, which probably marked the footpath to the church. It has neck projections under the cross head.

● St Nonna's Well, Altarnun

SX 226816. *Altarnun is just to the north of the main A30, near to Launceston. The well is found at the bottom of the field below the vicarage.*

Nonna is known at Pelynt as well as having dedications in Brittany. Non or Nonna is famed for being the mother of Saint David, the patron saint of Wales. A ruined Chapel of St Non and a holy well are to be found close to St David's, in Pembrokeshire. Altarnun is close to Davidstow, and the saint may be the origin of this name. Clearly, in the sixteenth century, the site at Altarnun was well-known, as the historian Richard Carew devotes a considerable portion of his *Survey of Cornwall* (1602) to it:

In our forefather's days, when devotion as much exceeded knowledge as knowledge now cometh short of devotion, there were many bowsenning places for curing madmen; and amongst the rest, one at Alter-nunne… called St Nunne's Pooll, which saint's altar it may be… gave name to the church. The water running from St Nunne's Wel fell into a square and close walled plot, where might bee filled at what depth they listed. Upon this weall was the franticke person west to stand, his back towards the poole, and from thence, with a sudden blow in the brest, tumbled headlong into the pond where a strong fellowe, provided for the nonce, tooke him and tossed him, up and down, alongst and athwart the water, until the patient, by forgoing his strength, had somewhat forgot his fury. Then was hee conveyed to the church, and certaine masses sung over him; upon which handling, if his right wits returned, St Nunne had the thanks; but if there appeared small amendment, he was bowsenned againe and againe while there remained in him any hope of life for recovery.

Bowsening was the act of ducking someone (probably from the Cornish *beuzi* [to dip]). It seems a common practice around this time and appears to be a cure for madness. Maybe St Nonna's well offered relief for such a condition.

● Bench ends, St Nonna's Church, Altarnun

SX 223813. *The church is at the northern end of the village.*

Often labelled, the 'Cathedral of the Moor', St Nonna's Church contains a collection of impressive carved, wooden benchends which give especial insight into Celtic Cornwall. The elaborate carvings were made by Robert Daye between 1510 and 1530. Among them are a variety of subjects including a green man, sheep on the moor, local worthies and a jester. Also featured are a fiddler and significantly, a man playing Cornish bagpipes. Such instrumentation was clearly common in Late Medieval Cornwall, since the 1502 play *Bewnans Meriasek* [*The Life of St Meriasek*] features such pipers:

Pyboren wethugh in scon	[Pipers, blow at once.
ny a vyn ketep map bron	We will, every son of the breast,
moys the donsya	Go to dance.
eugh bo tregugh	Go ye or stay,
wolcum vethugh	Welcome ye shall be,
kyn fewy sythen omma	Though ye be a week here.]

The wild Celticity of place is no better explored than in Daphne du Maurier's 1936 novel, *Jamaica Inn*, where the imagined villainous albino Vicar of Altarnun, one Francis Davey, is the smugglers' ringleader. The carvings of the font are also of interest.

● Crosses, Altarnun

SX 222 813, SX 213822, SX 217815, SX 206822, SX 223 817.

Several crosses may be found in the vicinity. In the churchyard, there is a tall wheel-headed cross, located close to the lynch-gate (SX 222 813). At SX 213822, close to the Rising Sun public house, is

Hockazenny or Occasiney Cross and near Trekennick Farm there is mounted wheel-headed cross (SX 217815). Tresmeak Cross is located in a lane around one and half miles north of Altarnun at SX 206822. Another is found at Two Gates – a road junction north of the parish church at SX 223 817.

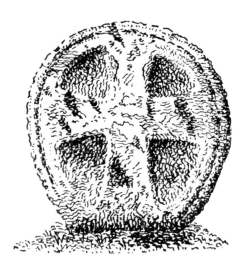

Cross head at Altarnun vicarage.

● St Anne's Well, Whitstone, near Launceston

SX 263985. *Whitstone lies on the Cornwall/England border between Marhamchurch and Launceston. The well is positioned in the south-east corner of the churchyard.*

Above the arched doorway of this well is this inscription 'Sancta Anna'. This is very likely the St Anne who was the mother of the more famous Saint Sampson. Of interest is a carving of what appears to be a crude, pagan stone head, which perhaps shows how Christian belief has appropriated the pagan past. A niche in the archway used to hold an image of the saint.

● St Michael's Well, Lezant, near Launceston

SX 337792. *Lezant is around five miles south of Launceston, just off the A388.*

The parish church at Lezant is dedicated to St Michael. His well is located by the side of a lane running north from the church. A small wooden door covers the well inside. The name Lezant is probably a derivation of *Lann sans* [holy church site].

● Launceston Castle, Launceston

SX325987. *The castle is found on the A388 close to the town centre.*

Major work began on the castle here in the aftermath of the Norman conquest, around 1067, possibly founded by Brian of Brittany (as part of the so-called 'Breton return', where the families of ex-patriot West Britons, who had travelled to Brittany in the wake of Saxon incursions, eventually returned home under 'Norman' occupation). The castle became the administrative centre for successive Earls of Cornwall, who controlled the estates of Cornwall. In the thirteenth century, the castle was rebuilt in stone, initiated by Richard, Earl Of Cornwall, the younger brother of Henry III. In the Tudor period, the castle took on a reputation as being the place where rebellion was dealt with in Cornwall, and was known as Castle Terrible. English aggression designed to create political and religious conformity had prompted the beginnings of the Prayer Book Rebellion, and many Cornish rebels were hung, drawn and quartered there. In 1646, it was used as part of the Royalist defence of Cornwall. The Cornish Gorsedd has been held at the castle on numerous occasions - in 1947, 1972 and 2003.

● Payment in Puffins, Launceston

SX325987. *The main gate of the castle is found to the south east.*

In the so called Caption of Seisin (basically a list of payments and resources seized), of the Duchy of Cornwall, dating from 1337, there is an intriguing reference in the *Redditus Forinc* [Foreign rents] section that the Islands of Scilly provided some 300 puffins to be eaten at Launceston Castle for the feast of Michaelmas, and that the islanders would be paid 6s. 8d. for them. This is an intriguing piece of trade in Celtic Medieval Cornwall. The puffins were delivered at the gate of the castle. In Cornish, the puffin is known as *nath*.

● Charles Causley, Launceston

SX 334847. *There are several points of interest in the town, which are related to Causley's work but begin at St Mary Magdalene Church.*

Born and educated in Launceston, where he was a teacher after serving in the Navy, Charles Causley (1917-2003) was an admired Anglo-Cornish poet, children's writer and dramatist, deeply influenced by Celtic legend. Causley began his career as a dramatist, much inspired by Cornish mystery play culture, but after the Second World War, began to develop a poetic career influenced by balladry and folklore. His apparently simple poems carry deep messages about innocence and experience. In his later work, his poetry embraced more modernist forms while he still developed children's literature and work with Cornwall's Kneehigh Theatre Company. The landscape of the Cornwall and England border, not to mention the town of Launceston itself form the metaphorical base of much of his poetry.

Charles Causley.

Launceston is littered with images and material from Causley's work. Start your walk at St Mary Magdalene Church (SX 334847). At the east of the church you will find a relief of a reclining Mary on the wall. Folklore says that if a stone or pebble pitched onto her back remains there, then it will bring you luck. Around the church are several memorials and buildings related to Sir Henry Trecarell who rebuilt the church in 1531. Outside of the church, turn right and then right again to find a path called Zig Zag, which features in Causley's poetry. Come back up into the town from the car park and turn right, heading toward the Eagle House Hotel. The two eagles in front of the hotel are featured in his poetry. From here enter the grounds of Launceston Castle (SX325987). The castle gives a good vantage point over Causley's landscape. Causley's grave is found around 100 yards from where he was born at St Thomas' Churchyard. The grave is simply marked 'Poet'. Causley's house (No. 2 Cyprus Well) is where the poet lived for most of his life.

● St Mary Magdalene Gothic Cross, Launceston

SX 332846. *The cross is located on the eastern side of the churchyard*

Mary Magdalene is an important figure within the Resurrection sequence of the *Ordinalia*, and it seems she was an important figure for the Cornish. The church is ornately carved, and the cross here reflects the ambition of that ornamentation. It shows Christ on the Cross with, probably, his mother and St John.

● Holyway Cross, South Petherwin

SX 272823. *This stands on the A30 from Launceston to Bodmin.*

The cross on the cross head here has expanded ends and there is sword-like band running down the shaft.

● St Catherine's Church, Temple, near Bodmin

SX 147733. *Temple is located just off the A30.*

St Catherine's Church stands on the site of what was an earlier Templar Chapel. The Templars may have realised that this location was a useful site to locate their Chapel because pilgrims travelling to the Holy Land or Santiago de Compostella from Ireland or Wales usually crossed Cornwall at this point in order to reach Brittany. After 1312 the Templars appear to have let the church go, and turned it over to the Hospitallers, but in the sixteenth century and succeeding centuries it became well known as place where couples could get married without the necessary banns or licence required elsewhere. It thus acted as a Cornu-Celtic Gretna Green. This is possibly from where the Cornu-English dialect phrase 'Get thee to Temple Moors!' is derived, used in response to a rebellious or insolent person. In 1753, an act was passed to make such marriages illegal. Both the layering of the Templar interest in the site and its status as a venue for alternative marriages in Cornwall have made it a significant site.

● Crosses, Blisland

SW 100731. *Blisland is found north of the A30 between Bodmin and Bolventor.*

The so-called Cross Park cross stands on the village green in Blisland (SW100731). Broken up during the seventeenth century, and stored partly in the meadow at Cross Park, the cross was reassembled in 1931. The churchyard holds a small wheel-headed cross on its western edge (SW100731).

● Tregenna Chapel Well, near Blisland

SW 095742. *From Blisland, take the minor road north east to Tregenna Farm. On a public footpath walk across four fields, to find the remains of the chapel.*

No saint's dedication is attached to this chapel, but it is obviously a significant site. The chapel is clearly more modern and was apparently built as a private chapel following a disagreement between the farmer and the local priest. The water here is very cold and clear.

South East Cornwall

● Trezance Well, Cardinham, near Bodmin

SX 125694. *Cardinham is found north east of Bodmin. Trezance is located on a road running north out of the village.*

It seems Trezance Well was in use in ancient Cornwall. The nineteenth-century historian Polwhele observes that 'the Holy well at Cardynham was sacred before the saints'. A baptistry once stood nearby, but this has long since disappeared.

● Churchyard Cross, Cardinham

SX 123686. *The cross is located on the south side of the churchyard.*

The complex design of this cross, and the proliferation of other crosses in and around Cardinham stand as testament to the spiritual significance of the area. This seven-foot tall cross has fascinating scroll and plait work upon it. For several years it formed the fabric of the building of the church. The Cross has a probable Scandanavian origin but that has not stopped observers linking it to native Celtic spirituality. There was, of course, an alliance between the Cornish and the Danes against the Anglo-Saxons in the ninth century. The church here is dedicated to St Meubred, who was a hermit.

Cross near the south porch of Cardinham church.

● Crosses, Cardinham

SX 123689, SX 113648, SX 110684, SX 130688, SX142680

Many significant crosses can be found in the area. Another tall cross is found in the churchyard (SX 123689) with an inscription on it reading RANOCORI FILI MESGI [Ranocorus son of Mesgus]. Part of the shaft of a cross (holding scrollwork) that possibly once stood in the churchyard is found at Glynn House (SX 113648). Higher Deviock Cross (SX 110684) is reached via a public footpath and is found a mile west from Cardinham churchtown. Treslea Cross (SX 130688) is a wheel-headed bound-ary cross located approximately half a mile east of the churchtown at the meeting of three roads. On Treslea Downs is another wayside cross (SX142680).

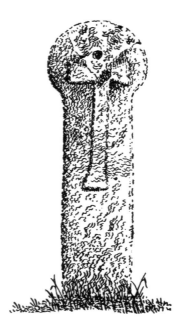

Carburrow cross, Warleggan.

● Plain-an-gwarry, Cardinham

SX 123697. *Just north of Cardinham may be found Lower Haygrove.*

The Tithe Map of 1839 refers to a field here as 'Place Green Field'. From Lower Haygrove, the field is the second one to the south-east. With such a distinctive name a playing place is a possibility.

● Carburrow Cross, Warleggan, near Bodmin

SX 156 690. *Warleggan is some six miles east of Bodmin. The cross is easily found on the south side of the churchyard, close to the porch.*

This thick-set cross appears very ancient and is of the wheel-headed type.

● Luxulyan, near Bodmin

SX 051581. *Luxulyan is reached by minor roads from St Austell, Bodmin or Bugle and is close to the Eden Project.*

Luxulyan's contribution to Celtic Cornwall is complex. St Sulien or Sulian was an abbot here sometime in the sixth century. We do find a similar name at locations in Wales and Brittany, and the church here may have originally been dedicated to him. It has also been argued by Gilbert H. Doble that Sulien may derive from the name of a Celtic solar deity. Now however, the church is dedicated to Saints Ciricius and Julitta. This rededication probably occurred in the fifteenth century when the church was rebuilt. A small holy well stands near to the church.

● Crosses, Luxulyan

SX 052580, SX 031613, SX 053579.

At the lychgate on the south side of the church is a wheel-headed wayside cross in good condition. Another cross may be found in the parish at Lockengate, between Bugle and Bodmin (SX 031613). It is known locally as Trevallan Cross. At SX 053579 is found a wheel-headed cross built into a stile on the Saint's Way footpath. It is approximately one mile south of Luxulyan.

● Jack Kerouac family history, Cliff Pill

SW 128558. *The Saint's Way runs across mid-Cornwall and its landscape can be viewed from Cliff Pill near Maneley Dunford.*

The American 'Beat generation' poet and novelist, Jack Kerouac (1922-1969) was very aware of his Brythonic Celtic routes. The author of *On the Road* (1957) and *The Dharma Bums* (1958) knew that his surname was Celtic, and in his own writings argues for a long-term Cornu-Celtic connection. In a drunken interview published after his death in 1971, Kerouac observed that "the Kernouacks went to Cornwall a thousand years before Christ… In the south-west country of England, inhabited by the

Jack Kerouac.

Celts, the name of the language is Kernouac… And something happened with the Cornish rebellion and they said, 'Let's get the hell out of here and cross the channel to Brittany, France'. They went there and their name was no longer Kernouac, it was Kerouac." Research by various biographers have shown that Kerouac's roots were from Brittany, and that he was descended from a merchant colonist, François-Urbain Le Binan, Sieur de Kervoac, whose sons married French Canadians. The original family may well have come from Cornwall however, or have passed through Cornwall from Ireland. Not only saints would have travelled along the old saint's way. Maybe this was the sort of path Kerouac's family once took.

● Arthur Quiller Couch Memorial, near Bodinnick

SX 131517. *From the Bodinnick Ferry, climb the hill. At the footpath turn left and walk to Penleath Point. The memorial is located there.*

Arthur Quiller Couch (1863-1944) was born in Bodmin – though he had family connections with Polperro. He was educated at Oxford, where he began writing under the pseudonym of 'Q'. In 1900 he edited *The Oxford Book of English Verse* and in 1912 became Professor of English Literature at the University of Cambridge. He will be ever associated with Fowey and its surrounds, where he often lived and set many of his stories and novels.

Quiller Couch was engaged with many aspects of the Celtic Revival in Cornwall, though at times, he seemed uncertain as to whether Celticity was still possible in the modern area. For example, he felt that reviving the mystery plays of Cornwall would be somewhat false, because the audience would have to act as much as the actors. However, Quiller Couch was very interested in local legends and stories, not least the narrative of Tristan and Yseult. In his *The Cornish Magazine* meanwhile, Quiller Couch did initiate much debate over the direction of Cornwall's future in the light of a Celtic Revival, as well as celebrating the work of cultural activists such as Robert Morton Nance. The Memorial looks across to Q's Fowey residence (The Haven) at SX 124515.

Sir Arthur Quiller Couch.

● Saint Winnow, St Winnow Parish Church, St Winnow

SX 116569. *The church town is on the east bank of the River Fowey, accessed via Lerryn.*

An ancient seventh-century oratory once sat here, which was dedicated to Saint Winnow. The church here was built in the twelfth century and its Rood screen has survived. Close by is St Nectan's Chapel, which lost part of its tower during the Civil War.

● Vivian family headstones, St Winnow Parish Church, St Winnow

SX 116569. *The headstones are easily located in the north-west corner of the churchyard.*

The Vivian family are a prominent Cornish family with long established roots in this area. Richard Hussey Vivian, was the 1st Baron Vivian living between 1775 and 1842. The headstones of later members of the family are completed in a Celtic style.

Aerial view over Polruan towards Fowey and Bodinnick which will forever be associated with Sir Arthur Quiller Couch.

● Saint Veep, St Veep Parish Church, St Veep

SX 140549. *St Veep is found on the eastern bank of the River Fowey close to Bodinnick. and Penpoll Creek.*

St Veep Parish Church is presently dedicated to Saint Quirieus and Saint Julietta, but it was once associated with Saint Veep. We know very little about the life of Saint Veep. In post-1549 Cornwall, one of the priests hanged for his beliefs was one Richard Bennett, the vicar of St Veep. He was dealt with under the direct orders of the Provost Marshall, Anthony Kingston.

● The Parish Church of St Wyllow, Lanteglos-by-Fowey

SX 144515. *Walk around Pont Pill and climb the steps to the church gate.*

The church here mostly dates from the late fourteenth century and it celebrates the life of St Wyllow – also know as St Willow, or St Wylloc. He was born in Ireland and was helpfully piloted by fish across the river and up Pont Pill, where he established a hermitage in the countryside. So it is said, he was killed by Melyn, who beheaded him. Some accounts suggest that Melyn was his own brother. Apparently after he was killed, the saint picked up his head and carried to the location of where the present-day church stands. There is a farm nearby called Lamellyon which marks the place of martyrdom and records the name of Melyn. Wyllow's feast day is 7 July. The church here is also famous as the location where Daphne du Maurier wedded Frederick Browning in 1932, travelling first in a boat to Pont Pill, then making the climb up to the church. It is renamed Lanoc Church in du Maurier's first novel, *The Loving Spirit* (1931). A walk to Polruan allows you to catch a passenger ferry back to Fowey.

● Crosses, at the Parish Church of St Wyllow, Lanteglos-by-Fowey

SX 144515. *These may be found in the churchyard.*

There is a tall lantern cross here on the south side of the churchyard which may well have been buried by local people to avoid its destruction during the Civil War. The lantern holds four images: a crowned Christ, the Virgin Mary, St Paul and St Peter. Near the entrance is another cross which may have once been located at Pont Pill.

● Tristan's Leap at St Catherine's Point, from Polruan

SX 125507. *Drive to Polruan via the Bodinnick Ferry. Park in the car park to the south of the village. The castle is viewed on the western side of the harbour entrance.*

In Béroul's narrative, at the point where Tristan is about to be burnt by fire, he makes a request to Mark's barons to make peace with God, and enters a chapel close to a cliff. Once inside he surmounts the altar, forces open the chapel's window and jumps, thinking that he might die through the fall; luckily the wind caught his cloak and bore him down unhurt to the rocks below. Geographically, a couple of locations might fit this moment in the narrative – one of them is St Catherine's Point. The castle that now stands at the Point is Tudor, but we know that a chapel stood there in 1390 so this

The lantern cross at St Wyllow's church.

might be a possibility. Another possible location is across St Austell Bay at Chapel Point, near Mevagissey (SX 028443) but this version is probably conflated with the story of Sir Henry Bodrugan, who also leapt from the cliffs here during Lambert Simnel's abortive rebellion (1487).

● Hidden corner, Polruan to Lansallos

SX 125507 to SX 173517. *Walk east on the coastal path and then return via the public footpaths.*

This corner of Celtic Cornwall is probably one of the least visited areas of the territory. Polruan possibly means 'St Rumon or St Ruan's Cove', but it might also translate to 'seal cove'. Pencarrow Head may translate to 'Stag's Head', while Lansallos probably means 'Selwyn's holy or church site'.

● The Parish Church of St Brevita, Lanlivery

SX 079591. *The church may be located just off the A390.*

Lanlivery was at one point an important centre of Celtic worship because the church here was enlarged in the fifteenth century and a magnificent tower constructed. We know very little about the life of St Brevita however, but there is some evidence of a dedication at Lanlivry in Brittany, which would support a connection.

Crewel Cross at Nomansland.

● Crewel Cross, near Lanlivery

SX 089590. *This is found at the junction where the B2269 meets the A390.*

Many drivers will pass this wheel-headed wayside cross. It was originally found embedded in a local stile, but was it was re-erected here in 1900. The area in which it is located is known as 'Nomansland'. In Béroul's narrative there is mentioned a writ that is hung on the so-called 'red cross'. The location of this stone, close to Lantyan and Castle Dore makes it a possibility, but of course, there are numerous other contenders.

● Restormel Castle, near Lostwithiel

SX 104614. *The castle is situated on the northern side of Lostwithiel, above the River Fowey.*

Standing in the middle of a large deer park, the original motte and bailey castle was built after the Norman Conquest, by Baldwin Fitz Turstain, the local sheriff, around 1100. However, the site had earlier fortifications upon it (further up the slope, there is a recently-discovered Roman fort). Subsequently, Robert de Cardinham, lord here from 1192–1225, constructed the surviving design. From around 1299 the castle passed to the crown, with Edward the Black Prince staying there in 1354 and again in 1365. In total however, the castle was not long occupied and many of its contents were stripped out and removed to other residences. A Parliamentarian garrison occupied the castle during the Civil War, and it is thought that much destruction was wreaked upon surviving Cornish-language manuscripts and documents held here and at the Stannary Palace. The castle was finally taken by Sir Richard Grenville on 21st August 1644.

The castle has long been associated with the *Tristan and Yseult* narrative. Some observers believe that the original commission for the tale was given by an early occupier of the castle site, in order to celebrate the south-coast of Cornwall and the River Fowey in particular. Other commentators argue that there may well be a connection between Isolda de Cardinham (married to Thomas de Tracey) who owned the castle until 1264. This date would certainly fit native storytellers or bards recounting the tale to a host named Isolda, though perhaps her name itself might have been inspired by the tale. The fact that Tristan is also presented as a skilled hunter of deer may also provide a link.

● *Antiquities Cornuontanic* by William Scawen, Restormel Castle

SX 104614. *The castle is situated on the northern side of Lostwithiel, above the River Fowey.*

One of the writers to comment on the loss of Cornish literature and documents at Restormel Castle was William Scawen (d. 1686). Scawen was Vice-Warden of the Stannaries – in effect, the Chief Justice of Cornwall. Scawen had an impressive understanding of how Celtic Cornwall was coming to be dominated by Anglicisation and how the process might be resisted. Although Scawen had some romantic notions of past Celtic Cornwall, he also had some very practical suggestions about what should be done in his *Antiquities Cornuontanic: The Causes of Cornish Speech's Decay*, published in 1680. Among the things that concerned him were the loss of interaction with Brittany, *guirremears* [the great plays] no longer being performed, the embracing of English by the gentry, and the suppression of

Aerial view of Restormel Castle.

Restormel Castle c.1910.

early 'Druidic' culture by Christianity. He was also concerned with a 'general stupidity' of the Cornish people in giving up the language and the 'want of writing in it'. Scawen's article was a visionary statement of what needed to be done to preserve Celtic Cornwall – a call which was taken up in the latter end of the seventeenth century and the early eighteenth century by a number of writers, particularly in the west of Cornwall. Some of Scawen's principles are as applicable today as they were in 1680 for he understood what socio-linguistics now call the 'ecological' conditions required for Celtic languages to survive.

● Stannary Palace, Lostwithiel

SX 104598. *Turn into the southern part of the town off the A390. The Palace is located close to the River Fowey.*

The Stannary Palace is one of the most significant survivals of Celtic Cornwall, and offers an insight into Cornu-Celtic independence through the centuries. The Stannary Parliaments and Stannary Courts were legislative and legal institutions in Cornwall. Special laws for tin miners were established before written law in Britain and so these institutions had their own jurisdiction, in effect – a kind of independence from the English system. Although the Stannary system evolved over time, in principle, Henry VII's charter of pardon of 1508 argued that no new laws affecting miners should be enacted without the consent of twenty-four stannators, six being chosen from each of the four stannaries: Foymore. Blackmore, Tywanhaile, Penwith and Kerrier. Thus the effects could be considered in the four regions of Cornwall, with stannators meeting locally but also meeting at the Stannary Palace in Lostwithiel – in effect, the Cornish Convocation or Parliament. Executive authority was completed

Duchy (Stannary Palace) in Lostwithiel sometime prior to 1878.

Duchy (Stannary Palace) Lostwithiel.

by the Lord Warden of the Stannaries. The surviving Stannary Palace and associated buildings are the only survivals of a very large complex, covering more than two acres, which consisted of the Great Hall (the Convocation Hall), Smelting Houses, the Coinage Hall, the Stannary Courts and the Stannary Prison.

At the height of the Civil War, Lostwithiel was taken by the Earl of Wessex who made it his headquarters, and he set about sacking the Stannary complex, destroying many documents. The part known as the Exchequer Hall was least damaged and this later became the Convocation Hall. The last Tinners' Parliament was held in the hall in 1751, but it is only through lack of use that the powers of the Stannary have been dissipated. The Stannary continued to have influence into the middle of the nineteenth century. In 1974, Cornish political activists revived the Stannary Parliament – in effect, giving them the right to veto British legislation. The revived Stannary Parliament works to support the wider aim of Cornish nationalism and the debate over the constitutional status of Cornwall.

● St Nighton's Cross, St Winnow, near Lostwithiel

SX 128599. *The cross is located on the southern side of the churchyard of St Nighton's Church. It lies just to the south of Lostwithiel.*

This is a wheel-headed wayside cross, which was probably much taller at one point in the past. Nearby is found on the north-western side of the Boconnoc Estate, a cross known as the Druid's Hill Cross. Although the Druid's Hill Cross has romantic overtones of the pre-Christian past, it was actually set up to record the loss in the aftermath of the battle at Braddock Down in the Civil War. Unfortunately there is no access granted to the public to the Druid's Hill Cross.

● The Giant's Hedge, Lerryn to Looe

SX 141572 to SX 247536. *This structure runs a considerable distance across south east Cornwall, though is best observed in Willake Wood (SX 153569).*

Remnants of this massive structure survive across much of south-east Cornwall, from the tidal reaches of the River Lerryn, to West Looe. It is generally thought to demark a sub-kingdom in the post-Roman period, and that it is the northern boundary. It must have required considerable people power to construct and suggests that whatever people or group were north of this boundary were not welcome below it. Most of the surviving hedge is about two and a half metres high with some sections still having a ditch in front of it. Many sections – particularly from Muchlarnick to West Looe - have been destroyed altogether. The name of the hedge demonstrates the giant feat in constructing the structure, but a popular folkloric couplet tells of another version of events:

> *One day, the Devil, having nothing to do*
> *Built a great hedge from Lerryn to Looe.*

One thing the Giant's Hedge proves is that Celtic unity in Cornwall was not always the case. This hedge is a good example of internal conflict and difference.

St Knighton's cross.

● Largin Castle Hill Fort, near West Taphouse

SX 169646. *On the A390 travelling east, turn left before West Taphouse. The fort is found in Largin Wood, accessed though Largin Farm.*

The oval fort consists of an inner and outer set of ramparts, constructed on a spur overlooking the River Fowey. It was constructed during the Iron Age, but was also probably used as a defensive structure during the Civil War.

● Sir Jonathan Trelawny, Church of St Nonna, Pelynt

SX 204551. *The church is found in the middle of the village on the B3359.*

Preserved in the church of St Nonna at Pelynt (pronounced 'Plint') are the chair and crook of Bishop Sir Jonathan Trelawny (1650–1721). Born at Trelawne in the parish of Pelynt, he was educated at Westminster School and Christ Church, Oxford. A staunch Royalist, he later became the Bishop of Exeter, and then at Winchester. Trelawny is famous for being one of the bishops tried under James II. Trelawny and other bishops petitioned against James II's Declaration of Indulgence in 1687 and 1688 (granting religious tolerance to Catholics). For this he was arrested and charged of seditious libel. He was imprisoned in the Tower of London. Eventually, Trelawny was acquitted and back in Pelynt, the community celebrated his victory – the church bells being rung. The incident was immortalised in 'The Song of the Western Men' by Robert Stephen Hawker, which has come to be known as 'Trelawny'. Some observers have pointed out that aspects of the song already existed in popular culture, and that Hawker merely formalised the lyrics. The urgent revolution alluded to in the song did not actually take place, but nevertheless the song represents a passionate, revolutionary and anti-metropolitan stance from Celtic Cornwall. It has continued to be sung at major gatherings, in pubs, and at rugby matches. Cornish language versions also exist.

From *The Song of the Western Men* by Robert Stephen Hawker

A good sword and a trusty hand!
A merry heart and true!
King James's men shall understand
What Cornish lads can do.

And have they fixed the where and when?
And shall Trelawny die?
Here's twenty thousand Cornish men
Will know the reason why!

Out spake their captain brave and bold,
A merry wight was he:
"If London Tower were Michael's hold,
We'll set Trelawny free!"

"We'll cross the Tamar, land to land,
The Severn is no stay,
With 'one and all', and hand in hand,
And who shall bid us nay?"

● Tregarrick, Tregarrick Farm, near Pelynt

SX 197554. *The farm is found along a minor road to the west of the village.*

The manor of Tregarrick belonged to the Winslade family. It was forfeited by John Winslade in the aftermath of the Prayer Book Rebellion of 1549, when ownership transferred to Sir Reginald Mohun.

Winslade was one of the leaders of the rebellion and lost his lands. Richard Carew says that 'Wideslade's sonne led a walking life, with his harpe, to gentlemen's houses, where through, and by his other active qualities, he was entitled Sir Tristram; neither wanted he, as some say, a belle I found, the more aptly to resemble his patterne.' The implication is that he became a kind of storyteller or bard, and was named perhaps ironically after the more famous Tristan.

● Bake Rings, near Pelynt

SX 187549. *On the B3359, in the middle of Pelynt, take the minor road east towards Headland Park. At a cross-roads, turn right heading north. The site is on the left-hand side.*

Dating from the Iron Age, this settlement is known locally as Bake Rings. It consists mainly of one circular rampart, but to the west of it is an additional, more rectangular enclosure. To the south east, on the other side of the road, is a further smaller embankment.

● Hall Rings Hill Fort, Pelynt

SX 214555. *Follow the B3359. The Rings may be reached by following a track turning east, just north of Pelynt Church,*

Prior to the twentieth century, the Rings here were in good condition but have since been ploughed out somewhat by agriculture. Hall Rings consist of an Iron Age hill fort with two banks and ditches. An additional banked area is found to the south west of the main fort.

St Nonna's Well, near Pelynt.

● St Nonna's Well, near Pelynt

SX 224565. *On the B3359, just before Pelynt, take the minor road east to Muchlarnick. Just before Sowden's Bridge, walk up Hobb Lane and find the well close to the hedge.*

Beneath a mature ash tree, this well is dedicated to St Nonna, who has a dedication at Altarnun on Bodmin Moor, Non being the mother of Saint David. The wellhouse is still in existence here, set back into the hillside The well has an intriguing well basin with carvings of a series of rings, each one of the rings containing a Celtic cross. These are still visible.

● St Cuby's Well, Duloe, near Looe

SX 241579. *The well is found on the main Looe road out of the village of Duloe, close to the sharp bend past the war memorial.*

This imposing, but very beautiful wellhouse is devoted to one of the Cornish-born saints who travelled elsewhere. Cuby supposedly hailed from Duloe (or perhaps Tregony) and travelled widely to Scotland, Wales, Ireland, Rome and Jerusalem. Cuby died on 5th November 555 and is buried at *Capel y Bedd* [the Chapel of the Grave] at his monastery on the island of Holyhead on Anglesey. Cuby may have been the son of Selevan. The wellhouse is well-designed with seating for pilgrims. Originally, it contained a granite bowl decorated with dolphins and a griffin. Anyone who stole it

St Cuby's granite bowl, Duloe.

would be cursed. Supposedly, one man tried to do so with a team of oxen, but on reaching the well, one of the oxen fell down dead, so he did not persist. The bowl can still be seen. It has survived in the nearby church and is used as a baptismal font. Moss and lichen have now taken hold of the delicately-carved cross which decorates the apex of the roof. Close by to St Cuby's Well is the Late Neolithic stone circle at Duloe.

Bosent cross.

● Bosent Cross, near Duloe

SX 222635. *This is found at a crossroads of minor roads between Duloe and Dobwalls.*

This cross is known locally as Bosent Cross and is thought to be in its original position. It is probably a boundary cross.

● Kilminorth Wood, near East Looe

SX 247538. *Begin your circular walk at the car park at West Looe.*

This is a section of very ancient woodland of some 45 hectares. It is composed of predominantly of oaks, though there are sycamores, birch and sweet chestnut. In the wood are to be found the badger and the fox. In Old Cornish these are *broch* and *louern*. Deer may also be observed: a stag was known as *caruu*, with a doe named a *da*.

● Tregoad Cross, Guildhall Museum, East Looe

SX 255533. *This is now located in the Guildhall Museum, in East Looe.*

This unusual wayside cross was found at Tregoad Farm in the 1930s. The monument was moved to the museum in 1973 and is cared for by Looe Old Cornwall Society.

● Portlooe Cross, near West Looe

SX 246528. *This cross stands at Portlooe Cross, just to the south west of West Looe.*

This is a slightly damaged wheel-headed cross, which has been cut square on one side.

● Neil Kennedy, Polperro

SX 212508. *Polperro is found at the end of the A387.*

One of the most prolific modern Cornish-language writers of Cornwall is Neil Kennedy. Kennedy was born in 1959, and grew up in Boscoppa, near St Austell and in Polperro. Kennedy now divides his time between Brittany and Cornwall, but has been a very active teacher of Cornish. The sea forms a metaphorical base for much of his poetry, as in the poem, titled *An Brennik* [*The Limpets*].

From *An Brennik* [*The Limpets*] by Neil Kennedy

Nag era ny war an doar,	[We aren't on the land,
na whath war voar,	nor yet the sea,
bes thera ny trega ter an deaw,	but we're between the two,
lebma'n tir a codha en moar,	where the land falls into the sea,
lebma'n bressel visquethak dirria,	where the everlasting war goes on,
ter an doar seh ha'n dowr gleb.	between the dry land and the wet water.
Gero ny gwitha gon leah cumpas,	Let's stand fast,
Ga peneek vel an brennik.	as unyielding as the limpets.]

● St Peter's Well, near Polperro

SX 205510. *At Polperro, take the minor road east to Lansallos. The well is located in the remains of quarry close to the main road.*

No well house remains here and the waters run into a natural stone basin. The rest of the water runs down to the village. The well was mentioned by Thomas Quiller Couch as being suitable for the treatment of 'inflamed eyes and other ailments'.

● Plain-an-gwarry, Talland, near Polperro

SX 211515. *The plain-an-gwarry is located in Pleaton Park opposite the caravan and camping site.*

Pleaton Park provides us with an interesting insight into its past. Pleaston may be derived from 'Plegian' which is Old English for 'play' and this would indicate that this was a former theatrical or sports location.

● Lammana, St George's Island, West Looe

SX 256514. *Access to the island may be gained a low tide, and there are occasional boat trips across.*

Looe or St George's Island is found about one mile off the coast and is around twenty-two acres in area, with a highest point of 150 feet above sea level. On a good day, the Lizard can be observed. The island was once known as Lammana. A Benedictine Chapel was built here in 1139 of which a few stones remain visible. Some observers have viewed this as the so-called Priory of Lammana. This was an outreach priory of Glastonbury, lasting there until around 1250. It is the belief of many that the chapel was established here because this is one of the locations around Cornwall connected with the coming to Britain of Joseph of Arimathea with the child Christ. Owing to Joseph's later returning to Britain with the holy thorns from Christ's cross, there was therefore a unique connection. Joseph is also said to have spat out apple pips from the tor, creating the orchards of south-west Britain.

Lammana may have links therefore with the legend of Avalon. Translated from Cornish, *Avalon* or *Avallen*, means 'island of apples', and it is the case that archaeologists have found a high proportion

Lammana, or St George's Island.

East and West Looe looking out towards St George's Island.

of apple seeds on the Iron Age lake village below the tor at Glastonbury, indicating the presence of such trees at one time. This could be before the Somerset levels were drained. Access to the island would have been permitted through waterways from the Bristol Channel. Arthur's body could therefore have been taken from Cornwall to Avalon by boat. The Cornish would have known the landscape following their surrender at the Battle of Dyrham, near Bath in 577. There is thought to have been the decisive battle which separated the Welsh Britons from the South West Britons. Remains of fortifications are to be found at Hinton Hill, just north of Dyrham in South Gloucestershire.

The place-name Glastonbury may be linked to the Old Cornish word *glastanen*, which translates to the oak, or more specifically the scarlet oak. This word is found in the so-called *Old Cornish Vocabulary*.

Excavations at Lammana Island in the 1930s.

● St Neot's Well, St Neot, near Liskeard

SX 183681. St Neot is found a little to the north of the A38 running through the Glyn Valley. The well is at the northern end of the village.

The place now known as St Neot was once the shrine to a Saint Gueyer. This was outlined in a text by Asser, a Welsh monk and friend of King Alfred the Great. Asser explains how he visited this location. St Neot is thus an addition to the layer of Celtic Christianity here. The precise identity of St Neot is difficult to determine. There are conflicting histories. He may well have been a monk who studied at Glastonbury, and then travelled west to Cornwall. He may also have been a relative of King Alfred the Great.

What is known is that he regularly took cold baths for the sake of his soul and had a clear affinity with wild animals. When living in the area he was once bathing when a doe appeared, chased by a pack of hounds. He gave the doe sanctuary and images of him are often pictured with the creature. Neot also used the deer of the area to pull a plough after the monastery's oxen had been stolen. Likewise, when his congregation complained that they were unable to attend mass because the crows kept eating their crops, he arranged for the birds to be captive until after the service. A story also lingers about him being given three fishes for his well. The supply would never end as long as he only took one to eat. Neot probably died around 877 and his remains were kept at St Neot until 974 when they were removed to Eynesbury in Huntingdonshire.

The well here is much altered from its Medieval origins. It was restored perhaps a little unsympathetically in a high Victorian manner in 1862. It is known for curing sickly children when visited in the first three mornings of May.

● The Windows at St Neot's Church, St Neot, near Liskeard.

SX 186678. *The church is located in the middle of the village.*

As well as being dedicated to St Neot, and containing some fascinating stained glass windows of him, the church also has a series of windows which present core images mirrored in the Medieval literary and theatrical culture of Cornwall. These are found in the so-called 'Creation' window. There is for example, an image of the Temptation, and the Holy Rood-related death of Adam. The latter is where Seth places the seeds of the rood into Adam's mouth – from which they will grow. Similar scenes are recognisable in the *Ordinalia*. In the detail of the Calloway window is an image of the Resurrection. There is also a fantastic image of all of the saints of Cornwall in God's lap.

● St Neot Cross, St Neot

SX 185674. *This cross is on the southern side of St Neot churchyard.*

If there is one cross which defines how interlaced knotwork should appear, then this cross is it. Knotwork is found on all fours side of the shaft. The cross head is damaged and is not original. Three other smaller crosses are to be found outside the southern porch of the churchyard. Trewarn Lantern Cross can be found close by and appears to depict St James the Greater as a pilgrim.

● Crowpound enclosure, St Neot

SX 176678. *This is located about half a mile due west of St Neot, next to a crossroads.*

This settlement enclosure is rectangular in shape with an entrance to the west of the structure. In the centre area is what appears to be a prehistoric round house, indicating long occupation at the site. The enclosure is difficult to date and could be variously from the Iron Age to the Early Medieval period.

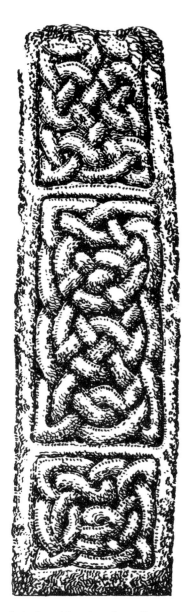

Interlaced knotwork on the cross shaft at St Neot.

● Goonzion enclosure, St Neot

SX 171677. *This is found a short distance away from Crowpound enclosure on the south side of the road.*

Once thought of as Roman, it is now accepted that this rectilinear enclosure is a native construction influenced by the Romans. On its eastern side are three lines of embankments, while entrance to the enclosure is from the south.

● Four Holed Cross, side of the A30, St Neot parish

SX 171749. *This cross is located on a band on the southern side of the A30. Care is required as this is fast stretch of road.*

St Neot is a large parish and on the northern edge of it is found a damaged Four Holed Cross. Due to its location it is probably one of the most viewed Celtic crosses in Cornwall. The upper part of the cross head is missing. The shaft is richly decorated. Further wayside crosses may also be observed at SX 184684, SX 188681, SX 21569, SX 196678 and at SX 166661.

● Golitha Falls, neat St Neot

SX 223685. *Off the B3360, park at Draynes Bridge and walk down the valley.*

At this point in the River Fowey's course from Bodmin Moor, the river drops quickly through a set of rocky outcrops and boulders. Beautifully situated, this woodland glade epitomises Celtic landscape in east Cornwall.

● Dozmary Pool, Bodmin Moor

SX 195745. *Turn off the A30 at Bolventor. Follow the road south to Dozmary Hill. A lane leads to the Pool.*

Dozmary Pool is a small lake found on Bodmin Moor. Through various versions of the Arthurian matter, this is one site that is claimed to be the home of the Lady of the Lake. Here, Arthur rowed out onto the lake and received the sword Excalibur from her. The pool is also the location where Bedivere returned Excalibur to its depths after Arthur's death at the Battle of Camlann. The earlier spelling of the location was Dozmaré. The pool has also been associated with the folktale of Jan Tregeagle. After he made his pact with the Devil, Tregeagle was punished with the task of dipping the water out of Dozmary Pool with a limpet shell, and then after his death, he was damned to its bottoms.

● King Doniert Stone and Half Stone, St Cleer

SX 236688. *The stone is found north west of the village of St Cleer.*

The remains of this stone have formed an iconic image of Cornwall over the years. In fact, the stone is divided into a memorial cross base, and another 'half stone'. The cross head and shaft have been lost. On the main face of the base stone is a Latin inscription in insular Celtic script which reads

DONIERT ROGAVIT PRO ANIMA. This translates to 'Doniert has asked prayers for his soul'. Doniert is generally thought to have been King Dungarth, who according to the Welsh Annals, drowned in 875 – probably in the River Fowey. The reverse of this inscription displays four knots, two of which have survived intact. There are further interlacing designs on the other panels. Next to it stands the other 'half stone' which is believed to be a separate monument. An eight-cord plait decorates the stone on one face.

● St Cleer Holy Well, St Cleer

SX 249683. *The chapel building is in the middle of the village on the road leading north east.*

St Cleer is probably St Clare or Clara. Confusion remains over whether the saint here was male or female. If he was male, then apparently, in his local monastery he was pestered by the attentions of a local noblewoman. This being the case, he then fled to an isolated hermitage in Normandy – now known as St-Claire-sur-Epte If female, then the same chase was enacted by a local chieftain. St Cleer's feast day is 4 November, and his/her well is covered by a fifteenth-century structure with an icon (more recently carved) in one of its nooks. The well was reputedly once used as a ducking pool by local people.

St Cleer Holy Well.

St Cleer Holy Well.

● Other crosses, St Cleer

SW 247681, SW 249683, SW 237704, SW 227685, SW 255703.

In the churchyard, there is a fragment of what was probably a much taller cross (SW 247681). It is found on the south side of the churchyard. Next to the St Cleer Holy Well is a large granite Latin cross (SW 249683) and north of St Cleer – on the road to Siblyback Reservoir – is to be found Crylla cross-shaft (SW 237704). North west of St Cleer – at the village of Redgate – is a another Latin style cross (SW 227685). The most striking of the other crosses found around St Cleer is the famous Long Tom close to Minions village (SW 255703). It may well have been carved from a menhir *in situ*.

● Stowe's Pound tor enclosure, near Minions

SX 258725. *Park at the car park at Minions. The Pound is around a mile to the north west.*

The lower and larger enclosure at Stowe's Pound dates to the Late Bronze Age. The upper enclosure ringing the tor is a Neolithic tor enclosure; at the top of which is located the curious stone structure known as the Cheesewring. To the south are the three Late Neolithic stone circles known as the Hurlers. A further two circles have been discovered, but the stones are no longer *in situ*.

● William Henry Paynter, The Cheesewring, near Minions

SX 258724. *The Cheesewring is located within Stowe's Pound.*

William Henry Paynter (1901-1976) was a folklorist and antiquarian, who during the middle decades of the twentieth century, collected much surviving witch-lore and pagan belief (rooted in the Celtic identity) of Cornwall. Paynter was instrumental in ensuring such activity was collected as part of the wider Cornish Revival. However, in a broadly Christian society, he still found material on pagan Cornwall difficult to place. Born in Callington, he eventually opened a small museum in East Looe, devoted to these interests, which ran from 1959 to the year of his death. He was a member of the Cornish Gorsedd and lead the Furry Dance at St Cleer in the late 1940s. Jason Semmens has recently drawn attention to Paynter's important place in Celtic Cornwall, labelling him the 'Cornish Witch-finder'. Paynter was fascinated with places like the Cheesewring and the cave of primitive mathematician Daniel Gumb, which is close by. After he was cremated, his ashes were scattered at the Cheesewring.

The Cheesewring.

● South Phoenix Mine, near Minions

SX 280716. *South Phoenix Mine is due north from the village of Minions.*

The South Caradon area has been heavily mined over the years, and the South Caradon Copper Mine, about one mile to the south west of the Caradon transmitter, was the largest copper mine in Britain in the middle of the nineteenth century. Caradon was truly a place where the industrial Celt excelled. South Phoenix Mine lies just a short distance from Minions village, and is now the Minions Heritage Centre. Much quarrying also took place in the local area. All across this region of Cornwall are aban-

doned engine houses, and their power and significance is expressed in the poetry of writers such as Edwin Chirgwin (1892-1960) who offers a lament to the industrial age in Cornwall. Chirgwin was one of the writers in Cornish who revived the composition of poetry in the post-war period.

From *An Jynjy Gesys dhe Goll* [*The Abandoned Engine House*] by Edwin Chirgwin

My a-gews hep let, my a-gan a goll,
War ow fossow los ydhyow gwer a dyf,
Lun a wakter of, ynnof lyes toll,
Genef bryny du powes whek a-gyf.

My a-lavar whath a'n bledhynnow pell
Pan o lun a whel pyth yu gwak yn whyr;
Kynth of trygva taw, gwyns ha glaw a-dell
Kepar del o tellys gans tus yn-lur.

[I speak without hindrance. I sing of loss,
green ivy grows on my grey walls,
I am full of emptiness, there are many holes
   in me,
and black crows get pleasant rest from me.

I still tell of the distant years
when what is now completely empty was once
   full of work,
although I am a dwelling place in silence, wind
   and rain
make holes in me just as men used to make
   holes in the earth.]

● Settlements. Craddock Moor, near Minions

SX 244724. *From Minions, walk to the disused quarry on Craddock Moor. These settlements are to the west of this.*

This complex site was probably first settled in the Bronze Age. The Iron Age sees only seasonal occupation with either some re-use of round houses or cairns as temporary shelters as people made use of the summer pastures. The interconnecting grazings and turbaries look to be shared amongst several households here, as well as the later Medieval settlement just to the north at SX 242729.

● Newel Tor Settlement, Newel Tor, near Minions

SX 239742. *From Minions, walk in a north-easterly direction across Witheybrook Marsh to Newel Tor.*

This is a post-Medieval farm whose fields appear to have reused prehistoric ones. There are still Middle Bronze Age round-houses scattered amongst these fields, with other round houses among unperpetuated prehistoric fields further up the slope. It is obvious that such settlements had a high degree of community cooperation and networking which is now again being considered as relevant in the twenty-first century.

● Hut Circles and Trewortha, Twelve Men's Moor, near Coad's Green

SX 255761. *This is best accessed off the A30. Follow the B3257 to Congdon's Shop, and then follow the B3254 to Berrowbridge. From Berrowbridge, walk through Rocky Wood up onto the Moor.*

Although off the beaten track, these Middle Bronze Age round houses have spectacular views of the surrounding moorland. To the south is another Middle Bronze Age settlement and field system at SX 257756. To the east is the so-called King Arthur's Bed (SX 248758), and close by is Trewortha – a ruined Medieval village (SX 225762). These are some of the best preserved Longhouses to be found in Cornwall. Just to the south of the Medieval village is another set of hut circles and further field systems. Some observers believe that this was once called Smallacombe.

⬤ Stannary Town, Liskeard

SX 252647. *Liskeard is located off the A38.*

Liskeard is known in Cornish as *Lescarret*, and it was one of Cornwall's coinage towns; its importance demonstrated by the fact that it had two Members of Parliament up until the opening of the nineteenth century. Of note there is Stuart House, used by Charles I in 1644 as a lodging house in Cornwall. The house is now used for community activities and arts. During the late twentieth century, a high number of revived Cornish speakers were clustered around the town. The Cornish Gorsedd was held there in 1969 and 1996.

⬤ Celtic-themed mural, Liskeard

SX 252647. *The mural is located on the Parade.*

The outer walls of the Co-operative food store in Liskeard are decorated with a Celtic-themed mural – of mosaic construction. The right-hand panel features a Celtic cross, while the left panel has a quoit (probably constructed before any Celtic language is attested) and an engine house.

⬤ Modern Celtic crosses, Liskeard

SX 243843, SX 259841, SX259653, SX 255650. *The crosses are found at all major entrances and exits of the town.*

To celebrate the millennium, the citizens and council of Liskeard have positioned a set of four Celtic crosses at the main entrances and exits of the town. This displays the continuum of this type of monument in Celtic Cornwall.

⬤ St Martin's Well, Liskeard

SX 252644. *The well is located at the back of the market where Well Street joins Market Lane.*

This well is also known as the Pipe Well because of the four pipes which carry water from it into the adjoining trough. The well had known healing qualities.

The Pipe Well, Liskeard.

● Plain-an-gwarry, Liskeard

SX 204638. *The field for the 'Play Park' is located close to Trevelmond Methodist Church. Take the lane by the Old Chapel. The site is just opposite.*

The surviving Tithe maps shows that a 'Play Park' was once owned by the tenement of Caduscott. Given the size of Liskeard as a settlement it would seem logical that it had its own drama, but we have no knowledge of what the subject matter would be.

● Culverland Cross, St Martin's Churchyard, Liskeard

SX 253644. *This cross is found in the north-west of the churchyard.*

This is a Latin style cross. On the monument is a plaque which reads 'This ancient cross probably the original Culverland Cross was found at land at Vensloe, Liskeard, the property of Samuel Bone, Churchwarden and Mayor of Liskeard and re-erected by him Sept. 1908'.

● Pro-Cornish graffiti, Liskeard.

SX 249641. *This is best seen by travelling east on the A38.*

Contemporary graffiti often expresses Cornish Celicity in the wake of seemingly unstoppable English cultural influence. The traces of a particularly fine work can still be seen on concrete panelling on the A390, commemorating the 1497 rebellion. Alternative readings of history are also found at key English Heritage properties, and over several bridges around Camborne, Hayle and Lelant, and at Botallack. Another particularly good example is found on the walls outside South Crofty in West Cornwall (SW 664412). It reads 'Cornish lads are fishermen and Cornish lads are miners too, but when the fish and tin are gone, what are Cornish lads to do?' This was daubed c.1998.

● St Keyne's Well, near Liskeard

SX 247503. *Follow the B2345 from Liskeard to the village of St Keyne. The well is at a road junction in the bottom of the valley.*

Saint Keyne was one of the many daughters of Brychan from Brecon in South Wales. There is a Late Medieval *Life* of the saint and we know that as well as initially settling on the left bank of the River Severn, she later travelled to Cornwall. She may be the same saint commemorated in Truro – at St Kenwyn (St Kenwyn here probably affixing *gwyn* [white, holy or virginal] to her name). A well there is named St Kenwyn's well and is to be found at SW 819458. Clearly Saint Keyne was a powerful saint because her life explains how she was able to turn snakes into stone. Despite this heritage, the well is perhaps best known for determining who will have the power in a marriage, famously versified by Robert Southey (1774-1843). Poetic interpretations of the legend have an earlier pedigree however, with east Cornwall Anglo-Cornish writer Richard Carew also writing about it in 1602. The custom is that whoever first drinks water from the well will have control. The well-advised will take a small bottle with them to sup of just after exchanging their vows. Although

St Keyne's Well.

The site of St Keyne's Well c.1890.

fanciful, interest of Celtic people and their important relationship with the power of water is embodied in this custom.

The Well of St Keyne by Richard Carew (1602)

In name, in shape, in quality,
  The well is very quaint;
The name to lot of Keyne befell,
  No over-holy saint.
The shape - four trees of diverse kinds,
  Withy, oke, elme and ash,
Make with their roots an arched roofe,
  Whose floore this spring doth wash.
The quality - that man or wife,
  Whose chance or choice attaines,
First of the sacred stream to drinke,
  Thereby the mastry gaines.

● Hendra Farm, near Liskeard

SX 268655. *Hendra Farm is located north-east of Liskeard.*

The practice of transhumance (the seasonal movement of people with their livestock over a short distance) has deep roots in Celtic Cornwall. Transhumance depends on the existence of hamlets, the practice of communal agriculture and large areas of rough ground. Not limited to upland areas, it permeated Cornish life from the Late Bronze Age to the Early Medieval period. An understanding of this practice may be fundamental to our awareness of the sophisticated inter-relationship between the natural world and the cultural world and the legacy of this for present day Cornwall. The place name Hendra is a compound of the Cornish *hen* meaning 'ancient' and *dre* meaning 'farming estate, or homestead'. *Havos*, as in the nearby Hammett at Quethiock, is derived from the Cornish *haf* meaning 'summer' and *bos* meaning 'dwelling'. Welsh has the equivalents of *hendre* and *hafod*. This linguistic connection suggests that transhumance was practised in both Cornwall and Wales by the late seventh century.

● Hendra Cross, near Liskeard

SX 268655. *The cross is on private property but can be viewed from a footpath.*

The cross here was originally part of a gatepost and has been restored. It displays a Latin cross.

● Padderbury Top Hill Fort, Doddycross, near Menheniot

SX 314611. *This is located on the east side of the road from Doddycross to the A390.*

Padderbury Top is an Iron Age hill fort, though much of it has been ploughed out. A concentric circle, the fort appears to have consisted of an inner and outer line of defence. Aerial photography has noted the presence of crop marks, indicating another smaller fort to the south west on the opposite side of the road. The Cornish Gorsedd conducted its ceremonies here in 1934.

● *Tyr ha Tavas*, Padderbury Top, Menheniot

SX 314611. *This is located on the east side of the road from Doddycross to the A390.*

One of the bards initiated at Paddersbury Top in 1934 was Cecil Beer (1902-1998). In the 1930s, Beer, alongside E.H.T. Hambly, E.E. Morton Nance and others formed a movement known as *Tyr ha Tavas* [Land and Language]. Intended as a pressure group and cultural organisation, the group had a number of clear objectives, which were to:

(a) Unite Cornish people throughout the world to strengthen the bonds of kinship in the building of a greater Cornwall.

(b) Preserve and develop in youth of Cornwall love and understanding of their country and history.

(c) Encourage an expression in Music, Drama, Literature, Art and other cultural forms of the innate Cornish instinct.

(d) Encourage the practice of typical Cornish sports, and the maintenance of particularly Cornish customs.

(e) Utilise the Cornish language as a visible sign of nationality, and as a means of helping Cornish people to realise their kinship with other Celtic races.

(f) Show Cornish people what Cornishmen have done, and what they can still do to help the world.

Although to an extent, London based, this short-lived movement initiated much conscience-raising with their motto being *Bedheugh Benytha Kernewek* [Remain forever Cornish]. The objectives of *Tyr ha Tavas* certainly influenced later political moves in Cornwall in the post-war period. In the 1970s, Beer moved to Australia, where he was closely involved in meetings of Cornish Bards there.

● Cadson Bury Hill Fort, St Ive, near Callington

SX 343674. *Travelling east on the A390 from Liskeard to Callington, park at Newbridge and walk up the track heading south. Cadson Bury is on the right-hand side.*

Composed of a large, single rampart, this elongated and sizeable Iron Age hill fort commands an impressive view of the local area. Two entrances break the rampart – one on the east, another on the west.

● St Ive Cross Chapel, St Ive, near Callington

SX 314672. *St Ive is on the A390 from Liskeard to Callington. The chapel is close by at St Ive Cross.*

St Ive Cross Chapel began in 1833 but was developed in 1860. Over the twentieth century there has grown a tradition of holding a Christmas service in the Cornish language. Nearby St Ive Church is dedicated to St Ivo, who was a Medieval English saint with no connection to St Ia.

● St Ive Churchyard Cross, St Ive, near Callington

SX 309671. *The cross is on the eastern side of the churchyard.*

This is a Latin wayside cross, for a long time used locally as a gatepost, but moved to the churchyard in the early twentieth century.

● Old Rectory Cross, St Ive, near Callington

SX 309671. *The cross is on the southern side of the churchyard.*

This cross was found in the old rectory and although now quite short in height, was probably once a wheel-headed wayside cross.

● Midsummer Bonfire, Kit Hill, Callington

SX 374713. *Follow the A388 to Callington. Take the B3257 around the north of Kit Hill. There are various parking places, with an easy walk to the summit.*

Kit Hill summit is dominated by an ornate mine chimney.

For much of the twentieth and twenty-first centuries Callington Old Cornwall society has lit a bonfire at the top of Kit Hill. Midsummer and midwinter bonfires were traditionally very popular in Celtic Cornwall. A chain of bonfires runs from Kit Hill, to St Breock beacon, Castle-an-Dinas, Redruth and Penzance. Robert Morton Nance has suggested some words for the benediction of the midsummer bonfires of Cornwall:

Herwyth usadaow afan hendasow yn termynyow kens, awotta n yow cul agan Tansys Golowan, haneth yn cres an Haf.

[According to the custom of our forefathers in days of old, behold us making our Midsummer Bonfire, this night in the middle of Summer.]

● How Culhwch Won Olwen, Callington

SX 358697. *Callington is on the A388.*

This is a text from the collection of Welsh Medieval tales known as the *Mabinogi* (c.1000). This segment portrays a Celtic-speaking Britain in which even the Romans have not yet arrived. In order to marry Olwen, the giant's daughter, Culhwch has to obtain the magical razor, shears and comb from the Twrch Trwyth, a giant boar. Arthur and his men help him, and during the chase pursue the boar to Cornwall where Arthur has a residence. Kelli Wig is traditionally identified as being Callington, although the village just north of Callington (Kelly Bray) may also provide a connection. The story runs as follows:

Twrch Trwyth went between Tawy and Ewyas. Arthur summoned Cornwall and Devon to meet him at the mouth of the Severn. And Arthur said to the soldiers of this island, "The Twrch Trwyth has killed many of my men. By the courage of men, while I am alive he will not go to Cornwall. I shall not pursue him further but strive with him soul for soul. You do as you may." What they did on his advice was to send out a troop of horsemen, with the dogs of the Island as far as Ewyas and he returned from there to the Severn and there, all the experienced soldiers of this Island ambushed him, and drove him by main force into the Severn, and Mabon son of Modron on Gwyn of the Dark Mane, the stallion of Gweddw, went with him into the Severn, and also Gorau, son of Cystenin, and Menw, son of Teirgwaedd, between Lake Lliwan and the Mouth of the Wye and there, Arthur and the champions of Britain fell on him. Osla of the big knife approached and also Manawydan, son of Llyr, and Cacmwri, the servant of Arthur, and Gwyn-gelli assailed him and grabbed hold first of his feet and ducked him in the Severn until he was covered by the billows. Mabon, son of Modron, spurred fiercely from one side and got the razor from him, and from the other side, Cyledr the Wild approached on his horse and took the shears from him. Before they got the comb he got his feet on dry land, and as soon as he reached the land, no dog or man or horse could keep up with him until he reached Cornwall. For all the evil they suffered trying to get those treasures from him, they got worse trying to save the two men from drowning. As Cacmwri was being pulled up two millstones dragged him into the deep. As Osla of the big knife was running after the boar, the knife fell from his sheath and he lost it. After that, his sheath was full of water: as he was pulled up, it pulled him into the deep. From there Arthur and the hosts went on until they overtook him in Cornwall. The evil that they had got from him up till then was like play compared with what they got from him in trying to get the comb. For all the evils the comb was got from him. From there, he was hunted out of Cornwall, and he was driven towards the sea. It was not known from then on where he went, or Aned and Athlem with him. And from there, Arthur went to bathe and to rest from his tiredness in Callington in Cornwall.

● The Battle of Hingston Down, Callington

SX 385713. *Hingston Down is located to the east of Callington, just north of the A390 between Callington and Gunislake.*

As Anglo-Saxon incursions into Cornwall became more common-place in the ninth century, we know of one major battle that occurred on Hingston Down in 838. Cornwall had resisted Anglo-Saxon advances fairly well until this point, when King Ecgbert decided to deal with the western Celts. It seems that the Cornish had formed some kind of alliance with Danish Vikings, which allowed them to conduct raids on Saxon ports in Wessex. Ecgbert decided to enact revenge and faced a combined Cornish and Viking army close to present-day Callington. Ecgbert won the battle but could not completely dominate the Cornish. A year later, he was dead.

An alternative suggestion for the site of this battle has been suggested. This is at Hingston Down – a spur hill, located just east of Mortonhampstead. Two reasons are offered for this location: firstly, it lies on an ancient trackway from Plymouth Sound (where the Danish fleet is believed to have landed); secondly, the Exe-Taw rivers were more likely a division between Cornish and Saxon lands. The Saxons would only have some ten miles to retreat to Exeter if this were the battle site.

● Inscribed Stone, South Hill, near Callington

SX 328726. *South Hill is around three miles north west of Callington. The stone is found on the south side of the churchyard.*

Decorated with a Chi Rho symbol at the top of the stone, it also holds a Latin inscription: CVMRECIN FILI MAVC. This translate to 'Cumregnus, the son of Maucus'. The stone is probably from the sixth century and these names appear to be Brythonic Celtic.

● Northcombe Farm Cross, near Linkinhorne

SX 294748. *The cross is on private ground but can be seen from the road.*

Although somewhat damaged, a distinctive cross can still be observed. The cross is mounted on an old millstone.

● Dupath Well, near Callington

SX 375692. *The well is located just off the A388. Follow the road to the farm and walk through the farm buildings. The well is on the right hand side of the path.*

Dupath Well.

The well at Dupath was designed and built by the Augustinian canons of St German's Priory in 1510 and they cared for it until the dissolution of the monasteries in 1538. The structure is built from sturdy granite blocks and features a bell-cote. There is a remarkable cruciform well basin inside, with the waters supposedly a cure for whooping cough. The four corners of the structure have crocketted pinnacles. It is said that it was constructed at the site of a duel between two Saxons: Sir Colan and Gotlieb over the hand of a lady. The lady had been in love with Colan since childhood, but her father much favoured the richer Gotlieb. Two different endings to the narrative are known. In one, both combatants die, the waters from the well could not save them. In another version, by imbibing the holy waters, Colan survived and built the wellhouse in an act of remorse over the death of Gotlieb. The Anglo-Cornish poet Robert Stephen Hawker who committed the story to verse, only names the two Saxons Siward and Githa. Despite the Saxon connection, the Well has come to represent much about the design and feel of wells in Celtic Cornwall.

From 'Dupath Well' by Robert Stephen Hawker

A roof must shade that storied stream,
Her dying lord's remember'd theme;
A daily vow that lady said
Where glory wreath'd the hero dead.

Gaze, maiden, gave on Dupath Well,
Time yet hath spar'd that solemn cell –
In memory of old love and pride:
Hear how the noble Siward died.

● Cotehele House and Wood, Cotehele

SX 422686. *Cotehele House and Wood are found off the A388 on the banks of the River Tamar.*

Cotehele House is a Medieval and Tudor house close to Calstock. Its main phases of building were completed by Sir Richard Edgcumbe from 1485-9 and his son, Piers Edgcumbe from 1489-1520. The family later moved south to Mount Edgcumbe across from Plymouth. Cotehele probably means *coes* or *cuit heyl* [wood on an estuary]. The woods here have a remarkable range of trees. Trees are well-recorded in the *Old Cornish Vocabulary*, and Celtic peoples often have an affiliation with them. Among the trees is the *onnen* [ash tree]. Celtic peoples accorded ash trees with magical properties. Folklore often records fairies living in ash groves.

Robert Hunt witnessed an ill child passed through a cleft in an ash. If the cleft tree reunited, then the child would recover, but only if he or she was washed in the dew from the branches of the tree on successive mornings. *Dar* means oak tree. Oaks have magical significance in many Celtic cultures. There is, as Nora Chadwick has noted, considerable folkloric evidence linking the stunted oak groves at Wistman's Wood on Dartmoor with druidic activity. It might have been a 'Nematon' - a sacred grove.

Hiven translates to yew tree. The yew symbolised immortality due to its incredible longevity, and was often planted in churchyards in Cornwall. Though an evergreen, the yew's berries are poisonous. Traditionally, yew was often used for furniture. *Colpiden* translates to the hazel tree. The hazel was also much associated with fairy activity. Hazelwood was sacred to poets in many Celtic cultures. In Cornwall hazel twigs were apparently used in the adder stones worn as amulets by Druids. *Guernen* is the elder tree. Elders were used in ancient times to diagnose illness. Elderberries were used to make wine, and as a 'dirty purple' dye.

● Plain-an-gwarry, Stoke Climsland

SX 361744. *This is located in the field immediately to the west of the original churchyard. It is now an additional graveyard.*

The Church Terrier of 1601 talks of a 'playing close' found here. If this were the case, this is interesting since playing places are generally less common in east Cornwall.

● St Mellor's Well, Linkinhorne

SX 319732. *Linkinhorne is located off the A388, via the B3257 to Bray Shop. The well is found to the south of the village via a public footpath.*

The environment of this well is much untouched, with the waters of the well running into the River Lynher. Mellor is probably the same saint as Mylor found in west Cornwall. A niche for an image of the saint remains. There are two lives which might provide the origin for this well. The first is the Breton abbot-bishop, but there is another Mellor who was martyred. His father was Melian, the Duke of Cornwall, and Melian was murdered by the last king of Devonshire, one Rivoid. To complicate matters, Melian was married to a woman who was Rivoid's sister. When the attack happened Mellor was just a child of seven years old, and he lost a hand and a foot in the attack. These were then replaced by a silver hand and a bronze foot which grew naturally with him over his life. This is a motif which occurs often in the lives of saints in Cornwall. However, Rivoid continued his murderous ways and had Mellor decapitated in 411. This was completed by his foster father. Such a story does fit the east Cornwall location of Linkinhorne.

St Mellor's Well, Linkinhorne.

● St Indract's Well, Halton Quay, near St Dominick

SX 417659. *On the A388, close to St Mellion, take the road to Halton Bardon and then on to Halton Quay. The well is found a little distance to the north of the quay.*

Marian associations have now supplemented the original saint associated with the well: St Indract, who arrived here from Ireland, travelling with his sister St Dominica up the River Tamar, to settle at Chapel Farm where there may be found the remains of a chapel. Nearby St Dominick is named after her. Indract meanwhile, is associated with Glastonbury in Somerset. The well was restored in the 1950s.

● The Well of St Mary the Virgin, Botus Fleming

SX 405614. *Botus Fleming is can be reached off the A388. On the road to Moditonham Quay, the well is next to the old school building.*

This well matches other Marian associations in south east Cornwall. The well is now dry though a statue of the Virgin is located inside. Botus Fleming, or more correctly Botusfleming, is an unusual Celtic place-name, probably composed originally of *Bod* [dwelling] but the rest of the name is unclear. It might be *Flumiet*; thus Flumiet's dwelling. Robert Morton Nance wrote a number of prayers for different occasions. One such prayer is '*Pysadow dhe Fenten Sans* [Prayer at a Holy Well]':

A Dhew, gans Nep us an fenten a vewnansm dre dregereth a Nep yu ny dhe vos dastenythys a dhowr ha'n Spyrys Sans, ha bos gwres dhe eva pup-oll a un Spyrys.

[O God, with Whom is the well of life, by Whose mercy we have been born again of water and the Holy Ghost, and have been made to drink of one spirit.]

● Churchyard Cross, Quethiock

SX 312647. *Quethiock is found four miles to the east of Liskeard, with access off the A38. The cross is easily located in the churchyard.*

This is the tallest cross in Cornwall and was re-erected in 1881. The cross and the shaft are heavily decorated, though somewhat worn.

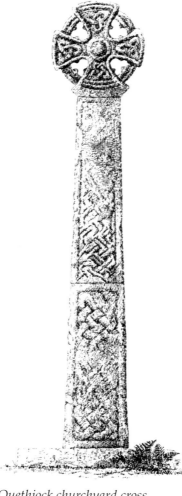

Quethiock churchyard cross.

● St German's Priory, St Germans

SX 359578. *St Germans is best accessed off the A38 at Tideford. The priory is close to the centre of the village.*

The present church is a large Norman building which replaced an Anglo-Saxon construction, which was the cathedral of the Bishops of Cornwall. The church is dedicated to St Germanus and in 926 King Athelstan appointed Conan as the bishop of Cornwall. The bishopric was short-lived however, with it being transferred to Crediton in 1042. A monastery developed along the church and between 1161 and 1184 operated as an Augustinian priory. After the dissolution, the priory was abolished and its buildings became a private house, part of the Eliot family. Before the development of Glasney College at Penryn, St Germans was likely to have been one of the major centres of Cornu-Celtic literary activity.

● *The Prophecy of Merlin* by John of Cornwall, St Germans

SX 359578. *A feel for the impact of Norman culture on Celtic Cornwall can see seen in the large, arched and ornate western doorway of the church.*

John of Cornwall, or in Latin *Johannes Cornubiensis* or Johannes de Sancto Germano was a Christian teacher and scholar, who we know was living in Paris in around 1176. Little is known of his life, but we may surmise that he was originally from St Germans. As was the trend during this period, John of Cornwall wrote a wild and imaginative interpretation of a prophecy of Merlin. We know such works were fashionable since a major prophetic section devoted to Merlin is also found in Geoffrey of Monmouth's *The History of the Kings of Britain*. Geoffrey died in 1155 so they were operating in a very similar time period. From his note and glosses it would appear that at one point this Prophecy of Merlin, was, in fact, written in Cornish, giving us a tantalising picture of Celtic literature in Cornwall during this age. Translated from the Latin, one section reads:

Learn the way at last, Cornwall, learn the work.
And our cradles shall bring back the Saxon mourning.
Why is our hand so generous? Who afterwards will be considered free?
Where the Great Bear looks, where the Tamar goes out into the South,
by the yoke of Brentigia the French lord it everywhere,
if you would continue to live, o queen, you so will so unplough,
out of which rodent-catchers and buck goats are multiplied in value.
The fury of the winds and every revolt against the citizens
will rage until the sad anger of the thunder ceases.

Some observers such as Paul Broadhurst have made connections with the rise of the Great Bear over Tintagel island at the winter solstice, so the piece is embedded with Arthuriana, while at the same time, there is clearly opposition to Norman rule. Several of the glosses on the text are interesting. One note talks of a location named Periron in the 'British tongue': 'a King grey like his mare. Of Periron. He says this about his arrival in Cornwall and because he then besieged the castle at Periron which is called Tintagel.' This would seem to be an alternative name for Tintagel castle. Also, we learn of another name for what is probably Bodmin Moor: 'Brentigia is a certain wilderness in Cornwall and in our language it is called the 'Down of the Tree', in the language of the Saxon's Fowey Moor'.

● Carracawn Cross, near St Germans

SX 321573. *This cross is found on minor road between St Germans and Hessenford.*

This cross was once located by the old Carracawn turnpike. It is a Latin type of wayside cross.

● The River Tamar, near Saltash

SX 435595. *There are good views of the river from both the Cornish and English side.*

Celtic Cornwall's isolation and difference has been reinforced over the centuries by the River Tamar. The Tamar's source is less than 4 miles from the north Cornish coast but it flows southward. At is mouth, the river flows into an area of water known as the Hamoaze before entering Plymouth Sound. Tributaries of the river on the Cornish side include the rivers Inny, Ottery, Kensey and Lynher, and on the English side, the Deer and Tavy. The east bank of the Tamar was fixed as the border of Cornwall by King Athelstan in 936, but in a few places along the river the border deviates slightly from the river. A good example of this is Bridgerule, which is on the Cornish side but is presently in England. The river is famous for its quality of salmon; salmon featuring often in Celtic folklore.

● Tamar Bridge, near Saltash

SX 430587. *Drive across the bridge and park at the service area near the toll booths.*

The Tamar Bridge is the major road bridge in south-west Britain carrying traffic from Cornwall into England. Construction of the bridge began in 1959, running parallel to Isambard Kingdom Brunel's Royal Albert Bridge. The bridge was needed because the ferries just downstream of the current bridge no longer had the capacity to carry all the traffic required. The bridge opened in 1961 with three lanes of traffic, but was modified in 2001 to include two additional decks. The bridge has bi-lingual signage on both pillars on the western side of the bridge. The signs read Kernow a'gas Dynergh [Welcome to Cornwall]. The bridge has often been the subject of Cornish protest through the years.

● Great Western Railway, Royal Albert Bridge, near Saltash

SX 435586. *The bridge can be observed from the service areas near the toll booths.*

The Great Western Railway (known popularly as 'God's Wonderful Railway') was a British Railway company that served south-west Britain and Wales. If was founded in 1833, and was finally amalgamated into the Western Region of British Railways in 1947. The Royal Albert Bridge, linking Cornwall to England, was designed by Isambard Kingdom Brunel (1806-1859) and was completed in 1859. The line was famous for its chocolate and cream coaches and, firstly, their holly green locomotive engines and later, Brunswick-green locomotive engines. The railway often promoted its links to Celtic Cornwall, and in tandem with the wider Celto-Cornish revival in Cornwall, marked Cornwall as an exotic destination. It also published booklets based on Celtic legend and lore. The Great Western Railway named a number of locomotives with Celtic-inspired names. Among these were Armorel, Avalon, Caerhays Castle, Camelot, Chough, City of Truro, Duke of Cornwall, Excalibur, Fowey Castle, Guinevere, Isle of Tresco, King Arthur, Lady of the Lake, Launceston Castle, Lyonesse, Merlin, Mounts Bay, One and All, Pendragon, Penzance, River Tamar, Tintagel and Tintagel Castle,

● The Story of Tamara, River Tamar

SX 440610. *There is a car park at the bottom of Saltash, on the western bank of the river. Look north to see where the two rivers converge.*

The River Tamar has its own origin story, recounted by Robert Hunt. The lovely nymph Tamara was born in a cavern. Her parents were spirits of the earth, but Tamara loved the light of day. Her parents warned Tamara about the dangers of the upper world but that never stopped her wanting to be there. Two sons of Dartmoor giants – named Tavy and Tawrage – wanted to possess her. Under a bush in Morwenstow they came upon her and tried to persuade her to declare which one of them she should prefer. Her parents missed Tamara, and when her gnome father searched for her, he found her seated between the two sons of the giants. He caused a deep sleep to fall on them and tried to persuade Tamara to return to the earth. She would not however, and so in his rage her father turned her into a river which would forever wind to the ocean. When Tavy awoke he instantly knew of the metamorphosis and transformed himself into a stream, running by her side, eventually mingling with her. When Tawrage awoke he thought she had been transformed into a stream by an enchanter. He prayed that he too would be transformed, but he mistook the road which Tamara travelled, and so he still flows – but away from Tamara, forever and forever. A recent Cornish language film, *Tamara* (2011), directed by Will Coleman, celebrates this legend.

● Carkeel Roundabout, near Saltash

SX 413601 *This roundabout is located a short distance from the Saltash tunnel, to the north-western side of the town.*

There have been numerous consultations about Cornwall constructing its own large-scale contemporary Celtic cross to welcome visitors to the territory. Following planning debates about the location of this, a compromise was reached by constructing the roundabout at Carkeel in the shape of a wheel-headed Celtic cross. The planting on the roundabout island symbolises the bosses found in real crosses. Carkeel probably means 'ridge fort'.

● Trematon Castle, near Saltash

SX 408581. *The village of Trematon is found a short distance off the A38 close to Saltash. The castle is one and half miles south east of the village near the hamlet of Tehan. The castle is owned by the Duchy of Cornwall and is leased to a private tenant, but is visible from the from the road.*

Trematon Castle.

Similar in style to the more famous Restormel Castle, this motte and bailey style fortification dates from soon after the Norman Conquest. The keep is oval and has a diameter of 21 metres. During the Prayer Book Rebellion, Richard Grenville, one of King Edward's key protestant supporters took refuge in the castle. He was captured by a party led by a rebel captain, Robert Smyth, one of Humphrey Arundell's neighbours. A group of Smyth's men stormed the gatehouse, captured Grenville and his men, while the women and children were locked in the keep. The rebels' capture of Grenville was part of Arundell's rear-guard defence strategy. He was making sure that Cornwall was secure and that all of the King's key men in Cornwall were locked up and unable to communicate with London. It was to Grenville however, that Arundell eventually surrendered.

● The Mermaid of Seaton, Seaton

SX 305543. *Seaton is located on the B3247 near Hessenford.*

Seaton in former times was an active port, Plymouth still being a tiny village. The town is said to have become over-run with sand, due to the havoc wreaked by a revengeful mermaid. She had suffered some injury from sailors who had put out from Seaton, and to curse them silted up the port. Mermaids are central creatures in the Celtic folkloric tradition of Cornwall.

● Richard Carew, Antony House

SX 418563 *The house is found on the A374 on the way to the Torpoint ferry.*

The present Antony House is an early eighteenth-century structure, built on the Carew family seat which they had owned since the mid sixteenth century. Richard Carew (1555-1620) was a poet, author, historian and soldier, whose portrait is held within the house. His greatest work was *The Survey of Cornwall*, published in 1602 but constructed towards the end of the previous century. Although Carew fully embraced the transition of Celtic Cornwall into the modern age (witnessed in essays such as *The Excellency of the English Tongue*), he nonetheless recorded much information about the Cornish language, as well as a somewhat sceptical view of how the great Cornish dramas were rehearsed. Carew mentions the skills and knowledge in the language of a Dr Kennel, as well as how to say 'I can speak no Saxonage [*Meea navidna cowzasawzneck*]. He also alludes to traits of naming Cornish people:

> Thomas they call *Tummas* and *Tubby*; Matthew, *Mathaw*, Nicholas, *Nicklaaz*; Reginald, *Reinol*; David, *Daavi*; Mary, *Maari*; Frauncis, *Frowncis*; James, *Jammez*; Walter, *Watty*; Robert, *Dobby*; Rafe, *Raw*; Clemence, *Clemmowe*.

In another work titled *A Herring's Tale*, he wrote a satirical portrait of Celtic Cornwall, in which a snail named Sir Lymazon is attempting to climb the tallest tower of an imagined Tintagel Castle. *The Survey of Cornwall* is highly useful document however, listing much of the Celtic language, place-names, customs and folklore which were disappearing from Cornwall as it entered the early modern period. The house also contains a portrait of Rachel Carew, seen by some observers as the inspiration behind Daphne du Maurier's 1951 novel *My Cousin Rachel*.

Inside St Julian's Well.

● St Julian's Well, Maker, near Torpoint

St Julian's Well, Mount Edgcumbe

SX 447521. *The well is found on the Mount Edgcumbe Estate. A large water trough sits next to it on the road in from the B3247.*

This dedication may be similar to the ones found at Boscastle and Lanteglos in North Cornwall. St Julian may be a male or female saint. The well is distinguished by a fourteenth-century pavement of red and green tiles, and within the walls are niches for icons.

● Lady Well, Sheviock

SX 374547. *The well is located close to the quarry to the south east of the village accessed from the A374.*

This Saint Mary-named well is almost indistinguishable from the surrounding rock, but the well itself is actually slate-lined. The place-name Sheviok (*Seivoch* or *Sevi* and *ek*) probably means 'place of the strawberries'.

● Rame Head Cliff Castle, Rame

SX 418484. *This is found off the B3247 from Millbrook. From Combe Farm, take a lane leading to Rame Head.*

On the neck of the headland a distinctive ditch with an entrance can be observed. Some small remains of the rampart can also be seen. Located at the summit are the ruins of a Medieval chapel devoted to St Michael.

● Plain-an-gwarry, Rame

SX 426491. *The church at Rame is in the south of the village.*

There is evidence in some thirteenth-century documentation that the area now called Church Fields was once known in French as 'La Plaistowe' [playground]. As plain-an-gwarrys were often constructed close to churches, this would fit.

● Gogmagog and Corineus on Plymouth Hoe, as seen from Mount Edgcumbe

SX 459524. *Drive to the end of the BS247 and park here. Walk through Mount Edgcumbe Park to Ravenness Point and look over to Plymouth Hoe*

This narrative about Celtic Cornwall is not actually set in present-day Cornwall. It concerns the arrival of the two Trojan refugees Brutus and Corineus. It is one of Celtic Cornwall's origin stories. After the end of the Trojan War, the two brothers made their way to Britain, and ended up landing at what is now Plymouth Hoe. On landing in Britain, they met a band of fierce local giants, the largest of which was known as Gogmagog. On first encountering the giants, the Trojans injured Gogmagog and took

him back to their camp to help him recover. In negotiating a settlement with the giants, Gogmagog apparently suggested someone 'try a fall' (or wrestle) with him, and that whoever should win, would become the King of Cornwall. Corineus accepted the challenge. A space was cleared on Plymouth Hoe and the two fought. Corineous somehow managed to knock over the giant and dragged him to the edge of the cliff, and threw him off; the giant's body breaking into fragments by the fall. Corineus then became King of Cornwall. So it is said the jaw of the giant is built into the foundations of the building known on the Hoe, as the Citadel. The place where Gogmagog entered the sea is known as Langoêmagog, or 'Gogmagog's Leap'.

● Celtic Cornwall in Devon, Devon

SX 459524. *Look across from Mount Edgcumbe to the South Hams and up to Dartmoor.*

Because of the westward retreat of the West Britons into present-day Cornwall, and particularly after the delineation of Cornwall by King Athelstan, aspects of Celticity remain in Devon. Indeed the folk-lorist Robert Hunt believed in the concept of what he labelled 'Greater Cornwall' (in effect Dumnonia). This has been borne out in a variety of ways. After the Battle of Peonnum in Somerset in 658, the Saxons arrived in Exeter. However the Saxons allowed the West Britons to continue living there in their own quarter of the city, under their own laws. This was in the locality of present-day Bartholomew Street. Until 1637, this street was known as Britayne in memory of the Britons who once lived there. In 928, King Athelstan repaired the walls of the city and at the same time made a decision to remove that 'filthy race' (meaning the Celtic speaking West Britons) from Exeter. According to William of Malmesbury, they were sent beyond the River Tamar. A plaque in Bartholomew Street records this expulsion.

Another aspect of Celtic practice continuing in Devon is where the Stannary convocation of West Devon sat. This is thought to have been on Crockern Tor – with representatives from Tavistock, Ashburton and Chagford meeting in open-air forum. Occasionally, the stannaries of both Cornwall and Devon would meet at Hingston Down near Callington.

Joseph Bidduph has made good argument for Old Devonian. This was the south-western Brythonic language spoken in parts of Devon, Somerset, and Dorset between the 5th and 6th centuries CE. It is clearly related to Old Breton and Old Cornish. Another way of looking at this is to consider it part of the retreating Old Cornish moving west. In relation to this several observers across the centuries have spoken and written about the possibility of Old Devonian or Old Cornish surviving longer in the South Hams region of present-day Devon; the isolation of this community being their reasoning.

Several Celtic narratives seem to have survived within the folklore of Dartmoor. These were written down by Eva C. Robert in her book *Dartmoor Legends* (1930). Among the stories are The Vengeance of Belus, The Bards of the Wood of Wistman and The Wrath of Taranis. The suggestion here is that such tales were part of a wider Dumnonian corpus of Celtic narrative.

Isles of Scilly

● Lyonesse, Isles of Scilly

SV 905105. *The Isles of Scilly may be reached by steamship, helicopter or aeroplane.*

An 'origin' story connected to Celtic experience is the flooding of Lyonesse. The full mythos surrounding the 'flooding' is recorded in several writings. The Cornish word for Lyonesse is *Lethowsow*, and according to Robert Hunt, Lethowsow was 'a region of extreme fertility... [which] once united the Scilly Islands with Western Cornwall'. One hundred and forty churches are supposed to have existed in the region, while the people there 'were remarkable for their industry and piety'. Hunt makes much of the fact that the flooding of Lyonesse supposedly occurred on 11 November 1099, drawing on evidence from the Anglo-Saxon Chronicle, but the actual entry says, 'In this year also, at Martinmas, the incoming tide rushed up so strongly and did so much damage that no one remembered anything like it before; and on the same day there was a new moon'. No actual location is given, and Hunt appears to assume this was the moment of flooding for Lyonesse.

View over St Mary's, Isles of Scilly.

Clearly, at the height of the Ice Age (18 000 years ago) the Islands were joined to the mainland. Since then, the sea levels have risen and separated them. The main islands of St Mary's, Tresco and St Martin were joined as one island called Ennor. Using the archaeological and place-name evidence, Charles Thomas suggests that this island broke up by about 1000CE. However, new evidence from Ratcliffe and Straker based on studies of intertidal peats suggests Ennor broke up around 1000BCE (in the Bronze Age). There remains on St Mary's a ruined castle called Ennor Castle.

Over time, there have been several folkloric notions of mariners hearing the bells of the drowned churches under the waves, and trawling up pieces of masonry. However, the Lyonesse myth is principally connected with two other components: the first is the story of how one of the ancestors of the Trevelyans (or Trevilians) escaped the flood, by riding on a horse and landing at Perranuthnoe. The second is related to St Michael's Mount. The old Cornish name for this location is *Cara Clowse in Cowse* [The Grey Rock in the Wood], and at one time, the Mount did stand in a shore-line forest, which was probably flooded, like the Isles of Scilly, at the end of the Neolithic Period. Evidence of preserved wood has been found in Mount's Bay, and local legend suggests that the full extent of this land area ran from Cudden Point to Mousehole, with Gwavas Lake (now the sea area just off Newlyn Harbour) a lake in the middle of that forest.

Of course, archaeology has shown that the Isles of Scilly are the relics of a much larger land area, but whether this is actually the Lyonesse imagined, is still conjecture. The Anglo-Cornish poet Thomas Hogg (1777–1835) wrote of Lyonesse:

> *Between Land's End and Scilly rocks,*
> *Sunk lies a town that ocean mocks.*

> *Where breathes the man that would not weep*
> *O'er such fine climes beneath the deep?*

Lyonesse has had a significance in Celtic Studies because Medieval, modern and contemporary writers have made Lyonesse the birthplace of Tristan. Again, the legend is significant. At once, it suggests that a more 'western' Celticity once existed in Cornwall, alongside a sense of loss over a greater territory and glory, reclaimed by nature. (In the contemporary context, it is perhaps a notable reminder of climate change on a cataclysmic scale). Though not always explicit in drama, Lyonesse nevertheless forms part of the Celto-Cornish imaginative construct of themselves – a projection of space and place further into the Atlantic – that is more peripheral, more magical, and is on-going, in the work of writers such as Thomas Hardy, Daphne du Maurier and Michael Morpurgo and Michael Foreman.

Other 'lost' Celtic worlds and territories are recorded in folklore. One of the most famous is Langarrow or Langona. This was a large city that once stood between the River Gannell and Perranporth. Catastrophe occurred when sand engulfed the city. The territory was thickly wooded, and so it was said, criminals were transported here from all parts of Britain. In Brittany, a tradition very similar to the lost land of Lyonesse exists. There it is related to the island city of Ys, which was located in the bay of Douarnenez. Apparently, the city was protected by sluice-gates, which only the King of Ys could unlock. The King's daughter – named Dahut – fell in love with a beautiful young man who was really the Devil in disguise, who persuaded her to steal the keys to the sluice gate. This she did, and the Devil opened the gates at high tide.

Oratory and Church, St Helen's

SV 902169. *St Helen's is located north of Tresco. The oratory and remains of the church are on the south of the island.*

Now named St Helen's, this island was once known as St Elidus – the founder of this religious community. The site contains a twelfth-century church which was destroyed in the dissolution of the monasteries. Stone walls enclose both the oratory and the church. Elidus might be a version of Eliud, known in Wales as St Teilo.

St Warna's Well, St Agnes

SV 880078. *The well lies above Porth Warna on Wingletang Down.*

Warna's origins are unclear. She may have Irish connections and have landed on St Agnes, travelling there in a wicker coracle. Much is known about the folklore surrounding her well however. Margaret Courtney, writing in 1890, observes that 'the superstitious families of St Agnes (five families in all),

St Warna's Well.

who enjoyed the reputation of being the most daring and unscrupulous amongst the Scilly wreckers of those days, threw three crooked pins into it, and daily invoked and prayed for her to send them a rich wreck'. Some have called her the patron saint of shipwrecks. The well is in good condition with three steps leading down to its waters.

Troy Town Maze, Castella Down.

● Troy Town Maze, Castella Down, St Agnes

SV 876077. *The maze is located on the western side of the island on Castella Downs.*

The current maze has modern origins. It is believed to have been constructed by a lighthouse keeper in 1729. However, so it is alleged, this maze was built on top of a much earlier one, and it is hard to view the design without thinking of the similar labyrinth designs found at Rocky Valley in north Cornwall. Walking the path of the maze is said to promote well-being. Regardless of its modern origin, the maze has come to be seen as a important spiritual site on the western edge of Celtic Britain. The maze is now very worn and in need of restoration.

● Pilot Gigs, St Agnes

SV 880083. *Races usually begin off St Agnes. For a good view, stand at the top of the island.*

The Cornish gig is a rowing boat with six oars. It is built of Cornish narrow leaf elm and is 32 feet long with a beam of 4 feet 10 inches. Originally pilot gigs were used to take out pilots from ports to incoming vessels coming to Cornwall and the Isles of Scilly from the Atlantic Ocean. They also acted as lifeboats. Although they declined in use in the opening years of the twentieth century, there has recently been a revival in their use for racing competitions and many modern vessels have been constructed, most based on the *Treffry*, built in 1838 and still raced by Newquay Rowing Club. Since 1990, the World Pilot Gig championships have been held annually on the Isles of Scilly on May Bank Holiday weekend. Gigs can be seen all around the islands and the coast of Cornwall, and many have Cornu-Celtic names such as *Avarack* (Pendeen), *Bryanek* (St Agnes), *Petroc* (Padstow), *Gwineas* (Gorran), *Kenza* (Mount's Bay), *Men-a-Vaur* (Tresco and Bryher), *Merthen* (Helford), *Morvoren* (Zennor), *Roscarrack* (Port Isaac) and *Sowenna* (Mevagissey).

● Shipman Head Cliff Castle, Bryher

SV 876161. *The castle lies to the far north west of the island of Bryher, close to Great Mussel Rock.*

On the neck of this peninsula is a large stone wall and ditch which once separated the rest of the island from this Iron Age cliff castle.

Armorel's Cottage.

● *Armorel of Lyonesse*, Samson

SV 876125. *The cottage is half-way up the slope of South Hill on the west side.*

What was once known as Holy Farm (the home of Edward Webber), is now the imagined home of the Celtic heroine Armorel, the central character of Sir Walter Besant's Scillonian-themed novel, *Armorel of Lyonesse* (1890). Besant, based in London, lived from 1836 to 1901. His novel is a typical

The view beyond the cottage of Armorel of Lyonesse.

insider/outsider narrative which dominates much late nineteenth-century fiction about Cornwall and the Isles of Scilly. Armorel is one of the last inhabitants of the island of Samson, but her life is overturned in the shape of a young artist from the mainland. The novel contains many brilliantly descriptive passages evoking the Celticity of the island, as well as presenting Armorel as a vibrant Celtic woman of some considerable independence living on the periphery of Britain.

● Round houses, Nornour

SV 944148. *Nornour is an uninhabited island joined to Great Ganilly in the Eastern Isles. The round houses are found on the path around the south of the island.*

There are a group of eight round houses here, which were occupied continuously from the Bronze Age into the Iron Age. It has a possible Romano-British re-use as a mariner's shrine, with the find of Goddess figurines – possibly Venus – who was a sea goddess in one of her guises.

● Arthuriana and Scilly, Eastern Isles

SV 943135. *Great Arthur and Little Arthur is a small island in the Eastern Isles. They can be viewed on the right hand side of the Scillonian III as she enters Crow Sound.*

In 1852, the Reverend Henry John Whitfield (1808-1858) travelled to the Isles of Scilly in order to record the islands' folkloric heritage. In search of the far Celtic West, Whitefield actually found very little in the way of folktales. Inspired by some of the landscape features of Scilly, he decided to set his own Arthurian epic based on the islands' heritage. Mordred and Arthur's final conflict therefore happens there, with Merlin causing a flood (based on the Lyonesse story) which destroys Mordred's army after he has slaughtered Arthur. The inspiration for much of Whitfield's work came from the barrows located on the island known as Great and Little Arthur – part of the Eastern Isles. Eventually, the survivors found a religious order on what is now the Island of Tresco, Whitfield neatly linking past and present, drawing on Tresco's history and the topography of the Isles.

● Tristana, The Longships rocks

SW 322253. *The so-called Longships rocks are visible from the Scillonian III travelling to the Isles of Scilly.*

In Béroul's version of the narrative of Tristan, we learn that he is the nephew of King Mark, and that his father was King Rivalin of Lyonesse. Rivalin was married to Blanchefleur, who was Mark's sister but she died in childbirth. It is with his wise tutor Governal, that Tristan departs from Lyonesse as a young man, travelling to the court of King Mark at Tintagel. The Longships may well be a relic of the former land surface of this imagined world of Rivalin.

● Giant's Castle Cliff Castle, St Mary's

SV 925101. *The castle is located just south form Porth Hellick on the coastal path around the island.*

This site has been dated to the Iron Age. It is a tall, rocky headland, surrounded by four lines of defen-

Giant's Castle.

sive embankments. The area at the top of the defences is very small indeed, though may once have been larger, its shrinkage due to erosion from the sea.

● Tresco Abbey Well, Tresco

SV 895144. *The well is located in the grounds of Tresco Abbey.*

Considering that fresh water would be difficult to obtain on the islands, wells were clearly of significance. The powers of this well must have been important, by the fact that it stands in Abbey grounds. The thick walls of the well are made of Scillonian granite.

View over Tresco c.1900.

Selected Bibliography

Angarrack, John, *Breaking the Chains: Censorship, Deception and the Manipulation of Public Opinion in Cornwall*, Camborne: Stannary Publications, 1999

_____ *Our Future is History: Identity, Law and the Cornish Question*, Bodmin: Independent Academic Press, 2002

Arnold, Matthew, *The Study of Celtic Literature*, London: Smith and Elder, 1867

Barber, Chris and Pykitt, David, *Journey to Avalon: The Final Discovery of King Arthur*, Abergavenny: Blorence Books, 1993

Besant, Walter, *Armorel of Lyonesse: A Romance of Today*, Felinfach: Llanerch, 1993 [1890]

Betjeman, John, *Collected Poems*, London: John Murray, 1988

_____ *Summoned by Bells*, London: John Murray, 1960

Blight, John Thomas, *Ancient Crosses and Other Antiquities in the West of Cornwall*, Whitefish, Montana: Kessinger, 2007 [1856]

_____ *Ancient Crosses and Other Antiquities in the East of Cornwall*, Whitefish, Montana: Kessinger, 2007 [1858]

Borlase, William, *Observations on the Antiquities Historical and Monumental of the County of Cornwall*, London: EP Publishing, 1973 [1754]

_____ *The Natural History of Cornwall*, Oxford: Oxford University Press, 1758

Borlase, William Copeland, *The Age of the Saints: A Monograph of Early Christianity in Cornwall with the Legends of the Cornish Saints*, Truro: Joseph Pollard, 1893

Bottrell, William (ed.), *Traditions and Hearthside Stories of West Cornwall: First Series*, Penzance: W. Cornish, 1870

_____ (ed.), *Traditions and Hearthside Stories of West Cornwall: Second Series*, Penzance: Beare and Son, 1873

_____ (ed.), *Traditions and Hearthside Stories of West Cornwall: Third Series*, Penzance: F. Rodda, 1880

Bowen, E.G., *Saints, Seaways and Settlements in the Celtic Lands*, Cardiff: University of Wales Press, 1969

Broadhurst, Paul, *Sacred Shrines: In Search of the Holy Wells of Cornwall*, Launceston: Pendragon Press, 1991

_____ *Tintagel and the Arthurian Myths*, Launceston: Pendragon Press, 1992

Broadhurst, Paul and Heath, Robin, *The Secret Land: The Origins of the Arthurian Legend and the Grail Quest*, Launceston: Pendragon Press, 2009

Brendon, Piers (ed.), *Cornish Ballads and Other Poems: Robert Stephen Hawker*, St. Germans: The Elephant Press, 1975

_____ *Hawker of Morwenstow*, London: Anthony Mott, 1983 [1975]

Buckley, Allen, *The Story of Mining in Cornwall*, Fowey: Cornwall Editions, 2007

Carr-Gomm, Philip (ed.), *The Rebirth of Druidry: Ancient Wisdom for Today*, London: Harper Collins, 2003

Chapman, Malcolm, *The Celts: The Construction of a Myth*, Basingstoke: Macmillan, 1992

Charters, Ann (ed.), *The Portable Jack Kerouac*, London: Penguin, 2007

Colquhoun, Ithel, *The Living Stones: Cornwall*, London: Owen, 1957

Combellack, Myrna (ed. and tr.), *The Camborne Play: A verse translation of Beunans Meriasek*, Redruth: Dyllansow Truran, 1988

Cooke, Ian McNeil, *Mermaid to Merrymaid: Journey to the Stones – Ancient Sites and Pagan Mysteries of Celtic Cornwall*, Penzance: Men-an-Tol Studio, 1987

_____ *Mother and Sun: The Cornish Fogou*, Penzance: Men-an-Tol Studio, 1993

Cope, Phil, *Holy Wells: Cornwall – A Photographic Journey*, Bridgend: Seren, 2010

Courtney, Margaret A. (ed.), *Cornish Feasts and Folklore*, Exeter: Cornwall Books, 1989 [1890]

Courtney, R.A., *The Holy Well and the Water of Life*, Penzance: Beare and Son, 1916

Cunliffe, Barry, *The Celtic World*, London: Bodley Head, 1979

_____ *The Ancient Celts*, Oxford: Oxford University Press, 1997

Davey, Merv, *Hengan: Traditional Folk Songs, Dances and Broadside Ballads collected in Cornwall*, Redruth: Dyllansow Truran, 1983

Davey, Merv, Davey, Alison and Davey, Jowdy, *Scoot Dances, Troyls, Furrys and Tea Treats: The Cornish Dance Tradition*, London: Francis Boutle Publishers, 2009

Day, Brian, *Chronicle of Celtic Folk Customs*, London: Hamlyn, 2000

Deacon, Bernard, *Cornwall: A Concise History*, Cardiff: University of Wales Press, 2007

Deacon, Bernard, Cole, Dick and Tregidga, Garry, *Mebyon Kernow and Cornish Nationalism*, Cardiff: Welsh Academic Press, 2003

Deane, Tony and Shaw, Tony, *Folklore of Cornwall*, Stroud: Tempus, 2003

_____ *A Cornish Christmas*, Stroud: The History Press, 2008

Doble, G.H., *The Saints of Cornwall: Parts 1-5*, Felinfach: Llanerch, 1997 [1960-1970]

Dudley, Peter, *Goon, Hal, Cliff and Croft*, Truro: Cornwall Council, 2011

du Maurier, Daphne, *Rule Britannia*, London: Arrow Books, 1992 [1972]

_____ *Vanishing Cornwall*, Harmondsworth: Penguin, 1972 [1967]

Ellis, Peter Berresford, *The Cornish Language and its Literature*, London and Boston: Routledge and Kegan Paul, 1974

_____ *Celt and Saxon: The Struggle for Britain AD 410-937*, London: Constable, 1993

Ford, John, *The Chronicle Historie of Perkin Warbeck: A Strange Truth*, London: British Library, 2008 [1634]

Fowler, David C., *The Life and Times of John Trevisa, Medieval Scholar*, Seattle and London: University of Washington Press, 1995

Fredrick, Alan S. (ed. and tr.), *Beroul: The Romance of Tristan*, Harmondsworth: Penguin, 1970

Fulton, Helen (ed.) *Medieval Celtic Literature and Society*, Dublin: Four Courts Press, 2005

Gendall, Richard, *1000 Years of Cornish*, Menheniot: Teere ha Tavaz, 1994

Goodrich, Peter (ed.), *The Romance of Merlin: An Anthology*, New York and London: Garland, 1990

Gray, J.M. (ed.), *Alfred, Lord Tennyson: Idylls of the King*, Harmondsworth: Penguin, 1983

Selected Bibliography

Great Western Railway, *Cornwall's Legend Land*, Vols 1 and 2, Penzance: Oakmagic Publications, 1997 [1922]

Green, Miranda, *Dictionary of Celtic Myth and Legend*, London: Thames and Hudson, 1992

Grimbert, Joan Tasker (ed.), *Tristan and Isolde: A Casebook*, New York and London: Garland, 1995

Hale, Amy, Kent, Alan M., and Saunders, Tim (eds. and trs.), *Inside Merlin's Cave: A Cornish Arthurian Reader 1000-2000*, London: Francis Boutle Publications, 2000

Halliday, F.E. (ed.), *Richard Carew: The Survey of Cornwall*, London: Melrose, 1953

Hardy, Thomas, *The Famous Tragedy of the Queen of Cornwall*, London: Macmillan, 1923

Harvey, David C., Jones, Rhys, McInroy, Neil and Milligan, Christine (eds.), *Celtic Geographies: Old Culture, New Times*, London and New York: Routledge, 2002

Hatcher, John, *Rural Economy and Society in the Duchy of Cornwall 1300-1500*, Cambridge: Cambridge University Press, 1970

Herring, Peter and Rose, Peter, *Bodmin Moor's Archaeological Heritage*, Truro: Cornwall County Council, 2001

Higgins, Sydney, *Medieval Theatre in the Round: The Multiple Staging of Religious Drama in England*, Camerino, Italy: Laboratorio degli studi Linguistici, 1995

Hingston, Francis Charles, *Specimens of Ancient Cornish Crosses, Fonts, Etc*, Penzance: Men-an-Tol Studio, 1999 [1850]

James, Simon, *The Atlantic Celts: Ancient People or Modern Invention?* London: British Museum Press, 1999

Jenner, Henry, *A Handbook of the Cornish Language: Chiefly in its Latest Stages with some account of its History and Literature*, London: David Nutt, 1904

John, Catherine Rachel, *The Saints of Cornwall: 1500 Years of Christian Landscape*, Padstow: Tabb House, 2001 [1981]

Jones, M. (ed.), *Traces of Ancestry: Studies in Honour of Colin Renfrew*, Vol. 2, Cambridge: McDonald Institute Monograph Series, 2004

Kent, Alan M., *The Literature of Cornwall: Continuity, Identity, Difference 1000-2000*, Bristol: Redcliffe, 2000

— (ed.), *Voices from West Barbary: An Anthology of Anglo-Cornish Poetry 1548-1928*, London: Francis Boutle Publishers, 2000

— (ed.), *The Dreamt Sea: An Anthology of Anglo-Cornish Poetry 1928-2004*, London: Francis Boutle Publishers, 2004

— *Ordinalia: The Cornish Mystery Play Cycle – A Verse Translation*, London: Francis Boutle Publishers, 2005

— *Nativitas Christi / The Nativity: A New Cornish Mystery Play*, London: Francis Boutle Publishers, 2006

— *The Theatre of Cornwall: Space, Place, Performance*, Bristol: Redcliffe, 2010

— *The Hope of Place: Selected Poems in English 1990-2010*, London: Francis Boutle Publishers, 2010

— (ed.), *Four Modern Cornish Plays*, London: Francis Boutle, 2010

Kent, Alan M. and Saunders, Tim (eds. and trs.), *Looking at the Mermaid: A Reader in Cornish Literature 900-1900*. London: Francis Boutle Publishers, 2000

Kent, Alan M. and Danny L.J. Merrifield, *The Book of Probus: Cornwall's Garden Parish*, Tiverton: Halsgrove, 2004

Kirkham, Graeme, *Managing the Historic Environment on West Cornwall's Rough Ground*, Truro: Cornwall Council, 2011

Koch, John T. (ed.), *Celtic Culture: A Historical Encylopedia*, Vols. 1-5, Santa Barbara, California and Oxford: ABC Clio, 2006

Hardy, Thomas, *The Famous Tragedy of the Queen of Cornwall*, London: Macmillan, 1923

Hancock, Peter, *The Mining Heritage of Cornwall and West Devon*, Wellington: Halsgrove, 2008

Hill, Kerrow, *The Brontë Sisters and Sir Humphry Davy: A Shared Vision*, Penzance: Patten Press, 1994

Hunt, Robert (ed.), *Popular Romances of the West of England: The Drolls: Traditions, and Superstitions of Old Cornwall (First Series)*, London: John Camden Hotten, 1865

_____ (ed.), *Popular Romances of the West of England: The Drolls: Traditions, and Superstitions of Old Cornwall (Second Series)*, London: John Camden Hotten, 1865

Laing, Lloyd, *The Archaeology of Celtic Britain and Ireland c.AD 400-1200*, Cambridge University Press, 2006

Langdon, Andrew, *Stone Crosses in North Cornwall*, Cornwall: The Federation of Old Cornwall Societies, 1996

_____ *Stone Crosses in Penwith*, Cornwall: The Federation of Old Cornwall Societies, 1997

_____ *Stone Crosses in West Cornwall (including The Lizard)*, Cornwall: The Federation of Old Cornwall Societies, 1999

_____ *Stone Crosses in Mid Cornwall*, Cornwall: The Federation of Old Cornwall Societies, 2002

_____ *Stone Crosses in East Cornwall (including parts of Bodmin Moor)*, Cornwall: The Federation of Old Cornwall Societies, 2005

Lane-Davies, A., *Holy Wells of Cornwall*, Cornwall: Federation of Old Cornwall Societies, 1970

Langdon, Arthur G., *Old Cornish Crosses*, Cornwall: Cornwall Books, 1988 [1896]

Langham, A.F., *The Island of Lundy*, Stroud: Sutton, 1994

Lattimore, Richard, *The Odyssey of Homer: A Modern Translation*, New York: Harper and Row, 1975

Le Braz, Anatol, *Le Theatre Celtique*, Paris: Calmann-Lévy, 1905

Lobb, R.R., *The Constitution of Cornwall or Kernow: The Country of the West Britons*, Cornwall: The Stannary Parliament of the Cornish People, 1993

Longsworth, Robert, *The Cornish Ordinalia: Religion and Dramaturgy*, Cambridge, Massachusetts: Harvard University Press, 1967

Lyon, Rod, *Cornwall's Playing Places*, Nancegollan: Tavas an Weryn, 2001

Cornish: The Struggle for Survival, Nancegollan: Tavas an Weryn, 2001

_____ *Gorseth Kernow: The Cornish Gorsedd – what it is and what it does*, Cornwall: Gorseth Kernow, 2008

Markale, Jean, *Women of the Celts*, London: Gordon Cremonesi, 1980

Matthew, John Hobson, *A History of the Parishes of Saint Ives, Lelant, Towednack and Zennor*, St Ives: St Ives Trust and St Ives Library, 2003 [1892]

Meryick. J., *A Pilgrim's Guide to the Holy Wells of Cornwall*, Cornwall: Meryick, 1982

Michell, John, *The Old Stones of Land's End*, London: Garnstone Press, 1974

_____ *The New View Over Atlantis*, London: Thames and Hudson, 1983

Miles, Barry, *Jack Kerouac: King of the Beats*, London: Virgn, 1998

Miles, Dillwyn, *The Secret of the Bards of the Isle of Britain*, Llandybie: Gwasg Dinefwr Press, 1992

Miller, Hamish and Broadhurst, Paul, *The Sun and the Serpent: An Investigation into Earth Energies*, Launceston: Pendragon Press, 1989

Selected Bibliography

Mills, Joseph and Annear, Paul, *The Book of St Day: The Towne of Trynyte*, Tiverton: Halsgrove, 2003

Miners, Hugh, *Gorseth Kernow: The First 50 Years*, Cornwall: Gorseth Kernow, 1978

Moore, David W., *The Other British Isles*, London: McFarland and Company, 2005

Munn, Pat, *Bodmin Riding and Other Similar Celtic Customs*, Bodmin: Bodmin Books Limited, 1975

Murdoch, Brian, *Cornish Literature*, Cambridge: D.S. Brewer 1993

Nance, Robert Morton, *Cornish in Song and Ceremony*, Cornwall: The Federation of Old Cornwall Societies, n.d.

_____ *A Glossary of Cornish Sea-Words*, Cornwall: The Federation of Old Cornwall Societies, 1963

Neuss, Paula (ed. and tr.), *The Creacion of the World: A Critical Edition and Translation*. New York and London: Garland, 1983

Newman, Paul, *The Meads of Love: The Life and Poetry of John Harris (1820-84)*, Redruth: Dyllansow Truran, 1994

Norris, Edwin, *The Ancient Cornish Drama*, London and New York: Blom, 1968 [1859]

O'Sullivan, Mark (ed.), *An Unknown Planet? Writings by Richard Ogden*, Warrington: Park Corner Press, 2008

Orme, Nicholas, (ed.), *Unity and Variety: A History of the Church in Devon and Cornwall*. Exeter: University of Exeter Press, 1991

_____ (ed.), *Nicholas Roscarrock's Lives of the Saints of Cornwall and Devon*. Exeter: Devon and Cornwall Record Society, 1992

_____ *The Saints of Cornwall*. Oxford: Oxford University Press, 2000

_____ *Cornwall and the Cross: Christianity 500-1560*, Chichester: Phillimore and Company, 2007

Padel, Oliver J. 'An Unprinted Scrap of Modern Cornish from Camborne' in *Journal of the Royal Institution of Cornwall*, 2007, pp.89-95

Pascoe, W.H., *Teudar: A King of Cornwall*, Redruth: Truran, 1985

Parker, Simon (ed.), *Cornwall Marches On! / Keskerdh Kernow*, Truro: Keskerdh Kernow, 1998

Payton, Philip, *The Making of Modern Cornwall: Historical Experience and the Persistence of "Difference"*. Redruth: Dyllansow Truran, 1992

_____ (ed.), *Cornwall Since the War: The Contemporary History of a European Region*. Redruth: Institute of Cornish Studies and Dyllansow Truran, 1993a

_____ 'a… concealed envy against the English': a Note on the Aftermath of the 1497 Rebellions in Cornwall' in Payton, Philip (ed.), 1993b

_____ (ed.), *Cornish Studies: One*, Exeter: University of Exeter Press, 1993b

_____ *Cornwall*, Fowey: Alexander Associates, 1996

_____ *D.H. Lawrence and Cornwall*, St Agnes: Truran, 2009

_____ *John Betjeman and Cornwall: "The Celebrated Cornish Nationalist"*, Exeter: University of Exeter Press, 2010

Pearce, Susan M., *Kingdom of Dumonia: Studies in History and Tradition in South West Britain, AD350-1150*, Padstow: Lodenek, 1975

Pennick, Nigel, *Celtic Sacred Landscapes*, London: Thames and Hudson, 1996

Peters, Caradoc, *The Archaeology of Cornwall: The Foundations of our Society*, Fowey: Cornwall Editions, 2005

Phillips, Andy, *Reclaming Cornwall's Celtic Christian Heritage: A Study Guide*, Portreath: Spyrys a Gernow, 2006

_____ *Lan Kernow: A Theology of Place for Cornwall*, Portreath: Spyrys a Gernow, 2006

Preston-Jones, Ann and Rose, Peter, 'Medieval Cornwall' in Whitaker, Rowan and Harris, Daphne (eds.), 1986, pp.135-85

Quiller Couch, Arthur, *From a Cornish Window*, Cambridge: Cambridge University Press, 1928 [1906]

Quiller Couch, Mabel and Lillian, *Ancient and Holy Well of Cornwall*, London: The Cornish Library, 2004 [1894]

Rastall, Richard, *The Heaven Singing: Music in Early English Religious Drama*, Cambridge: D.S. Brewer,1996

_____ *Minstrels Playing: Music in Early English Religious Drama*, Cambridge: D.S. Brewer, 2001

Ratcliffe, Eric, *Ithell Colquhoun: Pioneer Surrealist Artist, Occultist, Writer and Poet*, Oxford: Mandrake, 2007

Rawe, Donald R., *Petroc of Cornwall*. Padstow: Lodenek Press, 1970

_____ *A Prospect of Cornwall*, London: Robert Hale, 1986

_____ *Padstow's Obby Oss and May Day Festivities: A Study in Folklore and Tradition*. Padstow: Lodenek Press, 1990 [1971]

Roberts, Forrester, *The Legend of Tristan and Iseult: The Tale and the Trail in Ireland, Cornwall and Brittany*, Gloucester: Forrester Roberts, 1998

Rowe, John, *Cornwall in the Age of the Industrial Revolution*, St Austell: Cornish Hillside Publications, 1993 [1953]

Rowe, Laura, *Granite Crosses of West Cornwall*, Truro: D. Bradford Barton, 1973

Rowse, A.L., *Tudor Cornwall*, Redruth: Dyllansow Truran, 1990 [1941]

Roy, Rob, *Stone Circles: A Modern Builder's Guide to the Megalithic Revival*, White River Junction, V ermont and Totnes: Chelsea Green Publishing Company, 1999

Rule, John, *Cornish Cases: Essays in Eighteenth and Nineteenth Century Social History*, Southampton: Clio Publishing, 2006

Saunders, Tim, *The High Tide: Collected Poems in Cornish 1874-1999*, London: Francis Boutle Publishers, 1999

_____ (ed. and tr.), *The Wheel: An Anthology of Modern Poetry in Cornish 1850-1980*. London: Francis Boutle Publishers, 1999

_____ (ed. and tr.), *Nothing Broken: Recent Poetry in Cornish*, London: Francis Boutle Publishers, 2006

Seddon, Richard, *The Mystery of Arthur at Tintagel*, London: Rudolph Steiner Press, 1990

Shaw, Thomas, *Saint Petroc and John Wesley: Apostles in Cornwall – An Examination of the Celtic Background of Cornish Methodism*, Cornwall: Cornish Methodist Historical Association, 1962

Smith, A.S.D., *Trystan hag Ysolt*, Redruth: J. and M. Roberts, 1951

Spence, Lewis, *The Magical Arts in Celtic Britain*, London: Rider, 1949

Spriggs, Matthew, 'The Cornish Language, Archaeology and the Origins of English Theatre' in Jones, M. (ed.), 2004

Stokes, Whitley (ed. and tr.), *The Life of Saint Meriasek, Bishop and Confessor: A Cornish Drama*, London: Trübner and Co., 1872

Stoyle, Mark, *West Britons: Cornish Identities and the Early Modern British State*, Exeter: University of Exeter Press, 2002

Straffon, Cheryl, *Pagan Cornwall: Land of the Goddess*, St Just-in-Penwith: Meyn Mamvro Publications, 1993

_____ *The Earth Goddess: Celtic and Pagan Legacy of the Landscape*, Poole: Cassell, 1997

_____ *Fentynyow Kernow: In Search of Cornwall's Holy Wells*, St Just-in-Penwith: Meyn Mamvro Publications, 1998

Sturt, John, *Revolt in the West: The Western Rebellion of 1549*, Exeter: Devon Books, 1987

Thomas, Charles, *Exploration of a Drowned Landscape*, London: Batsford, 1985

‗‗‗‗‗‗‗ *Tintagel: Arthur and Archaeology*, London: English Heritage and Batsford, 1993

‗‗‗‗‗‗‗ *And Shall These Mute Stones Speak? Post-Roman Inscriptions in Western Britain*, Cardiff: University of Wales Press, 1994

‗‗‗‗‗‗‗ *Celtic Britain*, London: Thames and Hudson, 1997

‗‗‗‗‗‗‗ *Christian Celts: Messages and Images*, Stroud: Tempus, 1998

‗‗‗‗‗‗‗ *Penzance Market Cross, A Cornish Wonder re-wondered*, Penzance: Penlee House Gallery and Museum, 1999

Thomas, Charles and Mattingly, Joanna, *The History of Christianity in Cornwall: AD 500-2000*, Truro: Royal Institution of Cornwall, 2000

Thomas, Graham and Williams, Nicholas (eds. and trs.), *Bewnans Ke: The Life of StKea – A Critical Edition with Translation*, Exeter: University of Exeter Press, 2007

Thomas, Peter W. and Williams, Derek R. (eds.) *Setting Cornwall on its Feet: Robert Morton Nance 1873-1959*, London: Francis Boutle Publishers, 2007

Thorpe, Lewis (ed. and tr.), *Geoffrey of Monmouth: The History of the Kings of Britain*, Harmondsworth: Penguin, 1966

Tomlin, E.W.F., *In Search of St Piran: An Account of his Monastic Foundation at Perranzabuloe, Cornwall, and its Place in the Western Celtic Church and Society*, Padstow Lodenek Press, 1982

Tregidga, Garry and Crago, Treve, *Map Kenwyn: The Life and Times of Cecil Beer*, Cornwall: Gorseth Kernow, 2000

Walke, Bernard, *Twenty Years at St Hilary*, London: Anthony Mott Ltd, 1982 [1935]

‗‗‗‗‗‗‗ *Plays from St Hilary*, London: Faber and Faber, 1939

Watkins, D.H., *Trystan and Ysolt*, Camborne: An Lef Kernewek, 1973

Weatherhill, Craig, *Cornovia: Ancient Sites of Cornwall and Scilly 4000BC – 1000AD*, Wellington: Halsgrove, 2009

Whetter, James, *The History of Glasney College*, Padstow: Tabb House, 1988

Whitaker, Rowan and Harris, Daphne (eds.), *Cornish Archaeology / Hendhyscans Kernow*, Truro: Cornwall Archaeological Society, 1986

Whitfield, H.J., *Scilly and its Legends*, London: Timpkin, Marshall and Co., 1852

Williams, Derek R., *Prying into Every Hole and Corner: Edward Lhuyd in Cornwall*, Redruth: Dyllansow Truran, 1993

‗‗‗‗‗‗‗ (ed.), *Henry and Katharine Jenner: A Celebration of Cornwall's Culture, Language and Identity*, London: Francis Boutle Publishers, 2004

‗‗‗‗‗‗‗ *Edward Lhuyd: A Shropshire Welshman*, Oswestry: Oswestry Civic Society, 2009

Woodhouse, Harry, *Cornish Bagpipes: Fact or Fiction?* Redruth: Dyllansow Truran, 1994

‗‗‗‗‗‗‗ (ed.), *The Cornish Passion Poem*, Cornwall: Gorseth Kernow, 2007

Further Reading

Aughey, Arthur, *Nationalism, Devolution and the Challenge to the United Kingdom State*, London: Pluto Press, 2001

Carruthers, Gerard and Rawes, Alan (eds.), *English Romanticism and the Celtic World*, Cambridge: Cambridge University Press, 2003

Ellis, Peter Berresford, *The Celtic Revolution: A Study in Anti-Imperialism*, Talybont: Y Lolfra, 1988 [1985]

_____ *Celtic Inheritance*, London: Constable, 1992

_____ *The Celtic Dawn: A history of Pan-Celticism*, London: Constable, 1993

Jago, F.W.P. (ed.), *The Ancient Language, and the Dialect of Cornwall, with an enlarged Glossary of Cornish Provincial Words*, Truro: Netherton and Worth, 1882

MacKillop, James, *Dictionary of Celtic Mythology*, Oxford: Oxford University Press, 1998

Maclean, Magnus, *The Literature of the Celts*, London: Blackie and Son, 1908

Moffat, Alistair, *The Sea Kingdoms: The Story of Celtic Britain and Ireland*, London: Harper Collins, 2001

Padel, Oliver, *Cornish Place-Name Elements*, Nottingham: English Place-Name Society, 1985

_____ *A Popular Dictionary of Cornish Place-Names*, Penzance: Alison Hodge, 1988

Parsons, David N. and Sims-Williams, Patrick (eds.), *Ptolemy: Towards a Linguistic Atlas of the Earliest Celtic Place-Names of Europe*, Aberystwyth: Department of Welsh, University of Wales, Aberystwyth, 2000

Pittock, Murray G.H., *Celtic Identity and the British Image*, Manchester and New York: Manchester University Press, 1999

Pryce, Huw (ed.), *Literacy in Medieval Celtic Societies*, Cambridge: Cambridge University Press, 1998

Stalmaszczyk, Piotr, *Celtic Presence: Studies in Celtic Languages and Literatures: Irish, Scottish Gaelic and Cornish*, Łód : Łód University of Press, 2005

Toulson, Shirley, *The Celtic Alternative: A Reminder of the Christianity we Lost*, London: Century, 1987

Tschirschky, Malte W., *Die Erfindung der ketlischen Nation Cornwall: Kultur, Identität und ethnischer Nationalismus in der britischen Peripherie*, Heidelberg: Univesitätsverlaf Winter, 2006

Wakelin, Martyn F., *Language and History in Cornwall*, Leicester: Leicester University Press, 1975

Weatherhill, Craig, *Cornish Place Names and Language*, Wilmslow: Sigma, 1995

A Concise Dictionary of Cornish Place-Names, Cathair na Mart: Evertype, 2009

Whittaker, John, *Ancient Cathedral of Cornwall*, London: Stockdale, 1804

Wilhelm, James J. (ed. and tr.), *The Romance of Arthur: An Anthology of Medieval Texts in Translation*, New York and London: Garland, 1994

Williams, N.J.A., *Cornish Today: An Examination of the Revived Language*, Sutton Coldfield: Kernewek dre Lyther, 1995

Young, Simon, *The Celtic Revolution: How Europe Was Turned Upside Down from the Early Romans to King Arthur*, London: Gibson Square, 2010

Index of Places